THE BUSINESS OF SHIPBUILDING

OTHER TITLES IN THIS SERIES

Ship Management
THIRD EDITION
by Malcolm Willingale
(1998)

Ship Registration
THIRD EDITION
by N. P. Ready
(1998)

Farthing on International Shipping
THIRD EDITION
by Bruce Farthing and Mark Brownrigg
(1997)

Ship Finance
SECOND EDITION
by Peter Stokes
(1997)

Ship Performance
by Cyril Hughes
(1996)

Shipbroking & Chartering Practice
FOURTH EDITION
by Gorton, Ihre, Sandevarn
(1995)

Shipping Pools
SECOND EDITION
by William Packard
(1995)

Bunkers
SECOND EDITION
by Christopher Fisher and Jonathon Lux
(1994)

THE BUSINESS OF
SHIPBUILDING

BY

GEORGE J. BRUCE

*Lecturer in Marine
Production Technology,
University of Newcastle*

AND

IAN GARRARD

Partner, Curtis Davis Garrard

|L|L|P|

LONDON   HONG KONG
1999

LLP Reference Publishing
69–77 Paul Street,
London EC2A 4LQ

EAST ASIA
LLP Asia
Sixth Floor, Hollywood Centre
233 Hollywood Road
Hong Kong

First published in Great Britain 1999

© George Bruce and
Ian Garrard 1999

British Library Cataloguing in Publication Data

*A catalogue record for
this book is available
from the British Library*

ISBN 1–85978–851–3

Are you satisfied with our customer service?

These telephone numbers are your service hot lines for questions and queries:

Delivery:	+44 (0) 1206 772866
Payment/invoices/renewals:	+44 (0) 1206 772114
LLP Products & Services:	+44 (0) 1206 772113

e-mail: Publications@LLPLimited.com or fax us on +44 (0) 1206 772771

*We welcome your views and comments in order to ease any problems
and answer any queries you may have.*

LLP Limited, Colchester CO3 3LP, U.K.

Typeset by Interactive Sciences Ltd, Gloucester
Printed in Great Britain by
MPG Books,
Bodmin, Cornwall

PREFACE

The business of shipbuilding is one of the most misunderstood in many countries. In an era which has discovered "Globalisation" as a new force in international trade, the experience of the most global industry—an experience which stretches hundreds, even thousands of years—seems almost forgotten by many people. The simple fact is that a ship of quite modest size can, from any seaboard, reach any other seaboard. The role of the ship in exploration and world development is well-documented. But what is usually forgotten, or ignored, is the infrastructure behind the ships. Although a relatively simple wooden ship could be built almost anywhere, using local materials, to build and sustain a large fleet has always been a major undertaking.

The Arsenale in Venice is the most frequently quoted example of early industrial organisation. To first build and then maintain a fleet of ships, both for trading voyages and in case of war, required a large scale operation. The differentiation of warships from trading vessels—oared galleys for speed, rather than "round" ships for capacity—compounded the problem. All the problems that have beset the shipbuilding business in the modern era can be found in contemporary accounts, from the need to maintain a skilled workforce, to shortages of materials, to subsidies to maintain the infrastructure in case of emergencies. The problems of the US shipbuilders in the 1990s, struggling with a reduction in naval shipbuilding orders, find parallels in fifteenth century Venice.

But it is the scale of the operation and the excellent organisation that is of real note. Contemporary accounts describe the storage of galleys under cover, which could be launched into the canals and taken past a series of warehouses. Each warehouse held specific stores, organised in the required sequence of outfitting the galleys. One famous account describes the rate of completion of the galleys, as a fleet was readied for sea in a two-day period. The rate of production described equates to one galley ready for sea every 36 minutes over the period. All of which predates Henry Ford by 500 years.

Other locations also provide examples of early industrial scale shipbuilding operations. The mediaeval shipyards in Barcelona are preserved as the maritime museum, and demonstrate the use of undercover construction, and of a ship factory with all workshops organised in a single complex. Although contemporary ships were small by modern standards, they still represent considerable investment and technological achievement in the context of the times. The ship has always been the most complex technological artefact produced by the human race, and this continues to the present day. And once again, to build and support the ships has been the infrastructure behind them.

As ships slowly improved, becoming larger and more efficient, organisations grew. At the height of the Napoleonic Wars, the British navy had a fleet of over one hundred battleships, plus a myriad of smaller craft, all of which had been built and had to be maintained. Apart from the operational aspects of the global business that was the navy, the shore organisation, including construction and repair, was the largest organisation in the world at the time. Once again, the problems that are evident find modern parallels. The materials for much of the ship construction had to be imported (one aspect of the loss of American colonies that had a serious effect). The problems of supply chain management, which then had to be managed, to ensure the timely availability of suitable materials as required, are often seen as a modern phenomenon. The problems of dealing with private contractors, and especially ensuring adequate quality, also have modern parallels.

A visit to the historic dockyards, which grew rapidly in this period, demonstrates the size of operation that was undertaken. Materials shortages also provoked further industrial developments, perhaps most notably in the machinery for blockmaking at Portsmouth Dockyard. The craft production of blocks, needed in thousands for the rigging of large ships, could not match the requirements. As a consequence, Marc Brunel, father of the more famous Isambard Kingdom Brunel, developed machines for the purpose. In the process, he developed an early example of work breakdown, of mechanisation and the use of specialist equipment. The system pre-dated modern Group Technology by 150 years.

The shipbuilding industry has always been at the leading edge of technology. The ship is the largest genuinely mobile man-made artefact, and always will be. The offshore production industry has developed large structures which can be moved to a fixed location, but using much technology borrowed from shipbuilding. The largest ships built, loaded with oil cargo, exceed 500,000 tonnes displacement— equal to any offshore structure and capable of independent travel on a continuous basis.

The ship has also always been the most complex artefact produced by human effort. It has represented in every age the state of the art in technological development. There are many technologies which may be regarded as innovative, modern, advanced or which exceed the ship. But the ship absorbs them into ever more complex types. The shipbuilder has always managed complex projects, which combine numerous technologies to provide independently mobile, self-sufficient vehicles capable of a massive range of tasks. And, once again, the shipbuilder turns the latest concept into an operational reality.

The shipbuilding industry is also innovative. A major driver behind the development of the steel industry was the demand for ships, as the industry moved from wood, briefly to iron and then to steel.

In the UK in particular, shipbuilding is dismissed as a "smokestack" industry, although the importance of shipping to the nation is vaguely recognised. The experience of using cross-Channel and other ferries, the growing popularity of cruising and occasional views of other shipping is the experience of most people. That there is still, behind the appearance of the ships, a massive, world-wide industry to build and maintain the ships is lost sight of. Despite the relative decline of shipbuilding in the UK, and indeed in much of Europe, the industry is still surprisingly large. A major survey in 1996 and 1997 identified over 25,000 people employed in the business in the UK, including military construction. Subcontractors and suppliers increase that total. The Foresight Report on the whole maritime sector in the UK identified a total of 700,000 people gaining employment from the many aspects of maritime activity, including offshore oil and leisure, with the sector contributing around 5% of gross national product.

World-wide, several hundred thousand people are directly employed in building large, ocean-going ships, and when support infrastructure, sub-contractors and the supply chain are taken into account, and fishing and other local vessels, several million people depend for their livelihood on the business of shipbuilding. For as long as the people of the world continue to trade, to travel and to spend leisure time, there will be a demand for ships to be satisfied by the business of shipbuilding.

ABOUT THE AUTHORS

George Bruce began his career as an apprentice at Swan Hunter Shipbuilders. He worked as a Research and Development Manager for British Shipbuilders between 1978 and 1981 and subsequently joined A. & P. Appledore Ltd as senior consultant, becoming the company's technical director in 1989. From 1991 he has worked as a consultant with the Association of Independent Management and Maritime Services. Since 1996, he has been a lecturer in Marine Production Technology at the University of Newcastle. He acts as an adviser on development and manufacturing strategies to shipbuilders and repairers in the UK and abroad.

Ian Garrard is one of the founding partners of Curtis Davis Garrard, a specialist shipping practice located at London's Heathrow Airport. The firm acts for a range of international, primarily European and US, shipping and offshore clients, and is the only English specialist shipping law firm to have achieved ISO 9001 quality assurance accreditation.

He specialises in shipbuilding projects in the context of the shipping sector (including general cargo, LNG carriers, tankers, cruise ships) and the offshore (oil and gas) sector (including drilling rigs and FPSOs), from preparing invitations to tender to negotiating contracts to closing. He also has extensive experience of dispute resolution in relation to shipbuilding and has a wide perspective on all issues.

He was acknowledged as a maritime expert in "The World's Leading Maritime Lawyers" 1998, and has written various articles on shipbuilding.

TABLE OF CONTENTS

Page

Preface   v
About the Authors   ix
List of Tables and Figures   xix
List of Plates   xxi

1. THE MARKET FOR SHIPS   1

Dependence on trade   1
Development in size and types of ship over the last century   2
The impact of change on shipbuilders   3
The changing location of shipbuilding   4
Assessing shipbuilding production   5
Market shares   7
Labour cost   12
Performance   13
Exchange rates   14
Political support   14
Industry structure   15
The current market situation   15
Models of market demand   16
Short term demand   17
The outcomes of forecasting   23
Ship demolition   25

2. POLITICAL INFLUENCES ON SHIPBUILDING   31

Why politics matter in the shipbuilding business   31
An historical perspective   32
European subsidies   33
The OECD agreement   35
The excess of shipbuilding capacity over demand   35
Estimates of world shipbuilding capacity   36
Government-support measures   37

3. OTHER EXTERNAL INFLUENCES   41

"STEP" factors influencing shipbuilding   41
Economic environment   42
    Ownership of shipbuilders   42
    Exchange rates   45
The social environment   45
    The labour force   46
    Environmental issues   48

4. SUPPLY IN THE SHIPBUILDING BUSINESS   55

The industry world-wide   55
Government responses   56
The capacity of the world-wide shipbuilding business   57
Shipbuilding countries   60
Leading shipbuilders   60
    Japanese shipbuilding   63
    Korean shipbuilding   64
    Other Asian builders   66
    Europe   66
    The Americas   71

5. SECURING ORDERS   73

What is competitiveness?   73
    Strategy and corporate management   73
    Marketing and customer care   73
    Purchasing and material management   73
    Human resource management   74
    Design and technical capability   74
    Planning and organisation of work   74
    Production technology   74
Elements of technology   74
Technological generations   75
Generations of technological change   76
    First generation: up to 1950   76
    Second generation: 1950–1965   77
    Third generation: 1965–1975   77
    Fourth generation: 1975–1985   77
    Fifth generation: 1985–1995   77
    Sixth generation: 1995 onwards   77
Reviewing technology in companies   78
Numerical scoring   79
Using the scale   79
Competitiveness   80
The need to adapt for changes in products   82
Product life cycles   84

Securing orders   86

6. THE SHIPBUILDING CONTRACT   91

Introduction   91
  Legal framework   91
  Invitation to tender   91
  Letter of intent   91
  Interim agreement   92
  Contract form   92
Outline of standard terms   93
  Parties/Preamble   93
  Description and Class   93
  Contract price and terms of payment   94
  Adjustment of the contract price   94
  Approval of plans and drawings and inspection during construction   94
  Modifications (to the specifications for the vessel)   94
  Trials   94
  Delivery   95
  Delays and extension of time for delivery/force majeure   95
  Builder's warranty   95
  Rescission by buyer   96
  Buyer's default   96
  Insurance   96
  Dispute resolution   96
  Right of assignment   96
  Taxes and duties   97
  Patents, trade marks, copyrights, etc.   97
  Buyer's supplies   97
  Notice   97
  Effectiveness   97
Key aspects   97
  Parties/Preamble   97
    Parties   97
    Location of works   98
    Design responsibility   98
  Description and class   98
    Specifications   98
    Performance guarantees   99
    "Class" status   99
    Regulatory requirements   99
    Standard of works/QA   100
    Sub-contracting of works   100
    Registration and flag   100
  Contract price and terms of payment   101
    Lump sum price   101
    Adjustments   101
    Payment terms   101

Bank charges, currency, etc.	102
No set-off	102
Method of payment	102
Buyer's allowance	103
Adjustments to the contract price	103
Liquidated damages	103
Permissible delays	104
"Drop dead date"	104
Additional damages	104
Builder's bonus	104
"Cap" on liquidated damages	104
Approval of drawings and plans and rights of inspection and supervision	105
Buyer's approval required	105
Timing	105
Buyer's supervisors	105
Supervisors' facilities	106
Defects, ongoing process of review	106
Exclusion of liabilities	107
Substitution	107
Modifications to the works	107
Buyer's modifications	107
Compulsory modifications	108
Builder's modifications	108
Trials of the vessel	109
Sea trials	109
Acceptance or rejection of the vessel	110
"Punch" list	110
Conformity with the contract	111
Exclusion of implied terms	111
Buyer's right to rescind	112
Delivery	112
Protocol	112
Location	112
Times for delivery	112
Title to the vessel	113
Builder's lien	113
Risk of loss, damage	114
Extension of time for delivery	114
Force majeure	114
Notice requirements	114
Effect on "critical path"	115
Excessive delay	115
Builder's warranty	115
Scope of warranty	115
Nature and time of defects	115
Drydocking	116
Builder's liability extended	116
Design faults	116

Replacement parts   116
Sub-contractors' items   116
Notice of claims   117
Manner of repairs   117
Assignment of builder's warranty   117
Limitation on builder's liability   117
Exclusions from warranty   118
Rescission by the buyer   118
Recovery of instalments paid   118
Value of buyer's supplies   118
Refund guarantee   118
Builder's default   118
Insolvency of builder   119
Default interest   119
Where title passes as the vessel is constructed   119
Right to complete the works   119
Dispute as to rescission   120
Limitation on builder's liability   120
Buyer's default   120
Events of default   120
Rescission by the builder   121
Surplus/deficiency in sale proceeds   121
Other remedies   121
Insurance   122
Builder's risks   122
Partial loss   122
Total loss   122
Dispute resolution   123
Generally   123
Technical disputes   123
Arbitration   123
The courts   123
Assignment   123
Generally   123
Export licences/approvals   124
Taxes and duties   124
Responsibility   124
Patents, etc.   124
Builder's warranty   124
Indemnity   124
Builder's drawings etc.   125
Buyer's supplies   125
Responsibility   125
Notices   125
Effective date   125

7. SHIP DESIGN   127

The scope of ship design   127
Conceptual design   128
Preliminary design   128
Functional design   129
Transitional design   129
Detail design   129
Design for production   134
  Standards   135
  Prerequisites   136
  Application of design for production   138
  The effects of changes in technology   139
  Consequences of not designing for production   142

8. MATERIALS AND SERVICES FOR SHIPBUILDING   145

Development   145
Purchasing services and materials   146
  Supplier relations   147
  Inventory management   150

9. SHIP PRODUCTION PLANNING AND PRODUCTION
ENGINEERING   155

Production engineering and planning hierarchy   155
How planning and production engineering work   157
What is to be produced?   158
How will the ship be produced?   159
Product work breakdown structure   161
Build strategy   166
  Introduction   167
  Main production parameters   167
    Planned production rate   168
    Build location   168
    Launch conditions   168
    Key dates   168
    Labour resource requirements   168
    Potential bottlenecks   169
    Sub-contract requirements   169
  Build strategy—hull   169
    Erection sequence   169
    Initial process analysis—steel and outfit   170
  Build strategy—machinery spaces   170
    Identification of outfit zones   170
    Installation sequence   170
    Identification of outfit assemblies   171
  Build strategy—accommodation   171

Subdivision	171
Erection sequence	171
Identification of installation zones	171
Installation sequence	171
Planning framework	171
Building programme	172
Interim product groups and work stations	172
Work station load analysis	172
Main purchasing dates	172
High tensile steel	173
Mild steels	173
Profiles	173
High cost and long lead time equipment	173
When is the product to be made?	175
Where is the product to be made?	178
With what is the product to be made?	178
Progress monitoring	179
Productivity	184
Benchmarking	188

10. ORGANISATION OF SHIPBUILDING   191

Shipyard activities	191
Information flows	193
Organisation	197

11. THE PRODUCTION TECHNOLOGY   199

Introduction	199
Scope of production technology	199
Hull production	202
Steel treatment (levelling, shotblasting, painting)	203
Plate and profile cutting	204
Plate and profile forming	206
Assembly	208
Outfit production	210
Material receipt	214
Block assembly, outfitting and painting	215
Ship construction	216
Final outfitting	218
New production processes	219
Automation	219
Coatings	221
Environmental issues	225
Other production management issues	226

TABLE OF CONTENTS

12. THE DEVELOPMENT OF SHIPBUILDING FACILITIES — 227

The scope of recent development — 227
Shipyard location — 228
Shipyard facilities requirements — 231
Materials handling and transport — 235
The wide variety of facilities options — 237
The shipyard layout development process — 238

13. QUALITY ASSURANCE — 245

The need for quality — 245
  Product quality — 246
  Total quality management (TQM) — 247
  Standards — 248
  Inspection — 248
  Process stability — 250
  Quality control — 250
  Managing quality — 251
  Types of control charts — 251

14. THE FUTURE DEVELOPMENT OF THE INDUSTRY — 255

New products — 256
New materials — 257
The external environment — 259
The need for technological change — 261
Current technology — 262
New technologies and processes — 263

Index — 269

LIST OF TABLES AND FIGURES

Table 1   Change in per cent share of shipbuilding world-wide, 1980 to 1990   7
Table 2   World shipping on order in 1994 (dwt)   9
Table 3   Number of ships on order in 1994   10
Table 4   Labour costs ($US per man-hour)   12
Table 5   Typical average ship prices, 1990–1997   20
Table 6   Comparison of actual and expected scrapping, 1990–2000   27
Table 7   Main nations engaged in ship scrapping   27
Table 8   The gap between ship prices and costs (early 1990s)   34
Table 9   Shipbuilding employment in certain regions   36
Table 10   Estimated world capacity in CGT   37
Table 11   Docks for ships of 250,000 dwt   59
Table 12   Docks for ships of 100,000 dwt   59
Table 13   The world's leading shipbuilders by total order book   61
Table 14   The world's leading shipbuilders by compensated gross tons   62

Figure 1   Past forecasts and actual production levels (comparisons)   24
Figure 2   Performance trend comparison (Japan and Europe)   47
Figure 3   World shipbuilding capacity and production   57
Figure 4   Shipyard performance and technology   80
Figure 5   Relative performance of shipbuilding regions   81
Figure 6   Constant cost lines, linking shipbuilders of different performance and
               labour cost   82
Figure 7   Use of constant cost lines to identify performance gaps   83
Figure 8   Simplified catastrophe theory model   84
Figure 9   Product life cycle   85
Figure 10   Overlapping product life cycles   86
Figure 11   Model for managing inventory levels   152
Figure 12   Typical ship breakdown into zones   165
Figure 13   Outline structure of a strategic network   177
Figure 14   Simplified graph showing numbers employed on a ship over the con-
               tract period   182
Figure 15   Cumulative man-hours for a shipbuilding contract   183
Figure 16   Plotting actual man-hours against plan   183
Figure 17   Plotting progress and man-hours against plan   184

Figure 18   Highlighting variance from planned progress   184
Figure 19   Activity map for shipbuilding   192
Figure 20   Flow of design information   194
Figure 21   Flow of planning information   194
Figure 22   Flow of materials information   195
Figure 23   Flow of production engineering information   195
Figure 24   Work flow in shipbuilding   196
Figure 25   Ship construction from individual parts—flexible, but slow   216
Figure 26   Ship construction in units, requiring more investment and accuracy   217
Figure 27   Ship construction in blocks or rings   217
Figure 28   Introduction of additional stages of production to shorten construction
            cycle time   218
Figure 29   Reduction in construction time by overlapping hull and outfitting
            work   222
Figure 30   Relationship diagram showing interdependence between shipyard
            facilities   240
Figure 31   Pre-1950 layout—a direct descendant of wooden shipbuilding   240
Figure 32   1960s layout—developed from the older shipyard   241
Figure 33   1960s or 1970s layout—greenfield site   242
Figure 34   1970s or 1980s layout—undercover construction   243
Figure 35   The structure of a control chart. A process in control   252
Figure 36   A process going out of control   252

LIST OF PLATES

(between pages 138 and 139)

Plate 1   High volume steelwork — cutting steel plate parts in Japan.
Plate 2   The scale of large ship interim products — a 2000-tonne plate rolls.
Plate 3   Frame bending of complex profile shapes.
Plate 4   Mechanised assembly — flat panel production for large bulk cargo ships.
Plate 5   Assembly jigs for complex hull shapes.
Plate 6   Ship construction — accurate location of a structural unit.
Plate 7   Installing ship's equipment as ready-assembled packaged units.
Plate 8   Technology for positioning large structural blocks — saving cost and time.
Plate 9   Final outfitting for a cruise ship remains labour intensive.
Plate 10   Large-scale shipbuilding under cover — Meyerwerft.
Plate 11   The finished product — a cruise ship.

CHAPTER 1

THE MARKET FOR SHIPS

DEPENDENCE ON TRADE

Any shipbuilding business, in common with any other business, can only operate in the context of the market demand for its products. That is therefore an appropriate starting point for a consideration of the business of shipbuilding.

The demand for new ships is, in turn, dependent on the trade requirements of the global economy. This, in turn, is a function of the state of the world economy, and in particular its rate of growth.

Trade is cyclical. Nevertheless, there has been a steady, long term increase in the volume of goods traded around the world, of which the vast majority move, as ever, in ships. Despite the huge increase in air traffic, for moving people and other cargoes which require speed, most trade is simply too bulky for air transport to be cost-effective. And even in such trades as passenger carriage, the decline of passenger transport on the long haul routes and some shorter ferry crossings has seen a replacement by carriage for pleasure in cruising, along with a comeback in the form of faster ferries.

However, the trend of increasing trade has seen regular increases and decreases. The cost of shipping is elastic, and minor changes in demand for ships to carry trade result in large changes in the charges shipowners can make. When these are low, the owner is unlikely to order a new ship, unless artificially persuaded to do so through some form of external support. Therefore the demand for ships is very sensitive to small changes in trade. If demand for ships drops marginally, the demand for new ships should stop abruptly and the prices available should fall. Prices have fallen over the last decades to levels where demand is stimulated by the ability of a shipowner to pick up a bargain, which is then readily resaleable when there is even a short term upturn in freight rates. Trade thus goes in cycles, where price reductions in the wake of falling demand eventually result in speculative buying.

The effect of the market on demand, and hence prices, should result in the least cost-efficient producers ceasing to operate, and there are plenty of instances of shipbuilding companies ceasing trading as demand has dropped. However, the underlying demand is always there, so recovery in the shipbuilding market will happen eventually. There is always a possibility of staying in business, accepting losses in the short term, and then making profits again during the inevitable recovery.

There is another factor, in the shape of governments. This is considered later in this chapter as one of the key external influences on the current shipbuilding market. The political context of the business of shipbuilding also deserves a complete chapter to itself, and this discussion can be found in Chapter 2.

Before reviewing the current market in more detail, it is worthwhile digressing briefly into its historical development.

DEVELOPMENT IN SIZE AND TYPES OF SHIP OVER THE LAST CENTURY

Over the last 100 years, the annual production of ships, measured in gross tons, has increased from some three million to around 17 million. That there is long term growth is thus apparent, although there are remarkable peaks and troughs. The periods of the two world wars saw massive increases in shipbuilding to fill increased demand and replace losses. The rapid increase in oil consumption in the 1960s and early 1970s, allied to the increase in ship size, with VLCCs becoming the norm, resulted in an even greater increase in ship construction. That boom ended with the oil price hike of 1973, and the legacy of over-capacity has plagued the industry world-wide since then.

To go back to the early years of the century, the typical ship was of around 4,000 tonnes deadweight. The word "typical" is appropriate, since most cargo was break-bulk, and most shipping operated on a short term basis according to available cargoes. Ships can therefore be characterised, in modern terms, as small and relatively standard.

There were of course a number of much larger ships at sea. These included the fast passenger ships, in particular the transatlantic liners. There were also large fleets of battleships, which were larger than the typical cargo ships, although relatively small by the standards of today's VLCCs. But the industry was dominated by the smaller vessels, and there were relatively few large cargo ships. In fact, the *Great Eastern*, built half a century previously, remained the world's largest ship for most of that time, and dwarfed the average cargo ship well into the twentieth century.

Since then, there has been a steady growth in average ship size, from the 4,000 tonnes deadweight of 1900 to the current figure of around 12,000 tonnes dwt. This change in average size conceals a more spectacular increase in the size of some ship types, in particular the bulk carriers and oil tankers. These have increased from a modest 5,000 tonnes dwt for the tankers and 4,000 tonnes for the bulk carriers, to the modern 50,000 tonnes dwt and 45,000 tonnes dwt respectively.

The largest tankers are now typically around 250,000 tonnes dwt, with bulk carriers somewhat smaller at 150,000 tonnes dwt.

In addition to the increases in ship size, there have also been changes in the types of ships. From the relatively standard general cargo ships of 1900, with a modest

number of specialised types, there has been a proliferation of special pur[
Many trades and functions for which ships are built now simply did no
1900. There is a diversity of ship types, and a large number which are
specialist trades.

The world fleet is dominated by the large bulk carriers and tankers, at least in
terms of tonnage, and these are the types where the over-capacity is most acute.
There are also a number of very specialist niche markets, which have largely
developed in the last 20 years. As these specialised types have developed, a number
of shipbuilders have been among the first to construct them, often working in
conjunction with the shipowner to develop the type. This has given the particular
shipyards an initial competitive edge, which in some cases they have been able to
maintain.

Some specialist types have remained in niche markets, but others, notably
container ships, have generated a whole new set of trading patterns. In the development of this, the traditional dry cargo ship, which was the dominant type at the turn
of the twentieth century, has become all but obsolete in the face of competition from
the purpose-designed ships. These have far less flexibility, but their technological
advantages, in particular in cargo handling to minimise port times, gave them a huge
competitive advantage.

The changes in the shipbuilding market, in terms of the total tonnage, the
increasing size of ships and the development of specialised ship types, have had a
major impact on the shipbuilding business, as is discussed in the next section.

THE IMPACT OF CHANGE ON SHIPBUILDERS

The shipyards which existed in 1900 were designed to build the ships of their time.
They were typically located on river banks, near but not necessarily very close to the
sea. Location was partly dictated by access to a labour force, though to set up an
industry, the labour could be imported and then trained in a limited range of skills.
That was how the United Kingdom had initially gained the major share of the
market for steel ships in the second half of the nineteenth century. It was also
dictated by access to raw materials, particularly iron ore and coal, and to a modest
infrastructure. The shipyards typically had many building berths, so that work could
progress on many ships simultaneously. This was necessary, because the limited
capability to lift ship parts resulted in piece by piece construction. Taking the
numerous small parts to a building berth to be riveted into place one by one ensured
a lengthy building time.

Although steel and steam power had been around for 50 years, the ships themselves had much in common with their iron, and previously wooden, ancestors.
Apart from the materials, and the increase in size which this allowed (from a
maximum of about 70 metres for wood, to a more typical 130 metres for steel in
1900), the methods of construction were similar in terms of their organisation.
Specialised trades, based on a long apprenticeship, dominated each aspect of the

work. These specialised trades had grown out of the early, limited skills training given to the new labour force. The traditional shipwright had been partly superseded by the boilermakers, who were already trained to work in metal. These were the most important trades, with the specific skills to determine and achieve the correct shape for the hull. The others were essentially there for their support. They included riveters, caulkers, blacksmiths and others, each trade carrying out one of the key processes in the building of a ship.

The shipyards were ideal for the purpose, producing large numbers of relatively simple, standard ships at low cost. The low cost was achieved primarily because labour was cheap, and the differentiation of many trades provided specialisation and thus relative efficiency. At this time, the United Kingdom dominated world ship-building to an extent that has rarely been equalled before or since. But the techno-logy of shipbuilding has always been readily exportable, and many other nations had industrialised, and included a shipbuilding sector.

Shipbuilding has played a particular role in industrial development in many countries.

As an industry, it has been relatively straightforward to learn, it is a large user of skilled labour and needs a large industrial infrastructure of small and medium-sized suppliers. As such, it can provide a significant boost to the start up of industrial development in other sectors. The industry requires large quantities of basic mater-ials, especially steel, and this gives an underlying market for an indigenous steel industry. Finally, since trade is important to any maker of industrial and other goods (the products of industry), a country which provided the ships to carry its trade could gain a benefit. Throughout history, the development of shipbuilding has often been aligned with ship-owning and operation.

The effect has been that more and more countries have moved into the business of shipbuilding during the twentieth century. The increasing size of ships has required changes in the technology of construction, creating opportunities for newcomers to overtake existing builders whose competitive advantages derived from their existing skills. The increases have also created a need for brand-new facilities with the physical dimensions to be able to build the larger ships.

The increasing number of larger ships required to move world trade has thus created a climate of continuous change. This has led to threats to those unwilling or unable to respond to change, as well as opportunities for new participants in the business of shipbuliding.

THE CHANGING LOCATION OF SHIPBUILDING

As the demand for ships has steadily (or perhaps unsteadily) increased through the course of the twentieth century, the need for additional ship construction capacity has provided the final spur to new shipyard developments, often in nations with minimal traditions in this sector. Japan began its industrialisation, and was a relatively large-scale shipbuilder (within the context of UK market domination) from the early twentieth century. Korea began its industry in a small way, but its move to second place among shipbuilding nations only really took off from 1973, with the development of the Hyundai shipyards.

The nations that did develop a relatively large-scale industry did so largely as an instrument of national policy, which allowed significant spending on new sites and state of the art technology. Competition between nations, initially on the basis of colonial empires, more recently for trade, has had an influence on the development of shipbuilding in different parts of the world.

So the centre of gravity of world shipbuilding has moved, under the influence of the changes in the market, initially from the UK to other European nations. More recently, it has moved from the now long-established shipyards in Europe to the Far East. Within the Far East, the dominance of Japan has been challenged in the last quarter of a century by South Korea, and more recently in a more modest way by China.

The move has not been total. The impact of specialised types has left a number of European shipyards fighting a rearguard action against the wholesale transfer of the industry. In some niches, the European industry has a technological edge which has proved extremely difficult to overcome. Those European shipyards that have specialised, and developed a technology appropriate to their specialisation, have been able to compete very effectively.

ASSESSING SHIPBUILDING PRODUCTION

There are various measures of the volume of shipbuilding production. These are used in various ways in different reports, and can be a source of confusion. The measures are all based on ship tonnage, in some form. Ships are measured using various tonnages, which differ according to their intended function. The main measurements are:

Displacement. This is the total weight of the ship and any cargo which is loaded, and is equal to the weight of water displaced. It is generally only used for describing military vessels, which do not have a commercial payload.

Light displacement is the weight of the ship without cargo, but otherwise ready for sea. Again, it is mainly used for military ships, although it is relevant for dry docking of commercial ships.

Deadweight. This is the tonnage of cargo which can be carried, and is a measure of earning capacity. It is very close to the difference between light and load displacement. It is the tonnage usually quoted for cargo carrying ships (tankers, bulk carriers, dry cargo ships).

Gross tonnage is actually a measure of enclosed volume, at 100 cubic feet (or 2.83 cubic metres) equal to one ton. All the enclosed spaces of the ship, except for some working spaces above the deck, are included. It is the most usually quoted after deadweight, and is used to determine port charges.

Net tonnage is the same measure, but excludes machinery spaces, ballast and working spaces under deck. It measures the earning space of the ship, and is analogous to—but different from—deadweight. It is rarely quoted.

Compensated gross tonnage. This has been developed and used specifically for the measurement of shipbuilding capacity of shipyards. In order to make comparisons between shipyards building different types of ship, the gross tonnage is multiplied by a compensation factor (developed by the OECD). The compensation factors vary according to ship type and size, and give approximate equivalence. The compensation factors have been updated from time to time, most recently in 1992, and are generally accepted as the best available (albeit with reservations). The factors vary from 0.4 for large tankers, reflecting their relative simplicity, to 4.0 for some passenger ships, which are far more complex.

The *number of ships* is sometimes quoted, but is not a very useful measure unless a specific size and type is being considered.

Steelweight. The structural weight of a ship is determined by the design, although the final weight is dependent on steel and production tolerances. It does not always include some outfit steel items and there is no standardised measure. The actual ship steelweight is usually quoted as net (or finished) steelweight. The weight of steel purchased against a contract is usually quoted as gross (or invoiced steelweight). This is typically 8–20 per cent greater than the net figure, depending on ship size and production efficiency in the shipyard. Steelweight can be used as a measure of performance or capacity for comparisons, but only between ships of broadly similar size and type.

Other measures may be used, typically where the conventionally accepted measure does not give a realistic interpretation of ship characteristics. However, the conventional measures are still available. The main exceptions to the above are:

Passenger ships. Gross tonnage is more used than deadweight. Because the "cargo" of passengers is of very low density, the use of deadweight does not give a realistic indication of size. The number of passengers is also usually quoted.

LPG/LNG ships. The cargo capacity is usually quoted in cubic metres.

Container Ships. The cargo capacity is frequently quoted in TEU (twenty-foot equivalent units), that is, the number of 20 foot containers that the ship can carry. This is more useful than deadweight, again because the cargo density is relatively low.

Reefer Ships. May also use cubic metres as a measure of cargo capacity.

MARKET SHARES

It is instructive to look at the question of market share in the world shipbuilding industry, both as it has developed and, in a speculative way, as it may develop in the future. If the past market shares of the main shipbuilding nations are reviewed, trends can be identified, where these are apparent, and the factors which affect market share can be identified.

Within shipbuilding countries, political support may well be the most important factor in terms of the ability of an industry to maintain market share. Where there is real competition, labour cost and productive performance are the critical factors in the long term. Labour cost is affected by exchange rates, either through short term disturbances or as part of a long term trend.

The shipbuilding capacity in the late 1990s has been only around 85 per cent utilised, and it is suspected that there is more actual and latent capacity in the world, which will "emerge" if and when the market improves. A particular influence on capacity is the overall rate of performance improvement, which is estimated at around 4 per cent annually in the most efficient shipyards, which set the benchmark performance levels for the rest of the world.

The market for ships can be defined in a number of ways, either as the tonnage of ships or as numbers of ships, and either as the tonnage constructed or, for the future, tonnage on order. In this review, the primary basis is tonnage of ships on

Table 1. Change in per cent share of shipbuilding world-wide, 1980 to 1990

Country	1980 Output	% Total	1980 Rank	Country	1990 Output	% Total	1990 Rank	
Japan	6,094	46.52	1	Japan	6,824	42.96	1	(1)
Brazil	729	5.56	2	S. Korea	3,460	21.78	2	(4)
USA	555	4.24	3	Germany	856	5.39	3	(8)
S. Korea	522	3.98	4	Taiwan	667	4.20	4	(14)
USSR	460	3.51	5	Yugoslavia	457	2.88	5	(20)
UK	427	3.26	6	Denmark	395	2.49	6	(=15)
Spain	395	3.01	7	Italy	372	2.34	7	(13)
Germany	376	2.87	8	USSR	367	2.31	=8	(5)
Poland	362	2.76	9	China	367	2.31	=8	(–)
Sweden	347	2.65	10	Spain	363	2.29	10	(7)
E. Germany	346	2.64	11	Brazil	256	1.61	11	(2)
France	283	2.16	12	Finland	247	1.56	12	(18)
Italy	248	1.90	13	Netherlands	163	1.03	13	(–)
Taiwan	240	1.83	14	Romania	160	1.01	14	(19)
Norway	208	1.59	15	UK	131	0.82	15	(6)
Denmark	208	1.59	16	Poland	104	0.65	16	(9)
Buglaria	206	1.57	17	Bulgaria	80	0.50	=17	(17)
Finland	200	1.53	18	Norway	80	0.50	=17	(=15)
Romania	170	1.30	19	Portugal	73	0.46	19	(–)
Yugoslavia	149	1.14	20	India	70	0.44	20	(–)
Others	716	5.46	–	Others	393	2.47	–	–

order, and tonnage constructed. Where the data are in a different form, alternative measures have been used. Trends are looked at in terms of percentage share of the market.

Table 1 shows the leading 20 shipbuilding countries in the world, in 1980 and 1990. This shows that Japan maintained its lead as the largest builder over the decade. It also illustrates the very rapid rise of Korea into second place.

Brazil, forecast to be one of the leading nations during the late 1970s and early 1980s, has lost market share, as has the UK. The USA, a relatively large player in 1980, disappeared completely from the top 20. These provide useful illustrations of some of the key factors which affect market share, which are discussed in section 4.

Table 2 shows the more recent situation. This is in terms of total order book, and indicates that by 1994 Korea was close to equalling Japan as the leading nation with respect to order book, although Japan is still ahead in terms of tonnage. Table 3 shows the relative positions of the countries in terms of ships to be constructed. This clearly shows Korea's reliance on the large ship market. The competition between these two is squeezing the remaining nations. Added to this is the desire of the USA to rebuild its commercial shipbuilding and the increase in share for some of the former centrally planned economies.

The continuing dominance of Japan is clear, although its share has passed the previous peak of around 50 per cent of the market. The steady rise in Korean shipbuilding is also clear. The other two major Far East builders, China and Taiwan, have also increased their market shares steadily during the period, but remain minor players in world terms.

The status of European shipbuilding is also clear. Although the European market share has fluctuated widely, and different countries have been the regional market leader at different times, there has been an overall decline from 23 per cent to 18 per cent over the 1980s and 90s. This is based on ships completed. There has also been a trend away from the shipbuilders of Western Europe towards those further east. Thus, although the overall decline has been around 20 per cent, which represents a continuing position in terms of tonnage, it hides a number of significant changes in where the ships are being built.

Dramatic changes in the European market can be illustrated by the cases of the United Kingdom and Sweden, where government support to the industry was withdrawn in the mid-1980s. Other countries' governments provided some form of support to their industries to maintain them through the lean times, though few, if any, suspected at the outset that the lean times would continue for so long. There has also been relative success for the leading north European, high labour cost countries, compared with southern Europe, despite the latter's labour cost advantage.

The data from eastern Europe have not always been reliable in the past, but the indication is that these nations have collectively maintained around 10 per cent of the market over the decade. There has been a steady, slow decline in their share, but this may now have halted as their economies begin to recover from political changes.

Table 2. World shipping on order in 1994 (dwt)

Country	DWT	% Share
Japan	18,984,860	30.9
S. Korea	18,274,523	29.7
China	3,342,332	5.4
Romania	2,287,677	3.7
Denmark	2,257,520	3.7
Germany	1,994,606	3.2
Taiwan	1,890,460	3.1
Poland	1,696,496	2.8
Brazil	1,242,997	2.0
Ukraine	1,131,805	1.8
Italy	1,130,247	1.8
Russia	1,098,676	1.8
UK	1,015,023	1.6
Spain	950,985	1.5
Croatia	922,095	1.5
Finland	361,440	0.6
Norway	349,048	0.6
Singapore	242,398	0.4
Belgium	238,230	0.4
Netherlands	217,081	0.4
Bulgaria	171,957	0.2
India	151,075	0.2
Yugoslavia	117,450	0.2
USA	84,681	0.1
Indonesia	67,600	0.09
Malaysia	37,860	0.06
Egypt	37,040	0.06
Portugal	35,456	0.05
Slovakia	31,815	0.05
Sweden	30,650	0.05
Malta	18,140	0.03
Greece	15,150	0.02
Iran	11,437	0.02
Philippines	10,720	0.02
Australia	5,636	<0.01
Mexico	5,430	<0.01
Chile	5,274	<0.01
Thailand	5,160	<0.01
Peru	3,960	<0.01
Canada	2,849	<0.01
New Zealand	1,000	<0.01

Table 3. Number of ships on order in 1994

Country	Number	Total dwt
Japan	503	25,151,197
South Korea	251	22,672,922
China	125	3,931,540
Denmark	52	2,562,429
Taiwan	31	2,236,400
Romania	61	2,259,313
Poland	81	1,926,805
Germany	103	1,838,547
Spain	34	1,625,435
Ukraine	39	1,462,708
Italy	28	1,351,914
UK	12	1,157,500
Croatia	28	1,143,490
Brazil	21	863,400
Russia	60	654,944
Turkey	25	610,800
USA	13	587,836
India	16	448,225
Bulgaria	39	377,729
Singapore	36	333,810
Norway	16	329,500
Netherlands	56	307,915
Finland	5	299,150
Indonesia	30	189,500
France	3	186,000
Portugal	10	84,332
Yugoslavia	16	82,150
Malaysia	9	65,590
Argentina	4	51,550
Egypt	7	47,020
Slovakia	10	34,525
Sweden	1	24,200
Greece	1	16,000
Malta	2	15,500
Hungary	3	11,250
Philippines	2	10,000
Belgium	1	9,550
Iran	4	8,400
Czech Republic	2	7,400
New Zealand	1	1,000

Poland is the leading shipbuilding nation in the east of Europe, along
(part of the former Yugoslavia), and has had a steadily rising share of
Despite the conflicts in Croatia, and problems in particular with fin
country remains a major builder of ships, exploiting, along with the oti
European builders, a labour cost advantage.

Although Japan has maintained its position through the 1990s, the recent
increases in Korean capacity indicate that Korea's trend towards being the leading
shipbuilding nation is likely to continue. Korea's steady growth has continued,
while Japanese production has fluctuated around a steady level. In the future, other
nations are expected to be squeezed between these two. The various forecasts of a
massive increase in the market for new ships were the basis for South Korean
expansion. If it is accepted that the demand for new ships will not peak as had
previously been predicted by a number of commentators on the shipbuilding market,
it is not anticipated that market shares will change dramatically.

Japan and Korea will continue to dominate, with eastern Europe and China
making modest progress, at the expense of western Europe and minor builders. The
continuation of other nations in the industry will depend on political considerations
more than any others.

The future of the various leading shipbuilding nations is also dependent on
economic conditions, and their unpredictability is demonstrated by the Asian economic crisis which has developed during the writing of this book. How this will
develop, and its eventual impact on the business of shipbuilding, arc matters for
speculation. However, the most likely outcome is a continuance of the trends of the
1990s.

The brief review of market shares shows that there have been a number of
changes over the last 20 years or so. The reasons for changes in market share are
varied, and no single reason can explain the changes in any particular case. There
may be an overriding reason in each individual case, but the nature of that will vary
from case to case.

The key factors to be considered in trying to identify the reasons for fluctuating
market shares are:

— labour cost;
— performance;
— exchange rates;
— political support;
— industry structure.

Each of these is considered in turn.

Table 4. Labour costs ($US per man-hour*)

Country	1995
Finland	23.75
Germany	25.00
Norway	22.55
Italy	22.75
Japan	23.13
Canada	20.95
Denmark	21.25
Netherlands	21.25
Belgium	21.88
France	20.48
Spain	22.50
USA	18.14
United Kingdom	13.75
Greece	12.37
Korea	10.41
Portugal	10.40
Taiwan	9.29
Singapore	8.33

* Converted from national currencies at 1995 rates.

Labour cost

The cost of labour in main shipbuilding centres is presented in Table 4. This is in terms of the cost per man-hour, including social and other costs additional to basic labour rates per hour for skilled workers. The figures are in US dollars. Some caution must be observed in using them, as they are aggregate figures for the countries. They are also based on 1995 exchange rates, and so are subject to fluctuations in exchange rates. There have been wide variations in exchange rates experienced in the last few years. The remarkable swings in particular in the value of the Japanese yen against the US dollar far outweigh any changes in productivity or other factors. The figures quoted do provide some guide to the relative costs in the different shipbuilding centres.

Shipbuilding is a labour intensive industry, even where some degree of automation has been introduced. The introduction of automation also carries an investment cost, so the cost of labour is an important factor in determining competitiveness, and hence the ability to secure market share.

In general terms, countries with low labour costs are more able to remain in the shipbuilding industry, and to secure orders. However, they are often restricted to simple, large ship types, because low pay can be linked to limited training, and therefore a limited technical capability to manage more complex ships. This has parallels with the development of steel shipbuilding in the latter half of the nineteenth century. The initial development of a new shipbuilding industry tends to follow a similar pattern in each case. >

As the previous review of the trends in market share reveals, labour cost cannot be the only factor which influences market share. For example, on the basis of labour cost only, southern Europe should be able to secure more work than has been the case.

Performance

Shipbuilding performance is generally measured in terms of compensated gross tonnes (CGT) per man-hour, or a related measure. This is complementary to labour cost, and there is, for the more competitive shipbuilders, a very good correlation between labour cost and performance. Thus the relatively high labour cost Japanese are able to remain competitive with Korea, southern Europe and the even lower cost areas such as East Europe. (Again, it is important to take into consideration the effect of changing exchange rates.)

The trend in performance levels over the last decade has been one of constant improvement. This has been brought about in part by automation, more by improved organisation and methods, and also in many cases by improved flexibility of labour. In Japan, the improvement has been of the order of 4 per cent annually. This is measured relatively crudely, by taking into consideration overall production in terms of CGT, and the numbers overall employed in the industry (including subcontractors).

However, evidence from Denmark and from other relatively efficient European producers supports this picture of performance improvement.

Where the performance was below the competitive level, industries have closed unless they were in a position to benefit from subsidies, which might be either overt or in the form of subsidies to national shipowners. Some less efficient builders of ships are also able to benefit from above average financing arrangements.

The most competitive part of the overall shipbuilding market is in the area of greatest international competition, in particular for large, relatively simple vessels. In some niche markets, either for technologically specialised ships or for smaller vessels operating in a regional market, a higher level of cost can be sustained. This is because other barriers to competition exist, for example the need for specialised technology which cannot be bought. Regional markets also exist for smaller ships, where the costs of construction supervision at a builder on the other side of the world would be too great a proportion of the total ship cost.

The advantage that a technologically advanced and high performance industry can offer is difficult to sustain, because the technology of shipbuilding is relatively easy to transfer. On the other hand, many low cost nations may have only the low cost of labour as a competitive advantage, and fail to make the transition to higher performance.

Exchange rates

The volatility of currencies can have a far more dramatic effect on the cost structure of an international industry such as shipbuilding than, for example, performance improvement. Their impact has already been mentioned in the context of labour costs. For Japan, the key driver leading to the remarkable and sustained performance improvement has been cost, as a function of labour cost and the generally increasing value of the yen over the last decades. The more recent depreciation of the yen in the late 1990s, as the Japanese economy as a whole suffered recession, did bring a significant cost advantage to Japan. The variation in exchange rate between the US dollar and the yen in the late 1990s has been in the region of 30 per cent.

Short term volatility can also have an impact where shipbuilders are not shielded by some form of support. A temporary change in exchange rates can lead to an uncompetitive position and result in problems. In part, this can be due to a change in exchange rates in the short term for a shipbuilder that has a number of long term, dollar contracts. With very small profit margins, if any, in shipbuilding, a change in exchange rate of a few per cent can bring about a serious loss.

Political support

This may be the most critical factor of all. In the European context, the relative market shares shown earlier have a close correlation with government policies, whether declared or not. The decline of Sweden and the UK as shipbuilding nations is to a large extent a result of limited government interest in an industry perceived as labour intensive and therefore unable to compete with newly industrialised countries in the Far East.

By contrast, the German industry increased its share of the European market through government assistance at both national and state levels, at least until the demise of the Bremer Vulkan group. The extent of the support is becoming more apparent as time passes. In France and Italy, basically uncompetitive industries have been kept afloat in the same manner, until some belated changes in structure and organisation of the industries could finally be made. In other cases, government assistance has been used to restructure and support a programme of performance improvement, as in Spain. It is clear that an industry which falls off the pace has to make a massive and sustained effort over a period of years to be able to regain a competitive position.

In all such cases, without the political support, the industry would not be sustainable, because of the underlying international trend of improvement.

In the former centrally planned economies, shipbuilding has historically been a useful industry for providing hard currency. This situation has not changed substantially in some cases after the moves to market economies. These countries have been able to exploit low labour costs. However, their industries have been generally low performing, and tacit support is often needed to allow them to remain in business. Where a serious restructuring has not been achieved, eventually govern-ment support is likely to fade in favour of more sustainable industries. The decline of the Gdansk shipyard in Poland is one such case.

Industry structure

One of the findings of a 1992 study by KPMG into European competitiveness was that the Japanese structure, where the shipyards are vertically and horizontally integrated into large organisations, was a source of competitive advantage. By contrast the European industry was much more fragmented and the individual companies were vulnerable to the short and medium term instabilities in the market. Even where the European companies were part of a larger industrial grouping, the relatively low financial returns from shipbuilding place it in a weak position when competing for support.

There has been a recent trend in Europe towards larger groupings of shipyards, and in some cases towards increased co-operation. The Kværner Group has expanded into UK and eastern Europe, to take advantage of low labour costs. The Bremer Vulkan group followed a similar course, as well as expanding into related industries, until its demise. The state-owned AESA in Spain and Fincantieri of Italy also try to gain advantage from economies of scale and synergy. The majority of European shipyards are still small and independent, but the trend is towards the larger groups.

THE CURRENT MARKET SITUATION

The current market has, for around 15 years, been dominated by expectations for replacement of the VLCCs built in the 1970s. The unexpected longevity of those large oil tankers failed for a long time to dampen unwarranted expectations of a new peak in ship construction. Market forecasts predicated on their replacement kept many ailing shipbuilders in being, awaiting the boom. More seriously, capacity has even been increased in some areas, notably the Republic of Korea, on the assump-tion that the boom in large tankers was imminent. The availability of shipyards with an unwanted capacity for VLCCs, has led to them building smaller ships, to the detriment of the smaller facilities which also targeted those markets. A cascade effect has spread down through the entire industry, leaving only a few niche markets, where technological and other barriers to new builders limit competition, relatively unaffected.

There is, in simple terms, a serious over-supply in most sectors of the ship-building market. The extent of the over-supply has been estimated by different authorities, and their assessments of the extent of over-supply vary widely. A realistic view is that the world shipbuilding industry is operating at about 85 per cent of capacity. That capacity is around 20 million CGT annually, and with the combina-tion of new facilities coming into full production, and the increases in performance from technological advances, is set to increase further.

Other recent estimates of capacity vary from no more than 16 million CGT (an estimate based largely on past production levels and therefore depending more on the previous market conditions than real capacity) to over 20 million CGT. Capacity is in reality very difficult to measure. Many shipyards have not operated at full capacity in recent years. Some newbuilding shipyards have gone into the shiprepair, and more particularly conversion, market. Others have built different ship types, frequently ships smaller than the capacity of the facilities which are available. Although the annual production between the mid-1980s and mid-1990s has averaged less than at the peak of production in the mid-1970s, the number of shipyards which have been completely closed and are not able to be re-activated is relatively small. There has also, as has been noted, been some greenfield development as well as redevelopment of some existing facilities.

The industry world-wide has also improved its performance, particularly in terms of labour productivity, but also using such measures as the time taken to build a ship. The overall improvement for the pace setters has been close to 4 per cent annually. The effective capacity of those shipyards which are still in business, as well as the new and re-developed yards, has thus increased. Despite closures, the world is capable of building more ships now than has been the case previously. There are some restraints, in some areas of the world more than others. In particular, the quite severe shortage of skilled labour in some areas may be a factor, although training and retraining will be available once a definite increase in the market is apparent. If a real market exists, then shipbuilders are generally sufficiently resourceful to overcome such difficulties, so higher rather than lower estimates of capacity are generally regarded as more realistic.

MODELS OF MARKET DEMAND

A number of factors influence the demand for new ships. In most assessments of the shipbuilding market, these are usually accepted to be:

- replacement of ships scrapped due to age or loss; plus
- additional ships to support growth in world trade; plus (or minus)
- additional ships to support changes in trade patterns;
- new cargoes, new routes, changes in tonne-mile requirements;
- changes in technology in ports or ships.

The assumptions about scrapping of ships vary. In some cases, the assumption is made that ships will have a 25 year life. In terms of market forecasts, this leads to a prediction that previous peaks, and also troughs, in the market demand will be repeated. Other forecasts take different life times for different ship types, and work on a probability of replacement after a number of years. The probability rises as the ships age. However, this also tends to indicate a repetition of previous market cycles.

In reality, the market cycles are more dependent on destabilising factors in the general economy, of which the oil price rises of 1973, and then the early 1980s, are all recent major examples. Over a long time, based on the average ship life, the ships in the world fleet will be replaced, but that is inadequate for use as a predictor of demand.

Models of market demand generally start from an assessment of future world trade, based on economic growth forecasts, which is translated into the demand for shipping. The models make assumptions about the volume of trade to be carried by sea, allowing for the technological and other changes, which lead to an assessment of the future fleet requirements. Recent optimistic growth forecasts, showing long term economic growth in the world, are expected to be scaled down following the recent problems in many Asian economies.

Growth in trade follows a pattern over a long period, but the long term trend masks quite large variations in the short term (over typically two-year periods). Changes in trade patterns are difficult to predict except in the short term, and again are subject to unexpected events in the world.

Technological change is also difficult to predict, whether it affects new types of ship or changes in cargo handling, again except in the short term.

The existing fleet of ships, less those due to be scrapped (and a small allowance for casualties), is available to meet the demand, and the difference between supply and demand gives the future market for newbuildings.

The difficulty for all such forecasts in the last 25 years has been the existing over-supply of shipping to meet trade demands, and the over supply of shipyards to meet the new construction demand. If the difference between supply and demand is negative, rather than positive (that is, there is no real short term demand for new ships), then the world should stop production until the balance is restored. And in theory, shipowners will stop ordering new ships until the fleet has diminished to the point where there is also no more over-supply. In reality, ships have continued to be ordered and built, despite the continuous over-supply of the last 25 years.

In seeking answers to this apparent contradiction, it is necessary to look beyond the basic assumptions of unfettered markets into political and other external factors, and this is done in the next chapter.

SHORT TERM DEMAND

Whilst the models discussed above are looking typically at five to 10-year forecasts, the owner and shipbuilder are also very much interested in the short term demand, looking about two to three years ahead (which is the typical length of the world shipbuilding order book.) In the shorter term, the immediate ordering decision by the shipowner is influenced by more immediate considerations. These include:

freight rates, although the changes in rates occur in cycles which are often much shorter than the lead time for a new ship;

financing terms, where the availability of finance, often provided to support shipbuilders, may well trigger the ordering of new ships, because those ships can then be sold on at a profit;

political imperatives, where the ships are built because the objective of a government is to maintain the local shipbuilding industry, so ships are built irrespective of real, market-driven demand.

More subjectively, a shipowner may purchase a new ship on the expectation of an upturn in the demand for new ships. This may also create an opportunity to sell on a ship, once a position in an order book has been established.

In assessing marine markets, any individual shipbuilding company must also take into account the supply side which is, as indicated earlier, much more difficult to assess. This assessment of the supply depends primarily on an analysis of actual and potential competitors. This requires first a review of the capabilities of all production facilities which might be regarded as competition, to establish which is actual competition. This is then followed by a review of the capacities of those facilities which are capable of making the products which are under consideration, and finally an assessment of the availability of those facilities.

Once the potential supply—in other words, where the competition is coming from—is determined, other factors become important. To a large extent these are technological, since this determines what the shipbuilder can achieve in terms of delivery time, cost and quality. The ability to build ships at low cost, within the short timescales dictated by the current market and to adequate quality, is the outcome of the technological capability.

The other factors are circumstantial, and include location (in some cases), the level of political support and financing availability.

There are many sources of information about the shipbuilding business. A lot of information is available about the existing world fleets. Sources include:

Lloyd's Register of Shipping, which provides information on a regular basis, including fleet size and age statistics, shipbuilding statistics. In addition, the registers contain details of all existing ships, which are updated on a regular basis.

The United Nations is a source of trade statistics, through its various bodies.

The Organisation for Economic Co-operation and Development (OECD) makes regular economic growth forecasts, which are published, and these can form a basis for estimating future trade demand.

Trade associations: a number of the major trade associations in the shipbuilding business commission forecasts, as well as carrying out their own research into future demand. These include:
   — the Confederation of European Shipbuilding Associations (CESA);
   — the Association of Western European Shipbuilders (AWES);
   — the Shipbuilders Association of Japan (SAJ);
   — the Korean Shipbuilders' Association (KSA);

— the Association for the Structural Improvement of Shipbuilding (ASIS);
— the National Shipbuilding Research Program (NSRP), along with the Shipbuilders' Council of America (SCA) and the newer, breakaway American Shipbuilders Association commission work in the USA.

A number of *governments* also study the subject, and produce *ad hoc* reports. *The Commission of the European Union* also commissions reports. These reports have been for various purposes, including identification of the competitiveness of the industry, the relative costs and prices in the Far East and Europe of ship types, and the structure of the industry.

Finally, there are a number of *commercial organisations* which produce regular reports for sale which provide information about both the global and specific markets.

On a cautionary note, there have been a number of market forecasts which have produced diverging views. Most of these follow the outline model structure which was described previously. The reports often reach significantly different conclusions, from the same starting point. Some of the differences may be attributable to the intentions of the sponsors of the research, particularly to justify new or extended facilities. Actual shipbuilding production is usually also different again from any of the forecasts. A forecast based on the average of the forecasts may actually give a reasonable approximation to the true situation, so that some analysis, used with caution, is better than none. Certainly any shipyard is well advised to look at a number of alternative sources for its overall market forecasting requirements.

Given an acceptable (bearing in mind all the limitations of forecasting mentioned above) view of the future market, in the long and short terms, a company must then identify the most appropriate product mix for its capabilities. Factors to be taken into account include:

— The demand for the proposed products, and the competition. The ability to produce a particular ship type and size must be allied to an actual available demand for that type.
— The market price for the products, especially when compared to the company's production costs. It must also be within the capability of the shipyard to compete, primarily on price, with other shipbuilders who may be subsidised in some way. As an example, European shipyards which are capable of building large tankers have more or less withdrawn from that market in view of South Korean competition, which has been seen to be heavily subsidised.
— The product technology and complexity. The demand for ships does not necessarily mean a shipyard can build them successfully. Many shipyards saw fast ferries as a suitable market, and obtained licences to build particular designs, but few yards have actually succeeded in mastering the technology to produce ships economically.

— The company's past experience and ability to manage projects. Moving into a new market, particularly for complex ships, may strain the management resources of a company.
— The delivery and quality requirements. Many shipyards would be keen to build passenger vessels, but the quality of finish required, and the tight delivery schedules which are demanded, would create problems for them.

Other factors are wholly outside the influence of the company, although a view must be taken of their impact. These factors include some which have been referred to, such as exchange rates, interest rates and political influences. The political situation is discussed in subsequent chapters.

One aspect of the current, depressed market for new ships, which is a major concern for all shipbuilders, is that newbuilding prices have remained static or have even in some cases declined in US dollar terms since 1990. Table 5 includes a small selection of the most popular bulk cargo ships. It shows the average ship prices for each period in millions of US$.

Table 5. Typical average ship prices, 1990–1997 ($US millions)

Year	Dry Bulk		Tanker		Container
	70,000 dwt	120,000 dwt	80,000 dwt	250,000 dwt	2,500 teu
1990	30.5	50.0	44.0	90.0	—
1991	34.0	52.0	46.0	93.0	—
1992	30.4	43.8	41.7	86.3	58.5
1993	28.2	40.8	41.0	84.0	47.7
1994	27.2	39.5	42.0	82.0	41.1
1995	28.5	39.9	42.5	83.9	48.9
1996	27.5	38.5	42.0	82.5	48.5
1997	28.0	41.0	42.0	82.5	48.0

While there remains an excess of shipbuilding capacity over demand for new ships, there is unlikely to be a real recovery in the price of new ships. Some specialist markets, where there are real technological barriers to market entry, do provide acceptable prices for the shipbuilder, but these are not common. There may also be short term increases, if shipowners simultaneously believe in a coming market upturn. However, the prognosis at the time of writing is not good.

The forecasting which is needed by those engaged in the shipbuilding business, can be viewed as a hierarchy, in timescale and detail. It is first essential to take a relatively long term view, in order to maintain some long term strategy for the company. This is because the commitment to upgrading or changing facilities locks a company into a relatively long term investment. Even a decision to make other technological or organisational change is a long term decision, in terms of the impact on performance and capability. It is rarely practical to expect to make a significant change in less than one to two years, or to achieve a payback in less than five.

In the medium term, the markets of interest must be studied to identify the general trends and also specific opportunities. Once the facilities and technology have been determined, the focus is on detailed review of the chosen market sector(s). This is the basis for targeted marketing.

In the immediate future, the specific orders which are expected to be placed need to be identified, as a focus for the direct sales effort. The forecasting can then be extended into decisions about any short term facilities to be provided, make and buy decisions and ultimately into the loading on individual parts of the organisation. The forecasting can be summarised as an appropriate mix of:

— long range forecasts;
— medium term forecasts;
— product mix analysis;
— contract build strategies and planning.

There is a wide range of approaches to each forecast, for which the level of detail and rigour varies, along with the research and analysis cost. The perceived value of the analysis, as well as the level of resources available and the most useful point of their application, will determine what is actually done. In some cases, the additional effort associated with the more detailed approach will give an improved forecast, but it is important to take a realistic view of the accuracy of forecasts.

For long-range forecasts of the market, typical approaches are:

Market assessment, which is informally to seek opinions from customers, politicians and others connected with the industry. This approach is not particularly structured, and depends on *ad hoc* contacts with relevant individuals and organisations.

Market intelligence, which includes more formal contacts, including the use of questionnaires to seek information from a wider representative sample of the market players, and direct approaches to brokers and others with information. It is a more pro-active approach, but still depends on the opinions of others.

Market forecasts, which depend on using predictive models based on past market data and trends, and which have been described earlier.

A number of statistical techniques may be used. These include time series analysis and regression analysis, for long term trend analysis. These are based on the assumption that existing trends will continue, but this is dangerous. Instead, demand models may be set up, which try to relate the demand for ships to measurable factors in the economy. Such causal models may use multiple regression techniques, or possibly dynamic simulation. However, all models are only as good as the input assumptions, and these are a problem area. The need to model ship-scrapping is a good example. This is a critical element in many causal models, and a small variation in the assumptions made produces a large variation in the anticipated demand for new ships. Perhaps more critically, the actual scrapping rate may vary again, and have a further influence on new ship orders.

Considerable time and cost are therefore needed to develop the more complex models, which may then not always provide an accurate forecast. Some form of sensitivity analysis is usually performed on the outputs, to try and take account of possible variations in the underlying assumptions or the external forces.

Demand for marine production is, as has been discussed, derived from requirements of ship operators. The approach to forecasting demand is best based on answering three questions:

> *What demand will there be in the future for the services of the ship operators*? For example, how much oil extraction will there be or what volume of container trade can be expected in the future? But the answers to these questions are based on the assumptions about the future of trade, based on the developments of the world economy, and these can be unreliable.
>
> *What is the most efficient means of providing the services, taking into account changes in technology*? An example is the move to floating production systems, FPSOs, for offshore oil production. Another is the increasing use of high speed ferries to replace conventional vessels on some routes.
>
> *How will potential customers react to the expected market changes*? And from that reaction, what ships are they likely to require?

The market is about the balance of demand and supply. In the long run, markets should establish equilibrium, although the long term in the marine markets has been 25 years with no equilibrium yet. In marine production, the timescales for supply to react to market changes, which may require new or re-opened facilities, are longer than the timescales over which demand change, e.g. oil prices, rose rapidly at the time of the 1991 Gulf War, but fell again rapidly.

The demand is the requirement for new ships to be built, and it takes into account a number of factors, the most significant of which can be listed:

— the size and age of the current fleet, which indicate the current and future supply of ships to carry the trade requirements of the world;

— the expectations about trade growth, commodity values, freight rates, all based on some underlying assumptions about the growth in economic activity;

— shiprepair costs and capacities, changes in regulations, the scrap values for the older ships;

— technological changes which may encourage new demand, for example the size increases in container ships.

Supply is the current capacity of the shipbuilding industry to provide the ships which the model indicates are required in the forecast period.

THE OUTCOMES OF FORECASTING

It is instructive to make comparisons between the forecast and actual production levels in recent years. Many organisations produce demand forecasts for the shipbuilding industry, but the actual outcome is often very different. Figure 1 shows a comparison between some past forecasts and the actual production levels in the years immediately following the forecasts.

The data for Japanese shipbuilding have been plotted on the combined graph in Figure 1. This shows the actual production levels from 1975 to 1985, and subsequently extended to the end of 1993. These are shown against the forecasts which were made in 1985, 1988 and 1992.

In 1985, the forecast was for a relatively rapid upturn from the low point in 1987. Note that the production level in 1987 fell below the previous troughs in 1979 and 1983. This upturn was then predicted to peak in the early 1990s, at around five million CGT annually. This fits with the capacity of 5.6 million CGT, and the Japanese utilisation of 90 per cent of capacity.

Actual production in 1986 and 1987 was close to prediction (order books for shipyards are typically for a two-year period) but in 1988 production fell short of the forecast, and a revised forecast to the year 2000 shows a much more pessimistic outlook.

The difference in total between the two forecasts, between 1988 and 2000, is some 10 million CGT, or 0.75 million CGT annually over the period.

From 1989 to 1992, actual production recovered to a point midway between the two forecasts. A 1992 forecast shows a revised future production, which reduces the predicted shortfall by about half. The overall production is then predicted to peak at around five million CGT again, but the timing of the peak is five years behind the 1985 prediction.

In terms of overall ship demand, this difference would be explained by an increase in the life expectancy for large tankers of 25 years as against 20 years, with corresponding changes for other ship types. Forecasts in the late 1980s, and early 1990s were very much based on optimistic (from a shipbuilder's viewpoint) assumption of early scrapping for many of the 1970s-built VLCCs.

Looking at recent production and order book levels for 1993, the expectation was that the production for 1994 and 1995 would exceed the then current forecasts. When reviewed against the overall demand for ships, that implied that the peak predicted for 1998 and 1999 would not be as high as expected, but that production levels would instead be more consistent. This was because some of the ships which were to be built as replacements were actually built before the older ships were scrapped. In effect, some of the predicted peak of production was built early, perhaps as speculation, perhaps to ensure that owners had berths booked.

One definite effect of the predicted boom in orders was the increase in ship construction capacity in South Korea. This has had the effect of increasing capacity, and filling that capacity has influenced the market by bringing orders forward and

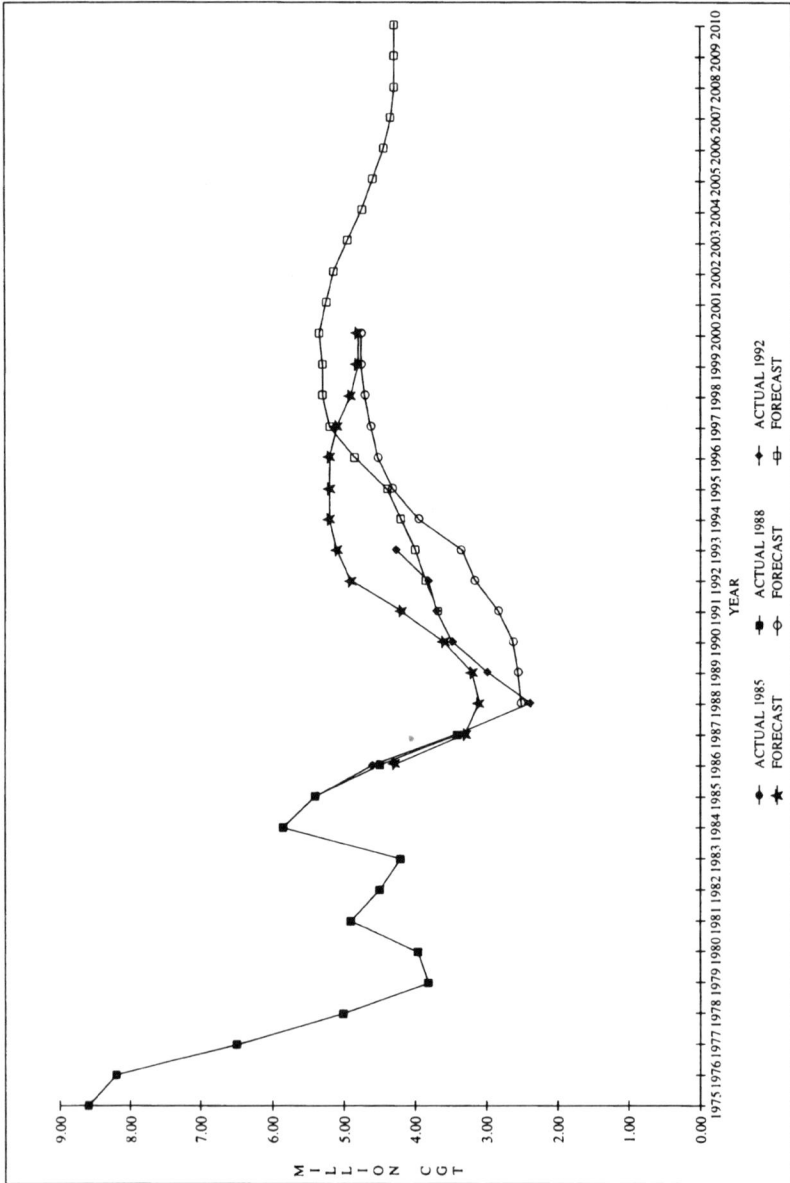

Figure 1. Past forecasts and actual production levels (comparisons)

reducing prices. That influence has perhaps also had the effect of reducing the size of the peak which was used to justify the expansion.

Ship demolition

Ship demolition—shipbreaking—has been referred to, and it is an important element in the market equation. Because all of the forecasts use demolition as their most important indicator of future demand, this aspect of forecasting is briefly discussed in this section. All forecasts make a number of key assumptions about ship scrapping and the validity of these is reviewed.

Demand for new ships is primarily based on the replacement of ships which reach the end of their useful life and are then demolished. This presupposes that the life expectancy of ships can be predicted, and also that there is a market for scrap. However, ship life is calculated differently by different forecasters, and this can have a large influence on the levels of future demand which are predicted. Also, at the end of its life, a ship's final owner will base his decision whether to continue trading partly on the ship's scrap value. If the ship can be disposed of for a reasonable sum, then it will be scrapped, but in a poor scrap market it may be more economic to continue trading, especially as there are only direct running costs and routine repairs to be considered.

The simplest assumption about scrapping is to give all ships a 25 year life. In the longer term, this is not unreasonable, but short term variations due to changes in scrapping and shipping markets can result in large short term variations in actual scrapping. These influence freight rates and thus affect the demand for new ships.

Other forecasters use a range of life expectancies, based on some analysis of the past life expectancies of different ship types.

It is also possible to make a much more detailed analysis, based on the probability of ships of different types and sizes reaching different ages. Curves showing survival rates are developed, and these are then used to predict the numbers of ships which will require replacement. However, any of these approaches can result in a larger than realistic demand, if they assume shorter lives for ships than is really the case.

During the late 1980s, life expectancies for VLCCs in particular were believed to be significantly shorter than for other types, and figures as low as 15 or 18 years were quoted on occasion. More recently 20 years was seen as a cut-off point. By the early 1990s, VLCCs were being sold for demolition at an average of 21 years. Later ships were being seen passing fifth special surveys.

The changes in forecasts, as shown in the analysis above, which compares forecasts with actual production, can largely be explained by changing assumptions about ship life expectancy. In simple terms, the life of large tankers is now expected to be nearer 25 years than 20 years, and the predicted peak in new tanker orders (the main driver for new ship demand) is now forecast to be later, around the year 2000 rather than 1995. However, once again it is important to point out that the excess capacity in the world shipbuilding business, coupled with a reduction in scrapping if an upturn in shipping markets is anticipated, has resulted in production running ahead of the predicted boom.

There are a number of other aspects of ship demolition that should be addressed. These can be summarised as:

— the capacity of the demolition "industry";
— the demand for the scrap steel;
— the need to differentiate between shipowners—the owners who scrap ships are not generally the owners who order new tonnage.

The rather mechanical approach to replacement in some forecasts assumes that ships are more or less automatically scrapped when they reach the appropriate age. However, this ignores the current over-supply of ships in most categories, which has been characteristic of shipping since the mid-1970s and is forecast, even on the most optimistic forecasts, to remain for several years.

Ships are being built by owners who require new ships to match changing trade patterns. Large container ships, gas carriers and passenger vessels have been the three key growth areas in the 1990s, where changes in trading, ship size and technology combine to create new demand.

In the case of tankers and other bulk ships, new tonnage is acquired by owners who operate large, modern fleets (including those who consider it to be necessary to comply with changes in regulation, in particular those required by OPA 90). There are also new ships acquired on a speculative basis, or because of low prices, typically from the re-emerging shipbuilders of the former Soviet bloc.

These groups are ensuring a steady supply of new tonnage, which is to replace or expand their existing tonnage, and is in many senses independent of any global replacement requirements.

The owners who scrap ships are generally second, third or later owners, who have acquired the ship at a relatively late stage in its life. They typically operate to lower standards, on spot or voyage markets rather than on time-charters, and will expect to sell the ship on at a favourable time. They will often scrap the vessel as it approaches a special survey, to avoid the large repair expense which can be anticipated (although more owners have taken to repairing older ships, because the repair costs prove to be lower than the cost of replacement with a new, or newer second-hand, ship).

At the present time, indeed for a number of years, the ship demolition market has been very poor.

There has been a steady increase in the numbers of old ships since the 1980s. The number of ships over 15 years old rose from 194 million grt in 1991 to 210 million grt in 1992. However, the numbers scrapped have been small, dropping from a peak in the mid-1980s of some 22 million grt. As a result, the age of the world fleet is continuing to increase, an outcome which was not considered as a possibility until it occurred.

The numbers scrapped in recent years have been as follows, compared with predictions based on ship ages and assumptions outlined above:

Table 6. Comparison of actual and expected scrapping, 1990–2000

Year	Millions dwt (Actual)	Various Forecasts		
1990	4.7	23.2	–	–
1991	7.0	25.3	17.6	–
1992	16.0	25.3	17.6	16.6
1993	17.3	25.3	17.6	16.6
1994	19.2	25.3	17.6	16.6
1995	15.5	25.3	17.6	16.6
1996	15.8	26.9	26.3	16.6
1997	16.8	26.9	26.3	43.2
1998	–	26.9	26.3	43.2
1999	–	26.9	26.3	43.2
2000	–	26.9	26.3	43.2

The very low levels in 1990–1991 reflect the rise in new ship prices at that time, and the effects of the Gulf crisis. Generally, the level has been below that forecast by the various organisations. It is in particular well below the levels forecast for the early 1990s, which fact demonstrates the longer-than-expected life of many ships.

It is clear that there is a large tonnage, if anything an increasing tonnage, which will reach the end of its useful life during the next few years. Countries which have been active in ship demolition, with their share of the 1995 market (in terms of ship numbers and tonnes dwt) are:

Table 7. Main nations engaged in ship scrapping

Country	Ship Numbers	Tonnes dwt
India	36%	18.0%
China	27%	22.0%
Pakistan	12%	26.0%
Bangladesh	13%	19.0%
Turkey	1%	0.5%

A few others carry out occasional work, but the five have been responsible for most, although Turkey has almost ceased shipbreaking activity. The capacity in the world is elastic, and depends very much on the available demand for scrap steel at an acceptable price. The annual scrapping capacity has been estimated at around 10 million grt (19.5 million dwt). This was adequate for past levels of activity, but is only about half that required for the forecast demolition levels for the next few years. The potential total capacity is up to some 20 million grt, which would cope with the forecast demand for the service, but the expansion is dependent on a demand for the scrap steel product. The peak for ship scrapping occurred in the 1980s, when a maximum of some 22 million grt of shipping was disposed of in one year.

The high proportion of VLCCs in the increase would also pose a problem, since these vary large ships are difficult both technically to dispose of and also generate a large quantity of scrap for which a market must be found.

The scrap steel from ship demolition is regarded as inferior, and usable only for reinforcement bars for civil engineering, and other less critical products. It is also in competition with conventional sources of material, and there is an over-capacity in world steel production.

Overall, the position of the demolition industry may influence the scrapping rate, through the value which is placed on the oldest ships in the fleet. This is expected to inhibit the demolition of those ships. A proportion of old ships will therefore continue trading, until environmental and other regulations positively prevent them from doing so. This will maintain an over-supply, particularly in the tanker market, which will have the effect of some dampening demand for new tonnage and restricting the forecast boom in new orders.

The impact of the low scrapping levels on the newbuilding market, and more particularly on the fleet size, is significant. All the main newbuilding forecasts which have been produced rely primarily on ship scrapping as the means of determining new demand, as mentioned previously, based on the assumption of straightforward replacement of old tonnage. The forecasts generally work on five-year periods, within which actual orders may fluctuate, and there is indeed no sound basis for developing a medium term year by year requirement. The short term fluctuations in the market determine actual ordering. The outcome of limited scrapping, coupled with increases in capacity which must be filled with orders, has been both an increase in the world fleet size beyond actual, or predicted, requirements, and an increase in the average age of the ships which make up that fleet.

It can be argued that the desire of Japan and Korea in particular to maintain continuity of production will have a smoothing effect, in that although orders may be placed in peaks and troughs, actual production will be relatively steady.

One common assumption in almost all forecasts of future demand for new ships is that, over a period of years, the demand and supply of ships are assumed to converge, so that the current fleet is gradually replaced by a new one which more nearly corresponds to transport needs. Over the life of the typical ship, therefore, the forecasts will reach a total which corresponds to the total fleet requirement for transport. This will depend on the economic growth and trading assumptions built into the particular forecast.

In practice, there is a very wide range of forecasts for the future newbuilding requirements. The differences are primarily due to differences in scrapping assumptions, so that the long term newbuilding requirements are much the same. However, in the medium term there is typically a time lag of two years between highest and lowest forecast outcomes reflecting different scrapping in the early years. The impact of relatively small variations in scrapping assumptions is equivalent to two years' annual production for the world's shipbuilding businesses.

If ship scrapping forecasts are compared with the actual figures over a period of years, the outcome typically fluctuates around the mean of the forecasts. Assumptions that supply and demand for ships would move towards balance relatively quickly have not materialised.

If an overall view of the forecast market for the industry is required, it is that the recent upsurge in orders, which has had the effect of maintaining the supply/demand imbalance, will result in there being no real boom in new building. Allied to the shortage of scrapping capacity, low prices both for scrap ships and for new ones, and the recent increases in world shipbuilding capacity, the result will be no more than a modest increase in new building. However, this will be absorbed by the new capacity, particularly in Korea, and there will be minimal impact on the fortunes of the shipbuilding industry.

Ship scrapping is a major element in the shipbuilding market, and some of the factors which affect scrapping are reviewed here. In particular, the capacity of the ship scrapping industry is critical, and a number of major considerations can be taken into account. These are:

The demand for steel. There is plenty of capacity in the world for new steel, and two fundamental problems with the recycled material. First, the re-rolled steel is cheaper than new steel, but is generally recognised as being of inferior quality to newly rolled steel. Secondly, ship scrapping is not a universally recognised source of the material.

Figures for past peak periods, which give an indicator of the industry capacity. Ship demolition is very basic in its methods, being almost entirely based on low cost labour, working on a beach. A number of proposals have been developed in the past for high technology scrapping, in effect a reversal of the construction process, but in reality the cost of the facilities is too great for the potential value of the product.

Domestic demand for rerolled steel. The steel which is produced is of low quality, and has very limited use once it has been recycled. Its primary use is in reinforcing bars for building construction. Domestic demand is important, because any use outside the country of demolition would be in competition with new steel supplies.

The number of suitable sites. These are essentially the sites that already exist, or have been used in the recent past. There is a supply of labour and the many sites exist so there is possibility of expansion in scrapping capacity. On the other hand, the value of the business is small, and the demand for the product is limited. This is reflected in scrap ship prices, which have been low for a number of years. The main nations involved in ship scrapping, China, India and Pakistan, all use the shore method of beaching vessels.

Productivity. As has been indicated, the process is labour intensive, and uses the most basic technology. The facilities required are no more than a suitable beach, with a reasonable tidal range, and access to basic steel processing for the re-melting of the recovered scrap. Productivity is very low, but without investment in some form of plant and equipment, there is no real means of improving the productivity. This is a limitation on scrapping capacity.

As an example of the productivity question, during the 1980s Korea and Taiwan could scrap a VLCC in something of the order of 25 to 30 days. In those areas currently engaged in ship scrapping, this process of completely dismantling a VLCC can take anywhere between six months and one year. The variation depends on the speed with which the large quantity of steel can be disposed of locally, and the actual productivity of the site. Raising the skill level of the workforce and also worker numbers could reduce this to three months. This would require no new facilities, but would still not increase the absolute capacity of the scrapping industry beyond previous levels, leaving a shortfall when set against the expected demand for scrapping of the very old ships in the world fleet.

The financial capability of the scrapping industry is important. There must be availability of ships to be scrapped for the industry to operate at all. The limited scrapping in the mid-1990s led to some stagnation, which inhibited any possibility of expansion in the last few years to meet anticipated demand.

Fluctuations in price exist so the profitability of the operation is very uncertain. The value of the scrap is such that a limited quantity only can be disposed of to maintain a reasonable price. A low price for the ships inhibits the scrapping decision by the shipowner, and the overall uncertainty about profitability causes a contraction in the market.

Effective capacity is estimated at, and expected to remain at, around 10 million grt *per annum*. During the period of scrapping of the majority of the large numbers of VLCCs built between 1974 and 1976, the scrapping volume is expected to reach 20 million grt *per annum*. When this period will be is a complex question. It had been assumed that it would fall in the mid-1990s, coinciding with a 20-year life, a special survey and some need to update in line with anti-pollution legislation. In fact, many of the ships have been through the fourth special survey, leading to a new estimate of a 25-year life.

Various estimates have been made of the volume of shipping which will be required to be scrapped, based on some estimate of the life of the ships. For five year periods, the consensus on volumes in gross tons was:

To 1995	10.9 million,
1996–2000	18.6 million,
2001–2005	15.9 million,
2006–2010	13.2 million.

With some ships being scrapped, and others continuing in service, the trend is to a longer average life, but with the effect of lowering the peak of scrapping.

CHAPTER 2

POLITICAL INFLUENCES ON SHIPBUILDING

WHY POLITICS MATTER IN THE SHIPBUILDING BUSINESS

In the market conditions that have existed for the last quarter of a century, political influences have played an increasingly important role in the shipbuilding business. The immediate reaction of most governments with a shipbuilding industry after the 1973 oil price increases was to offer support to the industry. This was done on the initial assumption that such support would be only a short term measure, until the problems caused by oil price increases were resolved. At the time, a number of governments were encouraging the development of new shipbuilding facilities, as a catalyst for industrialisation. The Republic of South Korea was the leading nation in this area at that time (and has continued to develop the shipbuilding industry ever since). Other countries which had embarked on an expansion of shipbuilding at the time included Taiwan, with a major shipyard at Kaohsiung, and Brazil. A number of other countries, including Iran, also saw shipbuilding as a sound basic industry on which to base development plans.

Even after the initial "oil shock" had subsided, some of the changes remained in place. In particular, the price of oil was expected to remain high, which resulted in serious inflationary and other pressures. These began to have a serious effect on the shipping industry, lowering freight rates and leaving an increasing number of effectively unwanted ships laid up. Despite these effects, a number of governments continued to pursue the ideal of shipbuilding as a leader in industrialisation. In part, the problem was compounded by the sheer scale of a major shipyard development. Apart from the sums of money already committed in some cases, the long term nature of the construction projects also made it difficult to stop. In addition, optimism about the future, that in the longer term the industry would stabilise and demand for ships would recover, played a part.

That shipbuilding is a sound industry on which to base a programme of industrialisation is not to be disputed. However, in reality (and even without the impact of increased oil prices) many countries were pursuing the same potential market. The ability to capture a share of a market where supply outstrips demand is a very daunting task, the extent of which was not fully realised in many countries at the time.

Apart from the drive in some areas to develop new shipyards, political influence has been a factor in several other aspects of shipbuilding, often in a different form in different regions.

In Europe, there has primarily been support for the industry to maintain employment. Immediately after the oil crisis, countries began to make provisions to support their shipbuilding business. The shipbuilding crisis lagged behind the oil price increase by around two years, as ships continued to be completed. Shipyards became effectively insolvent over a period, as orders were cancelled, or later as new orders could not be found. Solutions varied from nationalisation in the United Kingdom, delayed until 1978, through subsidies for private shipyards to the decision in Sweden, again taken after a delay, that mainstream shipbuilding could not be sustained in a high wage economy when prices were too low.

Support for marine production as a vehicle for industrial development, as noted above, has been predominant in Korea and China, with qualified success, and also in Latin America, with a lack of success. As also noted, the assumption that any one nation could secure a large market share was misguided. The exception was apparently South Korea until 1997, when the financial consequences of securing market share by simply building ships below cost were finally revealed.

The United States of America had only been a marginal builder of ships since 1945, except for specialised and local trades. Indeed, the USA had been a major user of subsidies for most of the intervening period. After the 1970s, the USA more or less disappeared from the international shipbuilding business. It re-emerged in the mid 1990s, as the realities of the end of the Cold War became apparent, and the flow of military ship orders which had sustained a large industry began to dry up. Government support had financed a vigorous research and development programme, and was now offered for the purposes of converting shipyards from military to commercial construction. This was partly in the belief that changes in relative wage levels could make the USA competitive, and also to be sure of maintaining a large-scale shipbuilding capacity against future military requirements.

In all cases, the political input has either increased or, at minimum, maintained the marine production capability of the world. This has been at a level which the demand for ships could not sustain. The current state of development of political influences dates from 1973.

AN HISTORICAL PERSPECTIVE

While the events of 1973 started the current problems of the shipbuilding industry, they were compounded by later oil price increases. The worst position was reached in shipbuilding in the early 1980s, particularly in 1984, when orders reached their lowest point.

It is important to state that although the events of the last 25 years have seen a major subsidy programme throughout the world, such political influence is not new. Economic depressions in the world, or in parts of the world, happen typically about every 50 years. In the United Kingdom, then the leading economy, there was a severe depression in the 1830s. There was a further case in the 1880s, which affected a wider area as more countries were developed, and more recently in the 1930s. In these previous economic depressions, it was largely politics that dictated whether industries in different countries survived. As an example, the UK industry suffered a dramatic reduction in its shipbuilding in the major depression of the 1930s, whereas most other nations protected their newer industries. In better times, politics also play a part. Japan used shipbuilding as the lead industry to rebuild industrial capacity in the 1950s. The rapid rise in oil prices in 1973 and subsequent turbulence led to more political influence than previously this century.

↑ In historical descriptions of shipbuilding and shipowning, subsidies are seen to be common. Many voyages of exploration were funded by rich private patrons, in the expectation of a share of substantial profits. This could truly be described as venture capitalism, as ships sailed over the horizon and might not be seen for years, if at all. The backers could make a fortune or lose all their investment.

But much of the exploration was also subsidised by government patrons. These voyages were intended to find and exploit natural resources, or to secure new trades. More recently, the development of fast passenger vessels, and in particular those for the transatlantic routes, was subsidised by means of mail contracts. Other ships were built with some provision for use as military auxiliaries, either as cruisers or troopships. Even the Royal Yacht, recently taken out of service and not replaced, was built under the polite fiction that it would have a potential wartime role as a hospital ship.

The need to maintain a shipbuilding capacity in case of war ensured subsidies in mediaeval Venice, during the centuries when that nation-state was dominant in maritime affairs in the Mediterranean. In order to maintain a fleet, both for trade and against the possibility of war, the state intervened. At some times, foreigners were forbidden to build ships for Venice, even if their prices were lower, which could often be the case, thus favouring the local shipyards. When this resulted in under-production—because there was no immediate demand for new ships—the state offered bounties for new construction. These were paid against ships constructed within a specified timescale. By 1533, there was a consistent policy of subsidising the construction of large ships in Venice.

In the longer term, the policy of subsidising private shipyards did not actually provide enough ships for the government's requirements, and they were then bought from foreign suppliers. The famous Arsenale, which was state owned and managed, became more and more important as the only means of providing and maintaining the fleet, which was required to be available for military purposes.

EUROPEAN SUBSIDIES

In the 1980s, some governments were providing large subsidies to shipbuilders. The competition directorate of the European Union (DG IV) recognised that subsidies were merely perpetuating surplus capacity at a very high cost. It therefore issued a Directive to manage the subsidies which could be offered. The intention was, first, to formalise the use of subsidies so that they could be controlled; secondly, to set standard subsidy rules which would have the effect of promoting fair competition between the Member States.

The long term objectives were to phase out subsidies entirely. In the process, there would be major restructuring of the industry in Europe, to leave fewer, more competitive shipyards.

To underpin the Directive, DG IV commissioned an annual study to allow a comparison to be made between the costs of constructing ships in Europe and the prices for which ships could be bought in the Far East. The European industry conducted its own study, and supplied evidence of ship prices below cost from some Far East suppliers.

Both studies used a similar methodology. First, they developed outline specifications for a number of agreed ship types. These could then be used to identify market prices, by seeking quotations and by study of the market. The specifications could also be used to seek cost quotations from European shipyards, for comparison purposes. The prices and costs were adjusted, to make allowance for financing packages and also to work to common dates to avoid inflation and other currency distortions.

The assessed cost–price gap was up to 30 per cent in the worst year. It decreased until 1994, when subsidies were expected to be phased out. The gap has since re-emerged, and subsidies will continue to the year 2000. Table 8 gives information from an earlier study, but is useful to illustrate the differentials which existed. It also gives evidence of the extent to which subsidies in overt or covert form existed in the Far East. Quite simply, the differences between prices and costs are not explainable in any other way. Table 8 also illustrates the relative advantage the European industry had in the more complex ship types.

Table 8. The gap between ship prices and costs (early 1990s)

Ship type and size	market price	adjusted market price	lowest quotation	lowest gap
Suezmax tanker	51.00	54.70	70.10	22.1%
3800TEU Container	50.00	53.60	80.80	33.7%
Panamax Bulker	27.00	28.90	36.50	20.7%
Day Ferry	72.00	77.20	80.00	3.5%
Chemical tanker	32.00	34.30	33.00	−3.8%
Multi-purpose 4200	8.00	8.40	8.70	2.9%

THE OECD AGREEMENT

There has for many years been a strong lobby from some nations to eliminate shipbuilding subsidies. The lobbyists have believed, in some cases rather naïvely, that they have some competitive advantage. Alternatively, the lobbyists may have had a more sophisticated, or less detectable, form of subsidy.

In Denmark, the efficiency of the industry was seen as providing the competitive edge, although the ownership or close relationship between major shipowners and shipyards played a part.

In the United States of America a belief grew in the late 1980s that their now competitive labour costs would give an advantage. As a result, the Shipbuilders' Council of America lobbied for many years with the Organisation for Economic Co-operation and Development (OECD) to phase out shipbuilding subsidies.

As a result of the lobbying and a general weariness of governments with the costs of the subsidies, an agreement was reached to phase out subsidies from the start of 1996. However, the agreement was never implemented.

By 1995, the larger United States shipbuilders had realised they were not competitive after all. (The reality of this has been emphasised by the decision, announced in early 1998, of Newport News to withdraw from the commercial shipbuilding market after sustaining heavy losses on its programme of *Double Eagle* tankers.) The larger United States builders then broke away from the Shipbuilders' Council, reversed their previous lobbying and delayed the agreement.

The United States also has a massive programme of investment and research to try to bring its performance in shipbuilding up to the best world standards.

Japan also delayed ratification of the agreement, leaving only South Korea and the European Union agreeing to ratify the new OECD rules. As a result, the agreement was not signed, and the process then ran into the US elections of 1996.

European Union subsidies were then scheduled to continue until the end of 1997. However, the continuing failure to agree on the removal of subsidies by the USA has resulted in a delay until the year 2000. Nevertheless, the Commission of the European Union has determined to stop the current subsidy regime at that time.

THE EXCESS OF SHIPBUILDING CAPACITY OVER DEMAND

The fundamental cause of the current industry position is the excess capacity, which has been caused by the failure (in some quarters it might be regarded as a success) of the industry to adjust sufficiently to the reduced demand for new ships. The dangers which were perceived by various governments to be inherent in localised loss of employment are one factor. A reaction to over-optimistic market forecasts is another, with shipbuilding industries and governments convincing themselves that the market upturn was due in another two years. Finally, there was, and still is, a strong reluctance to reduce capacity until someone else goes first. All of these dangers have contributed to an over-capacity in the shipbuilding business which has now endured for a quarter of a century.

Although the two major rises in oil prices, in 1973 and 1981, are largely blamed for the capacity crisis, the reality is that it would have occurred in a few years in any case. The 100 or so docks built, or converted to suit the VLCC and large bulk carrier market, eventually had the capacity to replace more or less the entire large ship fleet (those over 100,000 deadweight tonnes) at least every 10 years. And it is certain that the market for the large ships would have been saturated by 1980 at the latest.

Nevertheless, there has been a serious effort in some parts of the world to reduce capacity. This can be illustrated most readily by considering the total numbers employed in the industry over the period under consideration. Considering major shipbuilding regions, the total workforces have changed as shown in Table 9 below. There has been a major reduction in the AWES countries, a more modest but still substantial reduction in Japan, but in Korea there has been expansion, from a modest industry in 1975 to a major supplier of ships in the late 1990s. The USA has retained a relatively static workforce, demonstrating in some ways its relative independence from the international marketplace and high dependence on military ship construction.

Table 9. Shipbuilding employment in certain regions

Region	1975	1995
AWES	462,000	90,000
Japan	361,000	130,000 (includes sub-contractors)
South Korea	10,000	50,000
USA	100,000	100,000

ESTIMATES OF WORLD SHIPBUILDING CAPACITY

Given the improvements in labour productivity which can be identified in world shipbuilding over the period in question, it will be apparent that labour force is not an adequate measure of shipbuilding capacity. The alternative is to use compensated gross tonnes (CGT), as discussed in the first chapter. As an estimate of capacity, rather than a measure of production, estimates even using this measure do vary considerably. However, the figures provided by AWES can be regarded as reasonably reliable.

In 1975, the effects of the dramatic decline in ship orders were only just beginning to emerge, so the capacity surplus is relatively modest. Capacity reductions then lag behind the reduced demand, producing large surpluses. As the market begins to recover in the 1990s, the shipbuilding industry in the world anticipated the increase in demand, so the capacity began to increase ahead of the market. See Table 10.

Table 10. Estimated world capacity in CGT

Year	Shipbuilding Capacity	Production	Surplus
1975	22.4	20.5	9%
1980	17.8	13.5	32%
1985	17.2	14.2	21%
1990	15.0	11.6	29%
1995	17.5	14.3	22%
2000	20.8	16.0	30%

It is clear that there was a significant reduction in shipbuilding capacity. Some of this was managed, notably in Europe and Japan, and equally some of the reduction resulted from spectacular collapses of shipbuilding companies.

Only the most optimistic of market forecasts foresee demand and supply going into balance. The Korean expansion of the mid-1990s was based precisely on such optimistic forecasts. These anticipated a much greater demand for new ships, primarily to replace ageing VLCCs from the 1970s by the time they reached 20 years old. The forecasts were far more optimistic than Japanese, or particularly AWES, forecasts.

It is probable that shipbuilding capacity will continue to exceed demand into the future. As a result of this, continuing political influence is inevitable.

GOVERNMENT SUPPORT MEASURES

The support which is offered to shipyards takes various forms. These vary from the subtle, and sometimes more or less undetectable, to the very obvious.

In the latter category are such measures as market protection. This quite simply does not allow the construction of ships for domestic owners or trade to be built in any other country. This is the basis of the policy in the United States under the Jones Act. Its effect has been to drive United States shipowners offshore, to build ships only where a military input was available or simply not to bother. In earlier times, the more or less equivalent Navigation Acts, enforced by the United Kingdom for trade with its colonies, was a primary factor in the American revolution.

The same basic rules were also applied, as has been described, in the Venice of the fifteenth century. In all cases, the raw protectionism has not been a long term success.

A more subtle measure is the use of favourable tax treatment, again generally aimed at the shipowner, rather than the builder. However, the tax breaks are generally tied to domestic construction. The many container ships built in Germany in the 1990s were largely due to this type of measure. Numerous middle-class Germans were encouraged to invest their savings in the construction of ships, by use of tax advantages.

An increasingly popular form of support, notably in the large current programme of work in the United States of America, is investment in performance improvement and in research and development in recent years. Japan also uses this approach. Remarkably large sums can be channelled in this way, but are not really "subsidies", at least in the opinions of the givers and recipients. This is much more subtle than direct production assistance, which is the most basic form of subsidy. It may be hedged about by rules, such as those drawn up by the EU, but basically it provides a direct subsidy to cover the gap between production cost and market price.

Export credit assistance is a favoured means of support to shipbuilders. This provides guarantees against commercial loans, in effect underwriting the risk of a commercial bank lending to an overseas shipowner. In some cases, the government may provide direct credit, although this is rare. This type of assistance is governed by OECD rules, which stipulate that the loan is limited to 80 per cent of the purchase price, that it should be repaid in eight years and that capital repayment is in equal, half-yearly instalments. The interest rate varies, but is a commercial rate. Security is in the form of a first mortgage on the ship.

Many variations of the basic OECD scheme have been used. There may be a two- or three-year moratorium on repayments, which effectively ensures that the ship is trading before repayments begin. In some cases, the financing is remarkably generous. Again, the United States of America seems to offer the lead, with its "Title XI" finance, which gives low interest credit over a period up to 25 years. This is crucial in securing commercial orders against overseas competition.

Other subsidies are given in the form of direct assistance to the customers of the shipyard, the shipowners. These are generally tied to domestic owners, with the provision that the ships are built in the country's shipyards. They can take the form of direct aid, home credit schemes or especially favourable tax treatment, for example in the form of accelerated depreciation or carry-back arrangements.

All the forms of support are basically designed to encourage the production of ships, in a market which by definition is not encouraging such production for normal, commercial reasons. Their effect has been to stimulate over-production, and to retain capacity which would otherwise not be able to continue. All, or almost all, governments would wish to stop the use of subsidies, which are a direct subvention from the taxpayer to the shipbuilding business. However, few have done so, being unwilling to accept the situation that other governments will hang on to subsidies just a little longer until their shipyards are the only ones left in operation.

The Swedish government made this harsh decision a long time ago, but others have not been willing to follow that lead. The United Kingdom government of the 1980s inherited a recently nationalised industry. It neither fully supported it, nor pulled the plug, and the result was a slow demise for many of the shipyards. But few governments, heavily lobbied by their shipbuilders and regions, would be prepared to rely on others to play by the rules. Most shipbuilders would like their own particular system to continue, not indefinitely but for a short time, while of course all other nations cease subsidies and other support immediately.

As a result, instead of an international agreement to let the market rule, the subsidies continue.

The continuing support does have consequences. These are seen in the distortion of the market, and particularly in the massive shares built up in Japan and Korea.

It is unrealistic to try to argue that the Japanese shipbuilding industry is the leading builder of relatively standard ships for any other reason than that it is the most efficient producer by a large margin. But if the massive fluctuations of the yen in recent years are taken into consideration, it is apparent that other factors are also supporting this market dominance.

Japan has for many years had a home credit scheme for domestically built ships, which actively supports domestic builders and places barriers in the way of overseas competition. There are also cross-shareholdings between owners, builders and banks, overseen by the government, which also place barriers in the way of other shipbuilding nations. Non-tariff barriers do play an important role in some cases, and Japan is one of them. So is South Korea, and it would be almost unimaginable for an owner in either of these countries to place an overseas order.

The consequence is that of the total of Japanese-owned ships built over a particular three-year period, of 7,534,000 compensated gross tonnes, a mere 5,000 CGT, representing a single ship, was constructed in the European Union.

Korea has a similar approach. There are, for a start, specific government controls on purchase of ships, which provide a non-tariff barrier to overseas competition for Korean shipowner contracts. As in the case of Japan, there are very strong financial links between shipowners, banks and builders. The result in terms of Korean-owned ships is also similar to Japan. Of the total Korean-owned ships built in the same three-year period, of 1,284,000 compensated gross tonnes, none was built in the European Union.

At the start of this chapter, it was noted that state support for shipbuilding and shipowning is not a new phenomenon. Indeed a detailed study of the business through many centuries will reveal that such support has frequently been the normal state of affairs. The emergence of any market leader in the business of shipbuilding (and there has generally been a dominant producer, either on the basis of low cost or technological superiority) has always been followed by state support in competitor nations. As the leader has been overtaken, there has usually been some government support to try to stem the decline. In the interim period, as the battle for market share between the leaders takes place, support is one of the tactics in use. Other builders have to follow the same path or their small industry will simply be swamped in a price war.

Having outlined at least some of the ways in which shipbuilders are supported, it is worth mentioning in passing that the support given is modest compared to aerospace, as that industry has gradually resolved its structure into two major players for the large jet market. The parallels are remarkable. And support for shipbuilding pales into insignificance beside the money put into agriculture on a world-wide basis.

The motivation for using subsidies and other forms of support to the business of shipbuilding has frequently been political, whether to maintain a shipbuilding capability, for trade or military purposes, or to develop the industry. The business of shipbuilding has always been subject to major external influences, because of the global nature of shipping in general and its importance in trade, military and political affairs. The political dimension is arguably the most important in the present climate, but the others are discussed in the next chapter.

CHAPTER 3

OTHER EXTERNAL INFLUENCES

"STEP" FACTORS INFLUENCING SHIPBUILDING

Social, technological, economic and political factors (often described as "STEP" factors) form the environment in which shipbuilding, like any other business, must operate.

The political climate in which the shipbuilding business operates is the main external influence. In simple terms, if the political climate in a country is not supportive, the shipbuilding industry in that country cannot possibly survive. However, the external environment in which business operates is usually considered to have four main domains. These are the political domain, which has already been considered and, in addition, economic, social and technological domains. The environment, in the "green" sense, can be considered as a special case, and is considered independently later in this chapter.

Technology is the basis of the shipbuilding business, and the continuous developments in technology which have their origins in, or are readily transferable to, the shipbuilding business are the subject of much of this book. The industry is making continuous technological changes, with the technological leaders being those companies which are driven most by high, particularly labour, costs.

Economics clearly have an important role as part of the environment in which any business operates. The market-place in which that business operates is the main element of the economic domain. However, as has been seen, political considerations frequently override what would be considered normal market forces, and so the economic world in which the shipbuilding business operates is often distorted.

Social factors might not be an immediately obvious topic for a book on the shipbuilding business, but, as will be seen, they have an impact. In one sense, they can be thought of as part of the politics, in particular where employment is an issue, as it is in many shipbuilding regions. The strange economic and political climate in which the industry has operated for the last quarter of a century has also distorted the labour force in many areas, and this is also discussed later in this chapter.

Finally, the issue of care of the natural environment is increasingly impacting shipping and, by extension, shipbuilding. The industry suffers in a way from the sheer size of its operations and products, and therefore its high visibility. There is also its proximity to water, which is a highly sensitive environmental issue. While taking care of the environment is important to everyone, the shipbuilding business simply does not have the scale of environmental impact that might be assumed from some reports.

ECONOMIC ENVIRONMENT

The political climate has been reviewed, and its importance identified. Technology is discussed in detail in later chapters. Turning attention to the economic climate, this can be reviewed under a number of distinct headings. Previous studies of the industry have identified that the ownership structure is an important factor in competitiveness, and indeed survival, for shipbuilders. The strength of a large company or group structure, which includes financially sound businesses in different sectors, gives a company the chance to manage lean periods, where a small independent company might go under.

Exchange rates also play an important part in the industry. As it is one of the most truly global industries, the relative movement of currencies can have a dramatic effect. Certainly, a relatively modest short term change in exchange rate between two currencies can far outstrip the change in shipbuilding productivity which can be achieved by a company in the same time.

Another crucial factor is the ability to provide finance to shipowners. There are a number of sources of finance, and shipowners would not expect to pay any cash for a ship, but rather cover modest financing and repayment costs out of operating profits. Competitive financing terms are a key means of attracting shipowners, and a current clear example is in the United States, where the government-underwritten Title XI scheme offers very low interest rates over extended periods of time.

Competition between shipbuilders is very fierce in the current situation of over-supply of shipbuilding capacity. This has a clear economic impact. The market is truly global, and the price of a ship is relatively elastic. Given a small over-supply of shipbuilding capacity, the owner can take business anywhere in the world. As a result, ship prices are currently very low, and this makes reasonable profitability an almost impossible goal for a shipbuilder, except in some specialist niche markets. This lack of profit leads directly to the need for political support and to subsidies which have already been discussed.

Ownership of shipbuilders

The history of the shipbuilding business is in part one of numerous small companies, which often come into existence at a time when the market for ships is strong, and then disappear in depressions. The history is also one of very large organisations, most of which have flourished, or at least remained in being, for extended periods of time.

For many hundreds of years, ships were small, made of wood and, with the proviso of needing a number of skilled craftsmen, relatively easy to build. In particular, the facilities needed, and therefore the investment, was very modest. The acquisition or rental of a small area of waterside land, adjacent to supplies of timber and within a reasonable distance of the limited number of metal and other items required, would suffice. Such small firms could come into existence easily, with minimal barriers to entry into the market. Equally, they could wind up very easily.

Even in more recent times, some very basic successful shipyards can be found, with the waterside land as their key feature and use of an extensive network of sub-contract companies to supply most of the materials, equipment and services required. However, as ships have generally become larger, and as pressures on the cost and time to deliver have grown, the shipbuilding business has become more complex. Larger and more substantial investment has become necessary, particularly in the building berth or dock, but also in the workshops and equipment. The result has been, except for local, small vessels, to concentrate the industry in fewer, large companies.

There are opportunities, perhaps more in shiprepair then shipbuilding, for existing, possibly unused facilities to be acquired at low cost and for relatively small companies then to be developed. This does depend on the existence of the facilities, since the development of new docks and other major facilities is very expensive. The Kværner group has grown using this philosophy.

Large companies or organisations are not entirely new. The Arsenale at Venice in the fourteenth and fifteenth centuries has been referred to, and this was a large organisation, certainly by the standards of the time. The Admiralty in the United Kingdom in the eighteenth century has been described as the largest organisation in the world at the time. While its responsibilities ran to the entire operation of the Royal Navy, a substantial element of this was the building, refitting and repair of the ships, and the Royal Dockyards in the UK were substantially expanded at this time.

However, with the advent of steel ships, the use of machine rather than wind power, and the explosion in new developments in shipboard equipment since then, came the growth of large shipbuilding companies. Large companies could exploit economies of scale in production of ships and initially their equipment, and were better placed to survive in lean times. There has been a steady, if in some areas slow, trend towards larger companies.

This is a trend which is paralleled in other large-scale industries, notably motor car production and aerospace. Both are products of the twentieth century, and their development has been much faster than the development of shipbuilding. Both have moved much further down the path of a few, large companies dominating a world market.

There were some relatively large companies before the latter half of the twentieth century in employment terms, if not physical size. However, in absolute terms, really large companies have only been seen in the final quarter of the twentieth century. The really large single shipyards are to be found in South Korea, where the industry has developed as a major business only in the latest period.

Japan also has a number of large shipyards, although the large industrial conglomerates in Japan generally own several smaller shipyards (smaller is a relative term—small compared to the Korean giants). One of the reasons for the relative success since the 1960s of Japan and since the 1970s of Korea is believed to be in the ownership structure, where the large groupings (or very large shipyards) are able to make the economies of scale referred to earlier. The ownership structure, with the shipyards operating alongside other industry sectors, also adds to the strength, and makes the shipyards much less vulnerable to economic cycles.

Having said that, the situation in Asia which has developed during the writing of this book may gainsay the view expressed. Although the shipbuilding elements of the conglomerates have been caught up in the general economic problems, the realities of producing ships and selling them at prices which can hardly be considered to cover costs appear to have finally resulted in disaster. On the other hand, the existence of large, modern and well-equipped shipyards, along with a skilled workforce requiring employment will almost certainly see a continuation of the shipbuilding business in these two countries. To say that is to stray into the political domain once more.

In Western Europe, several groups have attempted to emulate the Far Eastern experience by forming large organisations with numbers of shipyards. The Fincantieri group in Italy is one, which has created a large organisation as a vehicle for modernisation. Its relative success owes much to the adoption of new technology and product development. It also owes much to strong government support, and it remains to be seen how viable the group will be in the longer term.

In Germany, the Bremer Vulkan group attempted to follow the same model, with a large portfolio of shipyards and related engineering companies. Its apparent success was also due to strong government support, which was being used in a highly "unofficial" manner. It is apparent that neither the product strategy nor the performance improvements were adequate.

The outstanding success, so far, is the Kværner Group. This has grown rapidly, acquiring shipyards beyond its Norwegian base. It has a product portfolio based firmly in high technology, value-added ships, which Europe is capable of constructing in direct competition with the Far East. Much of the success of the group is due to the acquisition strategy which is similar to that described for the smaller shipyard sector. That is, the shipyards have been acquired either from positions of bankruptcy or from grateful governments seeking an end to payment of large subsidies. In either case, the costs of acquisition have been minimal. In the most recent case, the move to acquire the Philadelphia shipyard, the proposed US$ 400 million cost of purchase and upgrading will be met 90 per cent by local and national government, and the remainder will be a loan. The shipyard is also expected to bid for US government contracts.

It remains unproven whether success is down to the existence of large groups which have the financial muscle to survive or to the existence of small, nimble companies which can enter and leave markets relatively cheaply. Both types of company have had spectacular success. Equally, both types have had casualties, and the casualty rate among smaller companies has been very high.

The ownership of shipyards as independent companies has been considered, as well as their ownership by large conglomerates. Ownership by shipping interests is another option. There is obvious synergy, in that the shipowner has control of the shipyard and the shipyard has a reasonably guaranteed flow of orders. The shipowner is unlikely to place orders elsewhere, so the benefits to the shipyard are clear. There is also potential for two methods of subsidy.

In all of the different forms of ownership, there remains the fundamental problem that both the shipping and shipbuilding markets have an excess of supply over demand. Except for the lowest labour cost or most efficient shipbuilders, the latter preferably working in high-value niche markets with technological barriers to entry, any form of ownership must ultimately depend on somebody to pick up the difference between the cost of production and the price which the market is prepared to pay.

Exchange rates

The shipbuilding business deals primarily in dollars, and the relative value of the national currency of the shipbuilder against the dollar is a major factor in competition, and sheer survival. The size of recent fluctuations is dramatic, as can be seen from the Japanese yen, which has varied from ¥90 to ¥140 against the US dollar during the 1990s.

The impact of these fluctuations in the value of currencies is potentially, and frequently actually, far greater than any aspects of cost which are directly under the control of an individual shipyard. Although the underlying improvement trend in labour productivity in shipbuilding is around 4 per cent annually, this represents only a 1–2 per cent improvement in total ship cost (allowing for overheads being improved in line with labour). Currencies fluctuate far more than this even in periods of relative stability. To be able to manage such variations, shipyards need to be part of a group, ideally with international elements, which can manage the changes, or needs the strength to take a long term view.

THE SOCIAL ENVIRONMENT

The social impacts on industry can easily be overlooked and therefore neglected, particularly where the industry is so much based in trade and industry, as is shipbuilding. The social impact on consumer goods, on fashion and retail industries, is clear to see. Advertising, the high profile of key brands and such issues as fashion, and even consumer safety, all ensure that the social domain is obvious. The social impact on shipbuilding may be less obvious.

It is however of major importance in one crucial area, that is the labour force which the industry requires. It is an obvious statement that people build ships (with the aid of machines and equipment), so the availability, skills and capacity of those people matter greatly to the industry. The industry has, in many developed countries, a "sunset" image. This is despite its size, its importance to economies and the remarkable new technological advances which have been made in recent years. Somehow, the connection is not made between the fast ferry on which someone may travel, or the luxury cruise liner (let alone the way in which an imported consumer item might have reached the local retailer), and the need to build the vessel and then maintain it for a life of 30 years or more.

Ageing workforces, skills shortages and a reluctance to work in an industry with, admittedly, poorer working conditions than most are problems encountered in a number of countries. These are driving some of the changes in the industry world-wide.

The labour force

The world-wide shipbuilding industry has had a sharply reduced workforce in most of the major, and minor, shipbuilding countries. Table 9 (see page 36) shows the total workforce in the major shipbuilding countries, and gives a reasonable indication of the world-wide total. It is apparent that there has been a decline in numbers, despite some increase in Korea, and smaller rises in a few other countries. Overall, the total volume of production has reduced. There is, however, another factor, which is the increase in labour productivity world-wide. This has been consistent with many other manufacturing industries, and is around 4 per cent annually. This has been the case for the last 20 years.

In fact, if the total output and numbers employed are looked at for a longer period, the rise in productivity has continued for longer, as Figure 2 shows.

In a situation where overall employment is declining, there are problems in managing the structure of the labour force. Although early retirement is a possibility, the demographics of the workforce are such that numbers of younger workers, typically the more mobile, skilled and assertive, will leave of their own accord. Equally, from a cost viewpoint, as well as because of labour opposition, the numbers who will be taken on as trainees will be very small. In some cases, training of young people in the shipbuilding industry has all but ceased. The net result is that the average age of the workforce in most of the world's shipbuilding industry has risen.

Available figures indicate that in most well-established shipbuilding nations, the average age of the workforce is now well over 40. This may not appear to be dramatic, and indeed only represents a rise in most countries of a few years. What the average conceals is a large number of older workers, who represent much of the skill base of the industry. They will retire soon, and in many cases are effectively too old for much of the outdoor and physically demanding tasks in the shipyards.

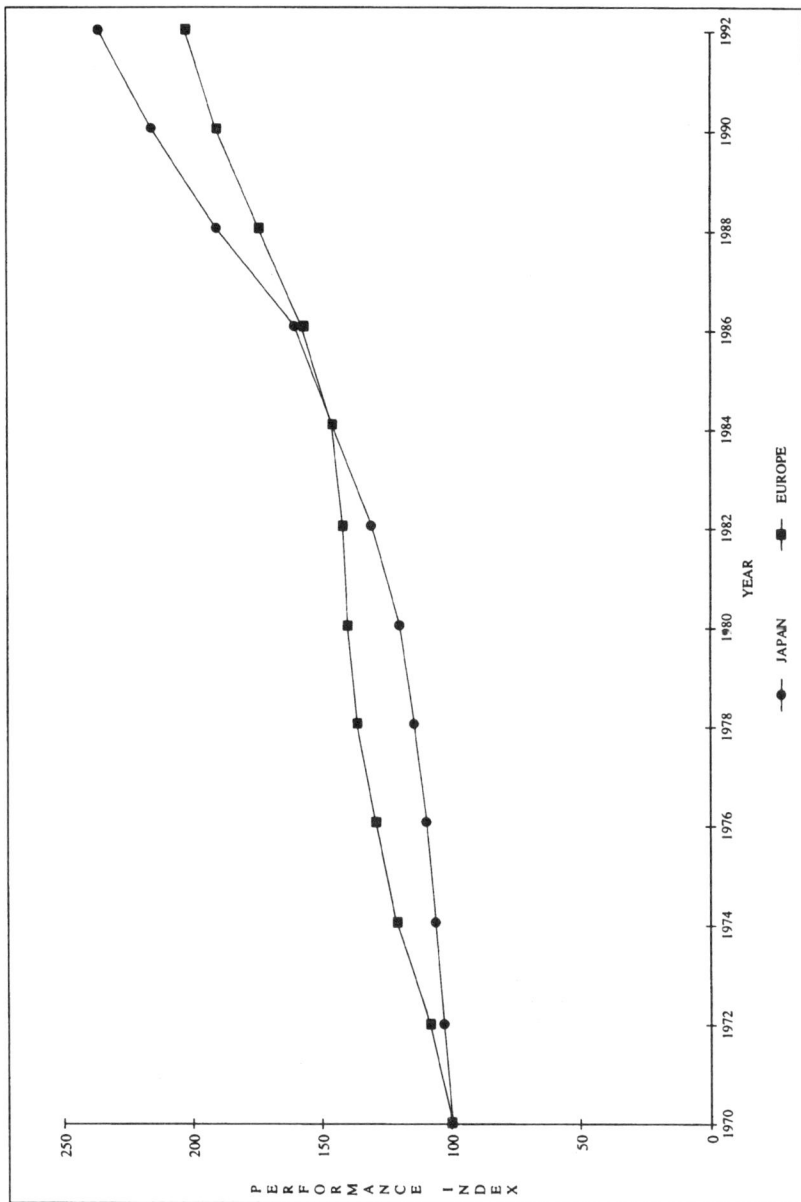

Figure 2. Performance trend comparison (Japan and Europe)

The typical pattern now is of a workforce with a large cohort of older workers, often the more skilled, who will soon retire, a limited number of middle-aged workers to replace them, and very few trainees to form the future of the work-force.

There are exceptions to the general pattern. In general, the industry has not recruited and trained young people to replace older workers, but has used this policy, alongside retirement, as a means of reducing the size of the labour force. Some companies have continued to recruit and train, as a matter of deliberate policy. These are often smaller companies, and those which have been able to develop into a defensible, niche market, and thus have perhaps felt more secure.

In most cases, there is now a problem of restructuring a workforce which has become unbalanced in terms of average age. Many countries have recognised this problem and the solutions being tried are varied. They include training of adults where younger trainees are not coming forward, the wholesale movement of the industry to new areas or even countries where labour is available, and the use of contract labour from other countries.

Table 4 (see page 12) presents data on comparative labour costs in different countries. The information presented is the hourly cost of labour, plus immediate costs of labour (social security, insurance, etc.). The costs given are aggregate figures for each country. They do not therefore take account of regional differences within countries, or different rates of pay in different companies. They are useful as a guide to the general ratio of labour costs between different shipbuilding locations, and can therefore be used to make broad comparisons of shipbuilding cost when combined with performance data.

Clearly, those countries with the highest wage levels have the most difficulty in recruiting people who wish to work in shipbuilding. The business does not fit with the lifestyle or the image which goes with high earnings. At the same time, those are also the countries where the wage costs have pushed companies into seeking alternative company structures, using lean methods, sub-contracting work where possible and automating processes. These approaches to operating the business of shipbuilding have an impact on people's perceptions. The industry is seen as uncertain, not offering job security, and that further fuels a reluctance to join.

The other issue which might be seen as in the social domain, although it is considered here as a separate item, is the "green" issue. Care of the environment is an agenda for many people, not always with a balanced view of the benefits of industry as well as its problems.

Environmental issues

There is increasing international concern about environmental pollution. As a direct result, there is increasing legislation to control or even ban some industrial activities which cause pollution. Within the shipbuilding business there are a number of production processes which can cause problems. One of the most significant of these is the preparation of (mainly) steel surfaces for paint coating. This requires cleaning and shotblasting. Some shipyards are moving to replace the shotblasting process with water blasting, but this still presents potential pollution problems. Another significant problem area is paint coating. This includes all stages from the application of a primer to retard in-process corrosion to the final painting of the external hull and the internal tanks and other spaces.

Most ship production processes result in waste, these two in particular, and the disposal of these is becoming increasingly difficult. Waste disposal is therefore a major issue for shipyards, certainly those in Europe, the United States and Japan. Other processes which cause problems include welding, which is a source of fumes, and noise, which is an outcome of many of the processes which are necessary in the shipyard.

Most countries have enacted environmental legislation to control the potential pollution from factories of all types. The shipyards, situated close to water, generally on a large scale (even a small ship is a major undertaking by the standards of most industries) and highly visible, inevitably attract a lot of attention. In the UK, in order to carry out an industrial activity which generates wastes, it is necessary to obtain a licence from the inspectorate (the Environmental Agency). Many other countries have similar requirements.

In general, the national objective is to ensure that pollution is minimised or avoided completely. The emphasis is on the management of waste, not on the processes to be used, but the processes may not be used if the environmental management is not in place. Typically, therefore, shipbuilding companies are expected to monitor their own performance, and to maintain detailed records of all aspects of their business which may have an environmental impact. There are inspections from time to time to monitor compliance with the appropriate regulations.

The principles are that the legislation is not prescriptive, that is, the shipbuilding companies may operate in any manner, provided they do not cause pollution. Where the regulations are introduced, with often onerous requirements, the companies are given time to achieve targets to reduce pollution. The expectation is that companies will basically monitor themselves.

There are several aspects of marine production which are affected by restrictions to avoid potential pollution of the environment. One of the most important concerns the use of paints which contain tri-butyl tin. This is used as an anti-fouling paint, and the tin compound acts as a biocide, preventing marine organisms from attaching themselves to ship hulls. However, because the paint is biocidal, and because of some, if limited, evidence that it can have detrimental effects on other forms of marine life, it has attracted attention.

Tri-butyl tin (TBT) in paint is restricted by the European Union through the Biocidal Products Directive. This has restricted its use. In particular it is not allowed for vehicles which are less than 25 metres in overall length. This prevents its use for leisure craft, which may well be the source of any actual problems associated with the use of the paints. This is because of smaller, pleasure craft, painted with TBTs being moored for long periods in harbours, resulting in pollution. Large, commercial vessels spend most of their time at sea, and the result is very dilute dispersion of the chemical into the ocean.

Larger ships may continue to use TBTs for a further 10 years from 1996, although the responsibility has been passed to the International Maritime Organisation (IMO) which is reviewing use of TBTs, and may produce rules in a shorter period which will have the effect of banning the use of TBTs.

Current use of TBTs is subject to strict regulation. In general, TBTs may only be discharged into rivers at a concentration of less than two nanograms per litre of water. In some cases, this may be more dilute than the water into which the discharge is made. At the same time, any shotblasting grit and debris contaminated with TBTs may not be disposed of in landfill. These regulations are of greater concern to the shiprepair business than to shipbuilding, but still are significant.

Alternatives such as copper-based paints will also be affected.

Volatile organic compounds (VOCs) which are present in most paints, inks and other solvent-based products react in sunlight with other pollutants and oxygen to produce ozone at ground level. Ozone is toxic, and the EU is keen to reduce the levels which are generated. In the EU, some 40 per cent of VOC emissions are attributable to paints and inks. As a result, a new Directive has been made which will require drastic reductions in the levels of VOCs over a 10-year period.

Shipyards generally use large quantities of paints containing VOCs, and as a result will be required to comply with the new Directive and reduce emissions. In order to comply it will be necessary to filter the exhaust from paint cells and to keep the level of VOCs in the exhaust to a set, low level. A plan for the management of emissions will be required, to demonstrate how the company will adhere to a set target to reduce the concentration of VOCs.

Alternative strategies for the shipbuilding business will be the use of low-solvent paints, which may have consequences in their ease of application and hence application cost. Water-based paints are another possibility, although all the alternatives available to date have disadvantages compared with current practice.

Surface cleaning and blasting is another area of concern. The process is necessary for the cleaning of steel materials on arrival at the shipyard, to remove millscale and prepare the steel for subsequent cutting, welding and painting. Further blasting may be required at later stages to restore the steel surface after some of the hot working processes, and to remove any corrosion which may occur to damaged paint surfaces during assembly and ship construction.

The volume of such cleaning is greater in shiprepairing and, as with the problems of painting, the shiprepair industry has a greater difficulty. Nevertheless, changes required are likely to result in an increase in ship construction costs. A number of processes are available for the cleaning process. These range from mechanical processes, which include small hand tools or portable machines, to fully automated dry or wet blasting. The mechanical processes are the easiest to manage with respect to avoiding debris and pollution, but are also the slowest. They are really only suitable for small scale repairs in limited areas.

In the shipbuilding industry, the commonest process is dry blasting. This uses a grit or steel shot which is thrown at the steel to be cleaned either by air pressure or by an impeller. For the initial preparation of the steel materials, the process can be enclosed in a chamber, which allows any polluting materials to be filtered and extracted. The reblasting of large steel blocks or units can be carried out in an enclosed workshop space—a blasting and painting cell—which again allows the potential pollution to be filtered and then safely removed although at a cost to the shipbuilder.

Any problems for the shipbuilder occur when blasting is carried out in the open, generally using a pneumatic system. This may be necessary prior to final painting on the building berth or in a dock. Enclosing the process is then more difficult, and to do so results in additional expense for the shipbuilder. The preferred approach is to complete as much of the blasting and the subsequent painting as possible before the ship construction stage, thus cutting to a minimum the danger of pollution. Whilst the facilities to do so are expensive, if they are properly used there is a cost saving potential from bringing the work to an earlier, more controllable stage of production. However, additional investment is required in the first instance, although there may be a long term return from improved efficiency.

Alternative processes are becoming available, including high pressure water blasting for cleaning and ultra-high pressure water blasting, which with entrained grit can even be used for cutting steel. These are of more significance to the shiprepair industry, which suffers the greater problem.

In making a choice of the most appropriate surface cleaning and blasting process, the primary concern is that the process delivers an adequate surface finish and a high rate of cleaning. It is also important that the waste generated by the process can be managed. This management is required to ensure that the outcome is to minimise the release of particulates into the air. It must also avoid the generation of large volumes of waste, identify if the waste contains harmful substances (more a shiprepair problem), and finally manage to dispose of the waste safely.

The traditionally favoured process is grit blasting, which is fast and provides a good quality finish. It does have disadvantages; in particular, there are large volumes of waste, except where the process can be contained in a chamber or cell. There are emissions into the air, again unless the work can be confined to an enclosed workspace, and the process will affect other work in the vicinity. At the end, even in a blast cell, the process requires a major cleaning operation. The debris from the process contains paint residue, and this can complicate the disposal requirements.

A number of methods for painting are available. These range from a brush or roller, either of which can have an extended handle for additional reach. Both are capable of producing good quality work, but cannot cover the areas required for shipbuilding in a reasonable time or at acceptable labour cost. Alternatives, in order of potential coverage in a given time, are a pressure-fed roller which provides a continuous supply of paint to the roller head, conventional air spray and airless spray.

Of these painting processes, the preferred option is airless spray, because it is fast, and it also provides a good quality of painting. There are some problems when the process is used outside, principally associated with overspray. If the process is used in windy conditions, there will be a serious increase in overspray, to the extent that operations may need to be stopped. Overspray from painting can be a problem, to the extent that it may be carried to adjacent property, with the result that, for example, cars are affected, or even local housing may be affected if close to the site. There is also a need for good operator training which is very important to manage the quality of the paint finish.

Waste disposal is a general problem for the industry, as increasing concern is found about the avoidance of pollution. Cleaning and blasting are the major sources of waste, although these problems affect repair more than new construction. Other processes also cause waste, including metals, wood, packaging, oils and so on, which must be separated and accounted for. The changes in legislation affect various aspects of operations:

— keeping contaminated waste out of rivers;
— avoiding atmospheric pollution;
— disposal of the waste excludes some alternatives;
— dumping at sea;
— landfill.

In general, all waste requires some form of treatment prior to disposal.

Welding in the industry is primarily a health and safety issue. Avoiding fumes close to the workplace is important, and the problem can in general be solved by the use of extraction systems within workshops, at work locations on the ship during assembly and final construction. The extraction may be made integral with the welding equipment, so that any fumes are extracted at source. The use of air-fed helmets is available for work in very confined spaces. In the long term, the use of automation, or remote control where possible, is a likely solution to the problems of welding fumes.

Noise is primarily a workplace health and safety issue, but may also affect the local environment. It is the most common cause of external complaints of nuisance caused by the shipbuilding industry. However, if carefully managed, noise can be controlled in the industry. It is possible in many cases to make a choice of quieter processes. The elimination of the use of pneumatic hammers and other tools for steelwork is one solution which has been adopted, particularly in enclosed workplaces. Once processes have been selected, it is necessary to ensure good management of them in use.

The typical noise sources in the industry come from a number of processes. First are the many services, including generators, compressors, pumps and frequency converters. The selection of quieter equipment, regular maintenance and, if necessary, some form of acoustic shielding is used to manage the levels of noise. Maintenance is also a means of dealing with noise due to leakages in compressed air pipes and also noise due to end-use consumption—making sure that the tools themselves do not cause excessive noise. The most noisy processes are blasting and noise from the use of impact tools, which can be largely eliminated by careful selection and grinding.

Grinding itself can be eliminated or at least drastically reduced by the quality of production. The need for grinding is largely a result of fairing processes which are used to align inaccurate components and structures. By ensuring that these items are more accurate, the need for temporary fixings, which must then be removed and dressed by grinding, is reduced and the problem thus largely overcome. There is often synergy between the reduction of re-work, which is wasteful, and the mini-misation of environmental effects.

CHAPTER 4

SUPPLY IN THE SHIPBUILDING BUSINESS

THE INDUSTRY WORLD-WIDE

Given the reality of a poor market for ships, at least in global terms, the question is then raised "who actually builds the ships?". The answer is partly to be found in the previous chapters, which have considered the external environment of the industry. In many cases, it is those shipbuilders whose government has been prepared to provide or condone the types of support which have been described.

In simple terms, there is in the world-wide shipbuilding industry an excess of supply over demand. Most, if not all, the troubles of the last quarter of a century stem from this basic imbalance. However, the global picture does disguise a wide variation between different regions, with the large commodity ships being built at rock bottom prices by builders with minimum costs or heavy subsidies, but in some of the more sophisticated categories, a surprisingly buoyant situation.

This chapter will therefore review the supply and demand situation in the shipbuilding business at the end of the twentieth century. It is worth first restating some of the causes of what has been, and still is, a traumatic situation for the majority of the world's shipbuilders. The historical dimension has been considered earlier, and the point made that such crises are not new in the global shipbuilding business. For present purposes, the events of the last 30 years will suffice.

The problem began with the development of large tankers, VLCCs, in the late 1960s and early 1970s. The size of these vessels resulted in a rash of new, or massively refurbished, shipyards with large facilities specially constructed to build these large vessels efficiently. That the facilities were needed could be demonstrated by reference to those shipyards which tried to build very large ships in old facilities. The ships could be built, but only slowly and at high cost.

The market at the time was seen as one which would continue to grow, and all the shipbuilding nations were keen to gain a share. The whole market was based on low oil prices, which at the time were effectively static or dropping in real terms. As a result the number of new shipyards far exceeded the market needs. The extent of the over-supply can be demonstrated by considering the number of docks potentially capable of constructing a vessel of 250,000 deadweight tonnes—effectively the standard of the early 1970s.

There are currently over 50 such docks in the world. Their numbers grew rapidly around 1970 in Europe, and subsequently in the Far East.

The reality of this situation is clearer when it is realised that there are only around 500 such vessels in the world. In total, only 800 have been built over the last 25 or so years.

Further, in 1973, following the Arab–Israeli conflict, the price of oil soared, disrupting economic activity for many years as inflation followed. The demand for tankers in particular sank rapidly, and other ship types were also in an over-supply position. There was a large backlog of existing orders, which continued to deliver new ships for three years, although many orders were cancelled. The outcome was an excess of ships, and that has been the position ever since.

The problem has not been homogeneous. It has affected the tanker market more than any other, and also other bulk trades. Equally, there have been niches which have continued to expand, almost throughout the 25-year period since. However, the effect of a rapid drop in orders for large tankers was a shift by the large, new shipyards into other markets. Thus, docks designed to build VLCCs could be found with a series of Panamax vessels under construction. The cascade effect passed down through all ship sizes, leaving very few sectors unaffected.

GOVERNMENT RESPONSES

The situation that was left after the demand for ships dropped was one where very few shipyards could expect to make money. In many countries, the industry was regarded as strategic, for economic or perhaps military reasons. In many countries also, the industry was a major employer, often in areas where unemployment was a serious problem. Very few governments where these conditions existed were prepared to allow the market to rule, thus destroying a major industry and employer.

So most governments in shipbuilding nations began to support the industry. This support took many forms, including direct subsidies to shipyards, and nationalisation in the UK. In some countries the government permitted expansion, despite the market conditions. The effects of this government support have been detailed previously. The impact on capacity is demonstrated by reference to Figure 3, which shows the level of production of ships in the world, over a 30-year period, compared with the capacity of the industry. Both are measured in CGT. What is apparent is that the decline in capacity, in response to the decline in demand, was not only smaller than would have been necessary to reach an equilibrium, it also lagged behind the declining orders. The time lag, as well as the excessive capacity, are both legacies of government intervention.

Millions of
gross tonnes

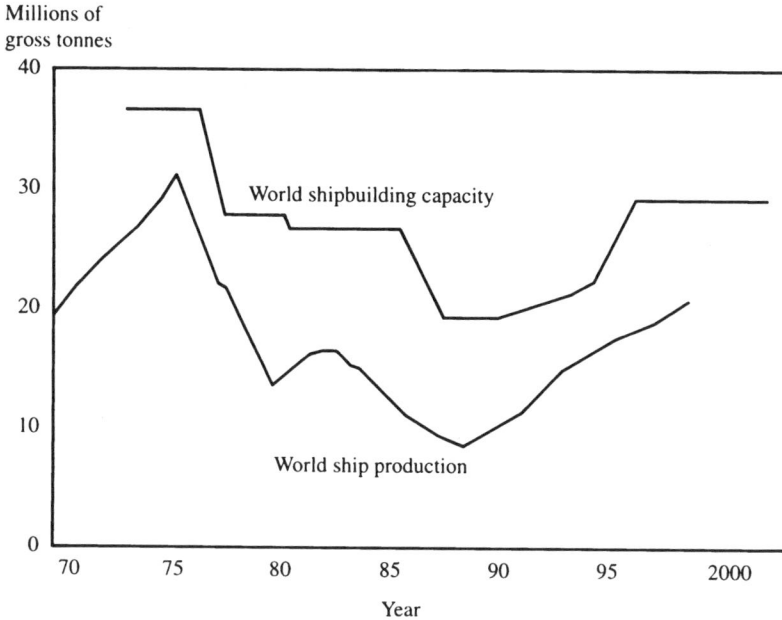

Figure 3.   **World shipbuilding capacity and production**

THE CAPACITY OF THE WORLD-WIDE SHIPBUILDING BUSINESS

There have been many estimates of the capacity of shipyards, and thus of the total world industry. The first question to be answered in assessing shipbuilding capacity, is "what measure of capacity is it best to use?" The various tonnage figures referred to in the first chapter have all been used at one time or another.

Deadweight is one of the easiest measures, but, as has been noted, it skews the capacity measure in favour of the very large vessels, particularly the oil tankers and bulk carriers. The alternative of gross tonnage is an improvement, principally because it is strictly a volume rather than tonnage measure. However, it still produces a skewed view which emphasises the production of large ships.

The preferred measure is the compensated gross tonne. Although the compensation factor can, probably rightly, be regarded as subjective, it is the result of a consensus of leading shipbuilding regions, and it is reviewed from time to time.

The capacity of the world's shipyards, even given the most suitable measure of compensated gross tonnes, is still a subject of debate. This is because the real capacity, as opposed to actual production, is hard to assess. Some reviews have taken the recent past production as their basic measure of capacity, assuming presumably that the capacity is rapidly adjusted to meet the real needs of the market. However, a review of the fluctuations of actual production will rapidly show that this view is flawed.

Actual production has varied considerably over many years but, most importantly, has increased in some years and declined in others. This indicates that there has always been some reserve capacity in existence, available to meet any upturn in the demand for ships. This view that there is reserve capacity is also consistent with the levels of government support which have been afforded to the shipbuilding industry on a world-wide basis over the last 25 years. It is therefore apparent that some other indicator of capacity is needed.

It has been noted that there is an ageing workforce in much of the shipbuilding industry. One view has been that the size of the available labour force might provide a more objective measure of capacity. However, if the size of labour force is considered against the output of the world's industry, it is apparent that the production levels vary. This supports the view of reserve capacity, in this case in the form of a workforce which is inactive, but presumably available for recall as demand rises. But what is also apparent is that the productivity of the world-wide labour force has been increasing over the period.

If the total labour force is plotted against the total output, although there are fluctuations due to ship demand, there is a definite trend of improvement in labour productivity. This needs to be taken into account in assessing the capacity of the industry.

Another approach is to take account of the physical facilities which are available. In effect, this approach considers the building docks, or berths, and assesses the capacity in terms of the number of ships each could produce. There are drawbacks, in that the docks have to be supported by other facilities, in particular large-scale steel production workshops for the larger ships. There is also a need for the workforce, or its substitution by investment in new, possibly automated equipment. There may also be disputes about the genuine availability of some of the docks, which may be in a state of disrepair, or may be in use for other activities, typically shiprepair or offshore work.

There is also the point that in circumstances where no large ship orders are available for construction, large docks may be used for smaller types. However, if just a part of the industry is considered, some indication of potential capacity may be gathered.

Considering only large tankers (over 100,000 dwt), analysis can be made of the docks available for their construction and the demand as forecast.

Capacity is measured in terms of dry-docks (and berths where appropriate) which are able to build such ships, and are potentially available for the purpose. The docks are broadly categorised as 250,000 dwt (over 300 metres in length and 50 metres in breadth), or 100,000 dwt (over 250 metres in length and 45 metres in breadth).

A number of docks are categorised as repair docks, or offshore docks (particularly in Japanese shipyards). Where these are in the same facility as a building dock, and there are the necessary support facilities for construction, these can be regarded as potentially available for construction, subject to the workforce and other considerations referred to above.

In Europe, a number of such docks have been in use for other construction, for example the Bremer Vulkan dock had been adapted for series building of container ships. These are left out of the immediately available capacity, but are again regarded as potentially available if market conditions are right.

The capacity in terms of the numbers of ships which could be produced from each dock is based on assessment of the national performance levels and known steel-work capacities associated with the docks:

Table 11. Docks for ships of 250,000 dwt

Location	Number of active docks	Ship production capacity	Potential extra capacity
Japan	8	40	20
Korea	6	30	20
China	1	2	
Taiwan	1	4	
Asia	16	76	
Europe	4	15	10
USA	1	3	6
Total	21	94	56

Table 12. Docks for ships of 100,000 dwt

Location	Number of active docks	Ship production capacity	Potential extra capacity
Japan	8	40	20
Korea	2	10	
Europe	4	12	8
USA	2	6	
Other	4	8	
Total	20	76	28

Overall, this represents a capacity in the world to replace all the ageing tankers without any additional needs. Taking into account additional Korean and other capacity, and the capacity potentially available for these large ships, the entire fleet could be replaced in a five-year period. This would create a shortfall in some other areas, but there is further capacity to be exploited, including Eastern Europe and the former Soviet Union.

There is a similar situation for all of the main ship types. There are a number of recognised, leading shipbuilders who will attract orders by reputation, price or other advantage. There are then a number of second-level builders who will attract orders in good markets, and may have some form of covert or other support. Finally there are shipbuilders who will be able to take orders in a very good market, or who will attract orders through direction of government or other non-commercial criteria.

In conclusion, some measure of capacity of the shipbuilding industry is required, and this is shown in Figure 3. This indicates the actual and estimated future capacity of the world's shipbuilding industry.

SHIPBUILDING COUNTRIES

Having identified, as well as can be done, the capacity of the world's industry to supply ships, it is appropriate to review how this capacity is divided between the different shipbuilding regions.

Dominating the world in terms of capacity to produce, as well as actual production, are Korea and Japan. As has been noted earlier, Japan has been the dominant shipbuilder since around 1965, and had 50 per cent of the market for a substantial period. Even into the 1990s, as Korea expanded, Japan retained a one third share of production.

Japanese industry has an awesome reputation, and the shipbuilding business in that country can justifiably be seen as the first of several sectors to achieve a dominant world position, and perhaps will be seen to retain that position for the longest. Any student of Japanese shipbuilding in the mid-1960s could find important lessons on how to operate a business. Equally, many other industries in western countries could profitably have seen shipbuilding as a warning for themselves, rather than dismissing it as a "smokestack" or sunset industry.

Although none of the individual Japanese builders can match the scale of the newer South Korean giants, the table of leading shipbuilders demonstrates how many companies are in the first division of shipbuilders. Although South Korea has from time to time taken more orders than Japan, the Japanese builders consistently produce the most.

LEADING SHIPBUILDERS

Table 13 lists the leading shipyards in the world, in terms of their total order book. The positions do fluctuate according to the order intake and deliveries, but the leading group of builders does not change very much. The order book is in terms of deadweight tonnes. The dominance of the small number of major Korean shipyards is clear, as is the position of the larger number of Japanese shipyards. A few other Far Eastern shipyards also appear as major producers, and the leading Europeans are well down the table.

Table 13. The world's leading shipbuilders by total order book

Hyundai Heavy Industries, Ulsan, South Korea
Samsung Shipbuilding, Koje, South Korea
Daewoo Heavy Industries, Okpo, South Korea
Halla Engineering, Samho, South Korea
Mitsubishi Heavy Industries, Nagasaki, Japan
IHI, Kure, Japan
Hitachi Zosen, Ariake, Japan
Kaoshiung, Taiwan
Nippon Kokan KK, Tsu, Japan
Namura Zonenshu, Imari, Japan
Stocznia Sczeczin, Poland
Kawasaki Heavy Industries, Sakaide, Japan
Dalian New Shipyard, China
Sumitomo Heavy Industries, Oppama, Japan
Tsuneishi Zosen, Numakuma, Japan
Imabari Shipbuilding, Marugame, Japan
Oshima Shipbuilding, Oshima, Japan
Stocznia Gdynia, Poland
Hitachi, Maizuru, Japan
Mitsui Shipbuilding, Chiba, Japan
Hanjin Heavy Industries, Busan, South Korea
Sanoyas, Mizushima, Japan
Shin Kurushima, Onshi, Japan
Halla, Inchon, Korea
Jiangnan, China
Sasebo, Japan
AESA, Puerto Real, Spain
Mitsubushi Heavy Industries, Kobe, Japan
Koyo, Mihama, Japan
Guangzzhou, China
Hudong, China
Keelung, Taiwan
Galatz, Romania
Dalian, China
Odense Staalskibsverft, Denmark

Many leading European shipbuilders do not appear in the list, including:

Kværner Masa Yards, Helsinki and Turku
Chantiers de l'Atlantique, St Nazaire
Meyer Werft, Papenburg, Germany
Fincantieri, Monfalcone, Italy
HDW, Kiel, Germany

However, if the table is re-ordered in terms of the yard orderbook, in compensated gross tonnes, the European shipbuilders, with their more generally more complex product mix, appear in higher positions. This is a better reflection of the value of the shipbuilding business in the different yards and countries, and also of the capacity of the shipyards.

Table 14. The world's leading shipbuilders by compensated gross tons

Hyundai Heavy Industries, Ulsan, South Korea
Samsung Shipbuilding, Koje, South Korea
Daewoo Heavy Industries, Okpo, South Korea
Mitsubishi Heavy Industries, Nagasaki, Japan
Halla Engineering, Samho, South Korea
Stocznia Sczeczin, Poland
Kawasaki Heavy Industries, Sakaide, Japan
Kværner Masa Yards, Turku, Finland
Chantiers de l'Atlantique, St Nazaire
Mitsubushi Heavy Industries, Kobe, Japan
Meyer Werft, Papenburg, Germany
Fincantieri, Monfalcone, Italy
Kværner Masa Yards, Helsinki, Finland
Hanjin Heavy Industries, Busan, South Korea
Stocznia Gdynia, Poland
IHI, Kure, Japan
Mitsui Shipbuilding, Chiba, Japan
Halla, Inchon, Korea
Tsuneishi Zosen, Numakuma, Japan
Sumitomo Heavy Industries, Oppama, Japan
Shin Kurushima, Onshi, Japan
Oshima Shipbuilding, Oshima, Japan
HDW Kiel, Germany
Odense, Denmark
Namura Zosen, Japan
MTW, Germany
Dalian New Yard, China
Kaoshiung, Taiwan
Imabari, Japan
Hitachi Zosen, Maizuru, Japan
Hitachi Zosen, Ariake, Japan
AESA, Puerto Real, Spain
NKK, Japan
Galatz, Romania
Sanoyas, Japan

The leading positions in the table will alter to some extent if actual production for any given year, or if a moving average of annual production, is used, but the same basic message will appear: that the dominant nation is still Japan, with around one third of the market. South Korea has a smaller order book and production than Japan, but these two account for around two thirds of the deadweight tonnage which is produced in the world.

The success of Japan has undoubtedly been built on a mix of overt and covert support, particularly in the early days of re-building, when local owners took the bulk of production. However, there is also no doubt that Japan has the highest shipbuilding productivity in the world, and that it strives continuously to improve. The Japanese industry has been the best managed, in that it has reduced capacity since the 1970s, although in a controlled manner compared to the fragmented western response to the supply and demand imbalance. It has certainly been more responsible than the aggressive and unjustifiable South Korean expansion over the same period.

Comparison of employment in the Japanese and European industries shows a similar decline in numbers, but also points to the remarkable improvements in Japanese productivity which have been a major contributor to the Japanese shipbuilding industry retaining its leading position.

Japanese shipbuilding

The Shipbuilders' Association of Japan has some 25 member companies, located around the country. Many of these companies have more than one shipyard and a number have both shiprepair and ship construction facilities. The shipyards are:

The Hakodate Dock Co. Ltd

Hitachi Zosen, with new construction shipyards at
  Maizuru
  Ariake

Imbari Shipbuilding Co. Ltd, which has new construction yards at
  Imabari
  Marugame

Ishikawajima-Harima Heavy Industries (IHI) at
  Kure
  Tokyo
  Chita

Kanasashi Co. Ltd, new building at
  Toyohashi
  Shimizu

Kanda Shipbuilding at Kawajiri

Kanrei shipbuilding at Naruto

Kawasaki Heavy Industries Ltd, with two yards
  Kobe
  Sakaide

Koyo Dock KK at Mihara
Miho Shipyard Co. at Shimizu

Mitsubishi Heavy Industries has three new building shipyards at
  Kobe
  Nagasaki
  Shimonoseki

Mitsui Engineering and Shipbuilding Co.
  Chiba
  Tamano

Naikai Shipbuilding Co. at Setoda

Namura Shipbuilding Co. Ltd at Imari

Narasaki Shipbuilding Co. at Muroran

Nippon Kokan KK at
  Tsu
  Tsurumi

Onimichi Dockyard at Onimichi

Oshima Shipbuilding Co., Oshima

Sanoyas Hishino Meisho Corp. at
  Mizushima

Sasebo Heavy Industries

Shin Kurushima has newbuilding facilities at
  Akitsu
  Imabari
  Hashihama
  Onishi

Sumitomo Heavy Industries at Oppama

Tsuneishi Shipbuilding Co. Ltd at Numakuma

There are in addition some 20 shipyards, not members of the association. They build smaller vessels, typically under 10,000 tonnes deadweight, and primarily for domestic shipowners.

Despite the rapid growth of South Korean shipbuilding in the last 25 years, Japan still retains the largest capacity for shipbuilding. That capacity is estimated at around 6.5 million CGT, or approximately one third of the world's total effective capacity.

The Japanese shipyards are capable of building all types of ships, but their production is centred on the basic types—bulk carriers, tankers and container ships. Some of the smaller shipyards specialise in other types, including liquefied gas carriers, chemical tankers and roll-on, roll-off vessels.

Korean shipbuilding

The rise of Korean shipbuilding has been as spectacular as was that of Japan in the 1950s and 1960s. Japan rebuilt and then massively expanded its shipbuilding as part of a national strategy to import raw materials and export finished goods. South Korea developed its shipbuilding as one of the foundations of a major industrialisation project, starting in the late 1960s, but expanding more or less continuously from 1970 to the mid-1990s.

The domination of the major South Korean companies can be seen from the table of leading shipbuilders, above.

The massive expansion in South Korea continued in the early 1990s. The most recent increases in capacity in that country were based on the market forecasts produced by the Korean Shipbuilders' Association. These took a very optimistic view of the future market, predicting the demolition of more or less all the 1970s-built VLCCs by the mid-1990s, and also taking a bullish view of future trade growth. These assumptions produced a very optimistic forecast, which was used as a justification for expansion.

That the forecasts were over-optimistic, and that this was a view taken by other forecasters at the time, is noted in Chapter 1. Even at the time the new shipyards were only at the planning stage, it was apparent that the world shipbuilding industry had more than enough large docks for almost any level of future demand.

The recent spate of expansion in South Korea can partly be explained by the regime of Kim Yung-San, which was much more liberal than those of his predecessors in allowing the chaebols their own decisions. Both the Halla and Samsung expansions were also linked to chaebol rivalry, and it was suggested at the time that the expansion plans were announced that it was more a matter of prestige for Samsung to build VLCCs than commercial possibilities. Although Samsung's plan to build a VLCC dock had been approved some years previously, the timing was surprising to most observers, at least if viewed in strictly commercial terms.

The development brought Samsung into major league shipbuilding because it could previously only construct vessels of Suezmax size. Hyundai had previously opposed both the Halla and Samsung expansions, but then it too announced plans for a further two VLCC-sized docks. Again this was probably based more on prestige than business reasons. The one group which did not plan to expand was Daewoo, which interestingly did not share the optimistic views of newbuilding demand. Daewoo more reasonably sought to expand through more efficient production, which would make it more resilient to a down-turn in orders, as well as more flexible and responsive to market demands.

The moves may have been caused in part by the success of the Korean yards over Japanese yards in 1993, when the Korean yards won 50 per cent more orders in terms of gt than the Japanese. At the time, the Korea Maritime Institute indicated that longer term shipbuilding capacity at a projected 7.5m gt could have surpassed Japan's at 7.0m gt by the year 2000. The implementation of the OECD agreement would have caused some problems for the South Koreans, on the grounds of subsidy and dumping. In view of this the commercial logic of their decisions at the time seems to have been bizarre.

Korean shipbuilding as a major player in the world market effectively began in 1972 with the first stage of development of the Hyundai shipyard in Ulsan. This shipyard, in common with many other new developments at the time, was specifically to build VLCCs. Both shipyard and the first ships were completed in a remarkably short time. The original shipyard with a single VLCC dock has since expanded, with additional facilities for both shipbuilding and shiprepair. Ulsan now has nine docks available, and is by far the largest individual shipyard in the world.

The development of Hyundai at Ulsan was followed by Korea Shipbuilding and Engineering (KSEC) with an ambitious development at Okpo. This ran into financial problems, and eventually the shipyard was taken on and completed by Daewoo Heavy Industries. The main dock is remarkable for its size, being over 500 metres in length and 130 metres wide. Although considerably lower in capacity than Hyundai, the Daewoo shipyard is the next largest in the world.

Once Hyundai and Daewoo were operational, other well-established but much smaller shipbuilding companies developed their own expansion plans. Samsung at Koje and Halla at Samho also developed new shipyards, in both cases larger than any others, apart from Hyundai and Daewoo. As a result, the four large South Korean shipyards are larger than any others, measured in terms of total deadweight which they produce. The Nagasaki yard of Mitsubishi is the largest of the Japanese shipyards in deadweight terms, and is the next after the Koreans.

In addition to the four mega-shipyards, there are a number of smaller South Korean builders.

Cheung Ku shipyard at Ulsan	Halla has a smaller shipyard at Inchon

Dae Dong has two yards at
    Busan
    Chinhae
	Hanjin has two shipyards
	    Busan, building ships typically up to pan-
	        amax size
	    Ulsan, building handy size bulk carriers

There are also half a dozen smaller yards, building ships of about 10,000 deadweight or less, primarily for local owners.

Other Asian builders

The other Asian country whose shipbuilding industry has been making inroads into the international market is China. Again, a small industry has been established for many years. Recent changes in the views of China's leaders, in particular a loosening of the constraints on industry and a wish to trade more, have led to a considerable increase in the country's shipbuilding capacity. On a deadweight measure, China occupies third place in the world, although a long way behind Japan and South Korea. China has had a considerable cost advantage, although investment is inhibited by the huge cost of new shipbuilding facilities. In a weak market, shipbuilding is not necessarily the most sensible investment area.

China has some 15 shipyards active in the international market. Most of them are building series of medium-sized bulk carriers, with some tankers and container ships.

Dalian New Yard is the only large shipyard in the country, in that it has a dock which can take VLCCs. So far it has not built such large ships, indicating some spare shipbuilding capacity, but has recently built 150,000 dwt tankers. Most of the other shipyards are limited to Panamax-sized vessels or smaller. The shipyards include:

— Bohai;
— Dalian (the old as opposed to the new yard);
— Guanggzhou;
— Hudong;
— Jiangnan;
— Shanghai;
— Xinggang Shipyard.

Others build vessels of typically below 10,000 dwt mainly for local owners.

Also in the far east, Taiwan has had a shipbuilding industry for many years. It joined the shipbuilding boom of the 1970s with the development of the large shipyard at Kaohsiung. The shipyard was designed for the construction of VLCCs, but in common with many others has built a variety of different ship types to maintain continuity of production. It has built bulk carriers and container ships more recently. The other shipyard of note, which is smaller, is at Keelung and builds a mix of bulk carriers and container ships. In both cases, the ships are built largely for domestic owners. The dwt on order in Taiwan has been around two million tonnes.

Europe

European shipbuilders have had a relatively lean time over the 25-year period which is the main interest of this book. The decline in European shipbuilding employment has been noted, and the position of the European builders too. There has been relatively little physical development of shipyards in Europe, although a lot of expenditure has been made on restructuring. Most of the leading shipyards, indeed the surviving shipyards, in Europe have engaged in major programmes of performance improvement.

There has been some development, notably in those sectors where the European builders are able to compete through technological advantages.

Germany has been the leading Western European shipbuilding country for a number of years. The position has been built largely on the production of container ships. There was a major setback when the Bremer Vulkan group collapsed, having diverted much of the funding given for restructuring the former East German shipyards into supporting its existing shipyards.

German shipbuilding has been very focused, with container ships forming the mainstay of the industry in recent years. Almost all shipyards have been engaged in this market. The major exception is the Jos L. Meyer company, whose Meyer Werft Shipyard in Papenburg has become one of the leading passenger vessel producers in Europe, and thus in the world. The shipyard has been in existence for many years, but has been transformed in the last decade into a major shipbuilding factory.

Other major shipyards include:

— Howaldswerke Deutsch Werft (HDW) in Kiel;
— J. J. Sietas in Hamburg;
— Thyssen Nordseewerke in Emden.

In what was formerly East Germany, a number of shipyards were rescued from the collapse of their former Soviet markets, and restructured. The ownership has changed from state to private. Some of the restructuring has been in investment in new facilities, notably at Kværner Warnowerft in Warnemunde, and Meeres Technik in Wismar, which has resulted in virtually brand new shipyards.

Other shipyards in the region include:

— Flender Werft at Lübeck;
— Volkswerft in Stralsund.

There are also a number of significant smaller shipyards in Germany. Overall, the shipyards have an order book around two million dwt tonnes.

The other leading West European nations include Denmark, Italy, the Netherlands, Spain and France. All have managed a radical restructuring programme, and all have had casualties along the way.

In Denmark, the leading casualty was the Burmeister and Wain shipyard in Copenhagen. B and W was one of the first shipyards to develop construction in a dry dock, for large ships, and was a leading innovator for many years. It eventually fell to financial pressures, unable to generate sufficient income from its ranges of standard bulk carriers to sustain the company.

The product strategy, of designing and building a very successful range of bulk carriers was radically different from that of most West European shipyards. The strategy was effectively competing head to head with the low cost Far Eastern producers. Eventually, as prices were at unsustainable levels, the company, lacking a financial backer or other support, was unable to continue.

The other major Danish shipbuilder is Odense, which is the leading large shipyard in Europe and has invested heavily in automation and other technology to maintain a competitive edge. So far it has been successful, along with the benefits of ownership by a major shipping company. Originally designed around 1970 as a VLCC shipyard, Odense has adapted to container and other higher value types.

Italy has a major state-owner group, Fincantieri, along with a number of successful private shipyards. The focus of Italian shipbuilding is on the higher value ships, notably, at Monfalcone. As in the case of Odense, Monfalcone was originally a VLCC shipyard, also newly developed around 1970. As the ability of European shipyards to compete with the low prices available in the Far East declined, the yard turned to alternative markets. It is now one of the four leading cruise ship builders in the world (that is, in Europe). Other shipyards in the group also build passenger vessels, including fast ferries. There is also construction of cargo ships, including bulk carriers for domestic ownership.

The smaller, independent Italian shipyards build primarily small, usually domestic tonnage, including fast passenger ships, chemical tankers and LPG ships.

The Netherlands has a relatively small, but very successful industry, with 12 larger shipyards and a number of smaller ones. Two of the 12 shipyards, Van der Giessen and de Merwerde, build reasonably large ships, but the majority build small ships, typically below 10,000 dwt tonnes. Many are for river-sea trades, and often for local owners.

Spain also has a nationally owned group in Astilleros Espanoles SA (AESA). This has a number of shipyards, of which the largest is Puerto Real, close to Cadiz. This again was a VLCC yard, and is one of the most modern. It continues to build large tankers and bulk carriers, and has invested heavily in up-to-date methods to improve its competitive position. The yard has also built passenger ships. Two smaller shipyards in the AESA group are at Bilbao (Sestao shipyard) and Seville, building medium-sized tankers and ro-ro vessels respectively. The AESA group includes other, smaller shipyards as well as repair and offshore sites.

There are also a number of smaller, privately owned shipyards in Spain which concentrate on the more specialised and smaller ship sectors. These include fast and conventional passenger ships, chemical tankers and refrigerated cargo ships.

France has the smallest number of shipyards of the five countries mentioned. The main shipbuilder is Chantiers de l'Atlantique, in Saint Nazaire in Brittany. This once again was a 1970 development for the then burgeoning VLCC market. Since that market diminished, and in its revival is effectively all but closed to European shipbuilders, the Saint Nazaire yard has moved into other markets, notably large passenger vessels. In this it has been successful, and is one of the four leaders in Europe.

The other shipyards are small and concentrate on passenger and other specialist types.

Finland retains a modest but specialised and successful shipbuilding industry. Although the shipyards have been spectacularly bankrupt on occasions, their technical skills and capabilities have been their saviour. The Finnish shipyards concentrate on niche markets, and include:

- Finnyards at Rauma;
- Kværner Masa Yards at
  - Turku, building LNG and other specialised vessels;
  - Helsinki, building large cruise liners.

The Helsinki shipyard is probably the world leader in its speciality market.

In Eastern Europe, Poland is the leading shipbuilding nation by a long way. Half of Poland's 24 shipyards are involved in newbuilding activity and have a newbuilding capacity estimated at around 625,000 CGT. The Szczecin yard is the leading shipyard, primarily engaged in the production of container ships which have been a Polish speciality for some time. The Gdynia shipyard also builds container ships. The Polish shipyards are relatively old, and have had little investment for many years. With new technology their production levels could be higher. More recent investment has been in computer technology and organisation, which is proving successful. The third shipyard in Poland was at Gdansk, but failure to modernise has led to a slow decline, and the yard is expected to close on completion of existing orders. The Gdansk Northern shipyard is the only other of significant size, but has limited production. Other yards build small vessels for local markets.

As an international competitor Poland is of increasing significance. In terms of export orders, container ships became the dominant ship type in the early 1990s. Poland has overtaken Germany as the leading shipbuilder in Europe, at least in deadweight terms, and is on a par with China in total production.

Other Eastern European shipbuilding nations of some importance are Croatia, Bulgaria and Romania.

Croatia inherited the three major shipyards of former Yugoslavia, the Uljanik yard at Pula, the 3 Maj yard at Rijeka and Brodosplit at Split. All are long-established yards, but have been modernised to a greater or lesser degree. They build a mix of ships, with tankers and bulk carriers predominant. There is a smaller shipyard at Trogir, which has built chemical tankers. The shipyards have had a lot of problems in maintaining production, suffering from the financial problems of other countries in the region and also the fall out from the conflicts in former Yugoslavia.

There are in total 18 shipyards in Croatia of which seven, including the ones mentioned, undertake newbuilding work. The overall capacity of the industry in Croatia is estimated at around 450,000 compensated gross tons annually. The order book has been around one million tonnes dwt, mainly of bulk carriers and oil tankers. The orders are generally for series ships, building for domestic owners and often for Russia.

Bulgaria has declined in ship production since the demise of the soviet bloc. The major shipyard is at Varna, and builds tankers and bulk carriers. There are a total of eight shipyards, six of which are capable of newbuilding with an estimated new-building capacity of around 200,000 CGT. The shipyards have operated well below this recently, with even the Varna yard only operating at around half capacity. The Bourgas yard has often carried out repair work due to problems with shipbuilding work. The other newbuilding yards are of only local importance.

Romania has eight yards which undertake newbuilding and they have an esti-mated capacity of over 500,000 CGT. The yards are all operating well below capacity. The Galatz yard has the largest theoretical capacity, but all the yards have experienced cashflow problems and find financing hard. The other yards include Mangalia and Constanza, which can build large vessels, including bulk carriers over 100,000 tonnes deadweight. The shipyards at Braila, Tulcea, Oltenita, Severnav and Giurgiu are all smaller.

The most common ship type built has been dry cargo ships, with a variety of other vessel types such as bulkers, ore strengthened bulk carriers, products tankers and tankers. Miscellaneous vessels ordered have also included a number of supply vessels and ro-ro ferries.

Of the former Soviet republics, only Ukraine has made a serious impact on the market with its shipyards situated in the Black Sea. The 61 Kommunar shipyard at Nikolayev is a reefer specialist, building large series of standard types. Also at Nikolayev is the Okean shipyard. This is the largest in the country, and is in overall scale a large shipyard by any standards. It is equipped to build the largest ships, although it has been limited to around 80,000 dwt vessels to date.

Other shipyards include Black Sea (Chernomorsky), Kherson Shipyard, Zaliv Shipyard at Kerch in the Crimea, along with a number of smaller, local com-panies.

With the exception of 61 Kommunar, the Ukraine shipyards concentrate on the bulk carrier and tanker markets, where their low costs give an advantage. The tonnage on order in the Ukraine has increased steadily to a figure in excess of 1,000,000 dwt.

Hungary has four small newbuilding yards and one small mixed yard with an overall newbuilding capacity estimated at 20,000 CGT. The shipyards are of limited and local significance.

Russia itself remains an enigma. In Soviet times, the Russian shipyards were largely focused on military and quasi-military vessels. Some of the very large shipyards in former soviet republics reflect this, but they also had a commercial shipbuilding role. The satellite countries within the soviet orbit built the merchant ships for Russia, then the Soviet Union.

There is a large reservoir of capacity, backed by considerable shipbuilding skills and a mix of western and Russian technology. Some estimates have put the latent Russian capacity at 10 per cent of the world total. However, since the fall of the previous regime in Russia, and despite a lot of Western interest in exploiting a new source of low cost ship construction, the shipyards have failed to make a serious impact in the world market. They have, in common with shipyards in many developing countries, been inhibited by problems of financing production. A perception of risk has also persuaded many western shipowners not to consider placing orders in Russia.

As a result, of the numerous shipyards to be found in Russia, only around 10 are active in the international market.

The Americas

In South America, a number of countries have engaged in shipbuilding. The government of Mexico promoted shipbuilding as a basis for industrial development in the late 1970s. Although a major development of the Vera Cruz shipyard was undertaken, it was relatively unsuccessful. Other proposals made around 1980, including a large shipyard development at Lazaro Cardenas on the Pacific coast, were not followed up because of economic problems. A few small shipyards operate in the country.

Venezuela also considered a major shipbuilding investment in the 1970s, but the ideas were not pursued. Argentina has had a small scale shipbuilding industry for many years, and remains a minor player in the shipbuilding business.

Brazil is the largest shipbuilding nation in South America. It developed shipyards during the boom times of the 1970s, but they have had considerable problems since that time. Four shipyards, CCN, Ishibras, Verolme and Caneco build mainly bulk carriers. They also build tankers for the national oil company, Petrobras. The total order book has hovered around the one million dwt tonne mark for a number of years.

The United States of America effectively left the international shipbuilding market in the 1980s, because of the high costs of production and poor market. There is a considerable industry which has been dedicated primarily to the needs of the United States Navy. There are several major shipyards:

— Bath Iron Works in Maine;
— Newport News Shipbuilding in Virginia;
— Avondale in Louisiana;
— Litton, Pascagoula, also in Louisiana;
— National Steel and Shipbuilding in California.

Led by these and other shipyards, the industry has had a sustained research and development programme, with the motive of improving its shipbuilding performance. The confidence given by this, along with lower relative labour costs, prompted forays into the market in the 1990s. The main outcome was a series of double hulled tankers—the *Double Eagle* class—ordered from Newport News. However, the probability is that this shipyard, along with others, will not make a major impact on the market, particularly if naval and other government orders continue.

In addition to the large shipyards, there is a very large domestic market for small ships and inland waterways, and a thriving shipbuilding sector supports this.

Although the world has several hundred shipyards capable of building ocean-going ships (and that excludes boatyards and smaller fishing vessel producers), the reality is that most of the production is concentrated in very few regions. The shares, measured in terms of deadweight are as follows:

— Japan, with around one third of the order book;
— South Korea, also with one third;
— China and Taiwan, with 10 per cent between them;
— Eastern and Western Europe, each with around 10 per cent.

The rest of the world contributes the remaining 2 or 3 per cent of all the ships.

It is difficult to see the picture changing in the near future. Despite the current turmoil in financial markets in the Far East and the rationale of closing some of the world's surplus capacity, it is hard to visualise significant closures.

CHAPTER 5

SECURING ORDERS

Within the context of the market, in particular the supply of shipbuilders and the demand for new ships, modified by the other external factors which have been referred to, the key question for any shipyard is "can we obtain new orders?". The questions of ability to complete those orders, and doing so at an acceptable cost, will also be reviewed. In essence, the point is to determine the competitiveness of the shipyard.

Competitiveness can be defined as the ability to win and execute shipbuilding orders in open competition and stay in business. For the moment, ignoring all the aspects of political and other external influences on markets, what aspects of shipbuilding technology deliver competitiveness? A number of reports have been produced over the years to address this question, and a consensus view appears to focus on seven key components of technology. These are:

WHAT IS COMPETITIVENESS?

Strategy and corporate management

Does the shipyard have a strategy, which is based on some vision of its future? Is this vision clear, and is it known to all the key staff? Is the consistent strategy which is designed to achieve this vision also in place and consistently applied?

Marketing and customer care

Does the shipyard have a coherent marketing strategy, supporting the overall strategy and based on a consistent product development? Is the shipyard aware of its customers' needs, and those of the market their customers serve? Does marketing extend as far as feedback on ships that have been delivered as a basis for product improvement and repeat orders?

Purchasing and material management

Given that materials and other services which are supplied to the shipyard by outside organisations will typically account for between 60 and 80 per cent of the value of the shipyard's products, how well organised is the purchasing strategy? And is it supported by a well-developed materials management system?

Human resource management

People build ships, and the industry worldwide is becoming critically aware of a major shortage of appropriately skilled people. Does the shipyard have a policy and strategy which recognise the need for skilled and motivated people? Are they supported by high quality recruitment, training and development programmes?

Design and technical capability

Is the product development strategy supported by a capable design process? Or is there a close relationship with an external supplier of design services, who is integrated into the shipyard's strategies and methods?

Planning and organisation of work

Given the ability to win orders, and develop the appropriate designs, how well does the shipyard prepare for production?

Production technology

Finally, how good are the production processes? "Finally" is appropriate, because much of the evidence available indicates that the actual production technology plays a lesser role in the success of a shipyard than might be supposed.

In this context, therefore, technology includes the whole set of processes in the industry, not merely hardware but also the people, operating systems and other "soft" issues.

ELEMENTS OF TECHNOLOGY

A number of the reports which have dealt with the question of competitiveness have addressed the question by looking in detail at the technology, usually, but not always, within the seven headings above. Taking these seven major components of the technology of the industry as a starting point, each of them can be subdivided into a large number of elements and a larger number of sub-elements. This breakdown into elements of technology can therefore be done in greater or less detail.

For a detailed analysis of production technology, two or three levels can be identified. Thus, within the component called "production", there are elements including:

— Steelwork production;
— Outfitting production;

— Construction;
— Installation;

and so on.

Within each of these elements, the sub-elements can then be defined. So for steelwork production, the sub-elements would typically be, depending on whether any of the production processes are sub-contracted:

— Plate and profile storage;
— Plate and profile cutting;
— Plate and profile forming;
— Assembly (which can be further sub-divided into different stages, minor assembly, sub assembly, unit assembly, block assembly and so on);
— Outfitting and painting (of the steel assemblies).

Similarly, outfitting production can be divided into different work types:

— Pipe storage, bending and cutting;
— Pipe fabrication;
— Sheet metal work;
— Machine shop;
— Electrical work;

and so on, bearing in mind that once again, any or all of these might be sub-contracted.

The chapter describing the production process in detail includes all the processes which may be found in a shipyard even though often some of them will probably be sub-contracted.

TECHNOLOGICAL GENERATIONS

Each element of technology which is identified can be at any stage along a path of development. There are some very advanced, computer-controlled, steel cutting systems within the industry, which represent the latest point on a path of development which started with a simple hand cutting torch. The use of oxygen and a fuel gas for steel cutting, supplemented by mechanical cutting systems, has been followed by plasma cutting and, more recently, laser cutting. There may be further, future developments using ultra-high pressure water jet cutting. However, some use of the original, simple hand cutting torch will still be found; indeed in some small shipyards it may still be the principal cutting tool in use.

There is a spectrum of technology, from the most basic systems to the most advanced. The advanced end of the spectrum is moving, as new technologies and processes are developed and adopted by the industry.

To continue with the example of steel cutting, it has been controlled in different ways:

— by hand torch;
— by mechanised cutting machine, controlled by hand;
— by optically controlled machine;
— by numerical control (using paper tape);
— by direct numerical control.

The steel cutting can also be carried out by different processes:

— by a fuel gas/oxygen process;
— by a plasma cutting process;
— by a laser cutting process.

And perhaps in the future, there may be water jetting or other processes which have become economic for plate cutting.

The shipbuilding industry is very wide ranging. Shipyards are found in most countries with a coastline or a large river. The industry ranges from the huge, modern South Korean shipyards, with a capacity for millions of tonnes deadweight annually, to small shipyards producing a few fishing vessels each year. This huge range of shipyards displays all the characteristics of all stages of development along the spectrum.

It is important for any individual shipyard to be at the appropriate stage of development. It is not necessarily better to be at an advanced stage, if labour costs and production volumes are low. The large South Korean shipyard will need advanced technology simply to manage the volume of production. On the other hand, the small fishing vessel shipyard may be able to continue in business, in its local region, using very basic methods.

GENERATIONS OF TECHNOLOGICAL CHANGE

The development of marine production can be expressed in terms of generations, with a significant change occurring approximately every 10 years since 1950. 1950 is taken as a convenient starting point for the shipbuilding industry. It is the time when the worldwide industry recovered from the 1939–1945 conflict. A primary reason is that it marks the effective introduction of welding of steel ships on a large scale, and it is also the time when the technology of shipbuilding began to develop in parallel with a massive increase in demand for new shipping.

So far, on this basis, six generations of current shipbuilding technology can be identified. These are very briefly summarised here, in terms of some of the key characteristics which distinguish one from its predecessor.

First generation: up to 1950

The main characteristic is fixed position working, where the individual piece parts—plates and profiles, cut and formed as required—are taken to the building berth, where all other hull construction activity takes place. Outfitting is all completed afloat, i.e. after the launch of the steel hull.

Second generation: 1950–1965

There is mechanisation of initial production processes, the introduction of early treatment lines for shotblasting and painting the steel plates and profiles, and of cutting machines for the plates. The piece parts are assembled into small units prior to transport to the building berth, which is now equipped with jib cranes of modest capacity. Outfitting is still largely completed afloat.

Third generation: 1965–1975

There is mechanisation of some assembly stages, in particular the development of flat panel assembly lines for larger ships which have significant areas of flat structure. The growth of ships in general, and the development of VLCCs in particular, leads to the development of brand new, specialist shipyards on greenfield sites for these large ships. Outfitting is developed, with many steel units having outfitting installed, and the painting of large blocks prior to their erection. This is now more likely to take place in a dock, rather than on a berth, and there are larger construction cranes.

Fourth generation: 1975–1985

The development of early ship factories for smaller ships, with most of the production processes completed within a single large building which also encloses the building dock. Group technology is adopted, leading to improvements in productivity for ships where the mechanisation of the large VLCC shipyards is not feasible.

Fifth generation: 1985–1995

There is some new facilities development, using product and group technology. The use of large cranes, mechanisation and under-cover construction is steadily expanded where markets or subsidies permit. There is emphasis on computers and on management of the processes, as much as on hardware.

Sixth generation: 1995 onwards

The shipbuilding industry is now in a sixth generation. This is still being developed and introduced into production, but some of the key features can be identified. These key features of the future technology which will define the next generation are expected to include:

— Undercover construction;

— Large, fully outfitted and coated blocks;
— Flexible automation;
— Integrated CAD and material management;
— Integrated planning and scheduling;
— Simulation of proposed production to evaluate schedules;
— Advanced cutting and welding processes (lasers, electron beam);
— Novel structural arrangements, benefiting from low distortion, etc.

REVIEWING TECHNOLOGY IN COMPANIES

Using the concept of succeeding generations of technology, the status of any shipbuilding company can be reviewed. A number of studies produced since the mid-1970s have made comparisons between shipyards to try to identify the level of technology (stage of development) which was in use, and particularly which elements or sub-elements of that technology contribute to good performance. The concept is essentially that of benchmarking, which is now an important activity in many industries.

Although the term "benchmarking" is relatively new, the process of analysing and comparing industries using some objective measure is not. In the shipbuilding industry, the pioneering work of Amos and Wilfred Ayre in the 1920s and 1930s used rivets as a basic measure, appropriate to the technology of the time.

In making the survey of the technology, the basic process is relatively simple. For each element of the technology, within the seven headings (or some other definition), a description of the processes and organisation is developed. This is then expanded to the number of sub-elements required, so that each process in the shipyard is identified and a description is available. The standardisation of the description allows consistent comparisons to be made.

The existing technology in the company under review is then assessed, sub-element by sub-element, and each is assigned to the appropriate generation. The systems can take account of the use of sub-contractors.

The assignation of each sub-element can be done using a simple, numerical scale.

- Level 1
  — Basic technology typical of shipyards in the early 1950s.
  — For example, use of manual cutting, small cranes, rudimentary planning.
- Level 2
  — Some mechanisation, typical of shipyards in the 1960s.
  — Mechanised cutting, small units, basic planning, and so on.

- Level 3
  — More mechanisation, larger blocks, typical of 1970s shipyards.
  — Panel lines, large cranes, docks rather than berths, some use of computers.
- Level 4
  — Most work under cover, e.g. newer shipyards of the 1980s.
  — Basic Computer Aided Design, good planning, early outfitting of blocks.
- Level 5
  — Ship factories, based on group technology, typical of 1990s.
  — Integrated CAD, planning, automation.
- Level 6
  — Is still being developed.

NUMERICAL SCORING

The use of the system to generate a score for each sub-element, element and for the overall level of technology is simpler. By comparing each sub-element which is assessed with the standard description and scale, a numerical score of one to six is obtained. The sub-elements can then be aggregated, and a mean found to give a score for each element of technology. Finally, taking the mean, within each of the seven headings, generates an overall score which can then be compared with other shipyards.

The scores can be weighted, to take account of the relative importance of the different elements, although in practice the effect on scores is not so large.

USING THE SCALE

It is important to note that the position of any particular shipyard on the scale is not any form of judgement. Again, considering the case of the small, fishing vessel shipyard, it may be appropriate to use technology at level 1 or level 2. This would be the case, for example, where the production is at a low throughput, perhaps for a single or two small vessels each year. It is also appropriate if the shipyard is in a region where the cost of labour is very low. It may also not be a problem to be at a low state of technology in a situation where time is not an important issue. That is, if the delivery date for the vessels being built is not critical.

However, most of the major shipbuilders in the world are generally at level 4 or 5. A few, where labour costs are lower, may be below level 4, but most of this group of shipyards are actively looking at further development, to maintain their dominant positions.

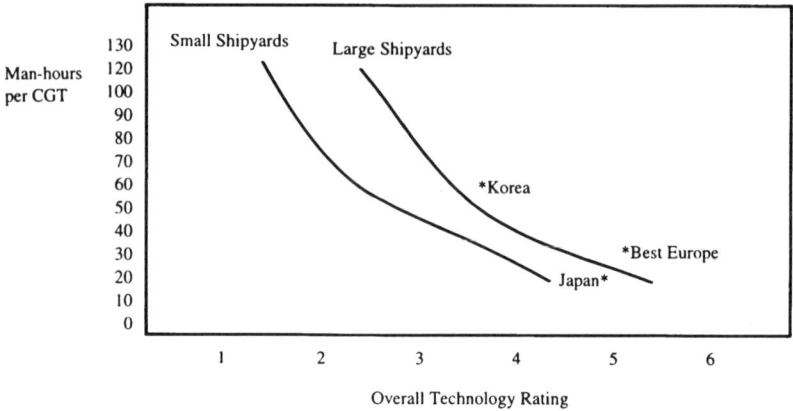

Figure 4.   Shipyard performance and technology

COMPETITIVENESS

The technology in use is not a perfect guide to competitiveness, but there is some correlation between the two. Figure 4 shows a curve of performance against level of technology for a number of shipyards, grouped into smaller and larger.

However, the ultimate measure for a shipyard, or indeed any production unit, is profitability. High performance in terms of technology, and hence in terms of productivity, is no guarantee of successful financial performance. Although money has generally been rejected as a usable performance measure for operational management and for benchmarking comparisons, it is still ultimately the most important measure of all.

An approximate cost comparison in money terms can be obtained, for any shipyard, using a combination of:

— CGT per man-year;
— Annual cost per employee.

The differential between the best and worst productivity is surprisingly large, and for identical products, the ratio between the best and worst can be as high as 6:1. This is to say that with the same product, essentially the same facilities and technology, one man hour in one company produces the same output as six man hours in the second company. This can only partly be explained by differences in wage costs.

Considering the key regions involved in maritime production, an approximate indication of the general levels of productivity is shown in Figure 5. The productivity levels are again in CGT per man-year.

Most of the required information for competitor analysis, in particular the information on throughput of shipyards and wage levels, can be obtained from published sources. The information for a particular shipyard, and that for its competitors, can be plotted as a line, or series of lines.

CGT per man-year

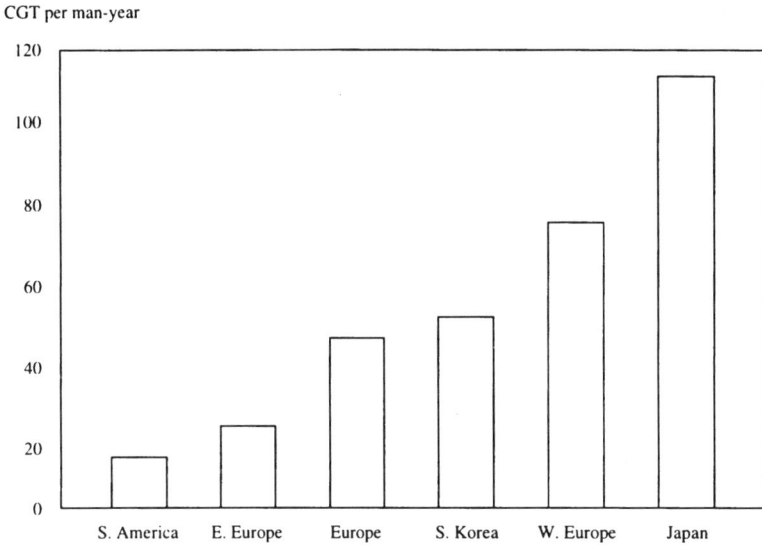

Figure 5.   *Relative performance of shipbuilding regions*

These are **constant cost lines**. In Figure 6, the vertical axis shows the productivity level for shipyards, measured in compensated gross tonnes (CGT) per man-year.
The horizontal axis measures the annual cost of each worker employed. If the
relevant productivity levels for a set of shipyards are plotted against labour cost, the
result is generally a line, or series of lines. These lines link companies with equal
costs, so that a company with an annual wage cost per employee of 20,000 US
dollars, and a productivity level of 40 CGT per man-year, will lie on the same line
as a company with annual labour cost of 40,000 US dollars and a productivity level
of 80 CGT per man-year. In each case, the cost per CGT would be 500 US
dollars.

In general, competitive companies will lie on the same line, and less competitive
companies will be below the relevant line. The difference between a company below
the line and one on the competitive line is a measure of the gap in performance
which would need to be closed for the shipyard to become competitive.

The alternative lines in the figure represent different markets. For "commodity"
ships, for example basic bulk carriers, the upper line would be appropriate, since the
price available in the market will be lower and a lower cost per CGT is essential to
compete.

For niche markets, different cost structures may be viable. If there is a technological barrier to entering the market, either some specialist knowledge or previous
experience of a special ship type, then a higher cost per CGT may be available. In
this case, the lower line would be the appropriate target.

In addition to identifying the requirement to improve performance, by identifying
the gap between a shipyard and its competitors, the impact of subsidies can also be
deduced. If a shipyard needs to reduce costs, and that implies that a subsidy is not

CGT per man-year

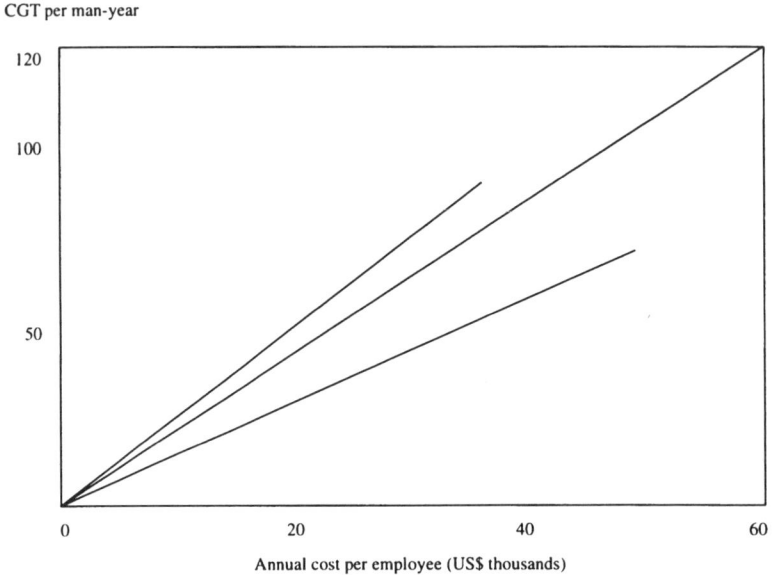

Annual cost per employee (US$ thousands)

*Figure 6.   Constant cost lines, linking shipbuilders of different performance and labour
cost*

available, changes are required to reduce the expenditure of resources. Even if a
company is competitive, the general trend in the world is to improve productivity
annually by around 4 per cent. Thus a key objective for any shipbuilding company
is to minimise the work content, resources and time spent in producing its products.

Figure 7 shows the situation. A shipyard at position A is essentially competitive,
that is, it is on the relevant line for the particular market in which it operates. A
company at position D is not competitive because it has a higher labour cost and the
same productivity and the gap between D & E identifies the change that is needed
to reach a competitive situation. This would be at position E.

Shipyards B and C are less competitive than A and E. The situation can be
explained in two ways. B and C may be in a different market that the other shipyards
cannot compete in for other than cost reasons and can afford higher costs. The
alternative is that B and C are benefiting from some form of support which
compensates for the gap which is apparent.

THE NEED TO ADAPT FOR CHANGES IN PRODUCTS

For an existing facility, new products must be selected to suit the production
facilities, with the proviso that selection of a product depends on the market. Over
time there will be a change in product, as technological and trade changes occur.

CGT per man-year

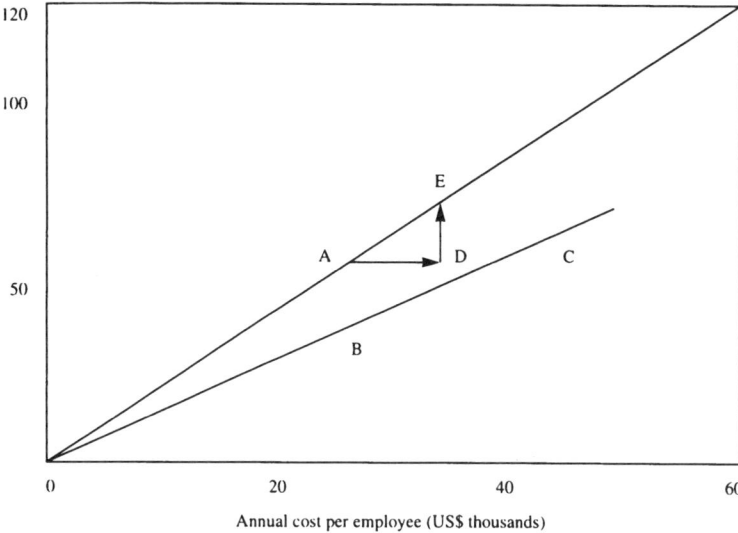

Figure 7.   Use of constant cost lines to identify performance gaps

There should be a corresponding adaptive change in the facilities, as the range of interim products changes and production technology improves.

All organisations should adapt over time, as their environment changes. This may be interpreted as the need for continuous improvement, which is one aspect of change. But it is also about adapting, for example, the size and skill mixture of the workforce. This may require re-training and upgrading of existing workers to make them adaptable. More commonly, shipbuilders will use sub-contractors to supply intermittent or new needs for particular skills. The shiprepair industry, which suffers from very short term volatility in the demand for different skills, has generally moved further in this direction. The Dutch shipbuilding industry has developed a very highly structured sub-contracting culture.

It is observable that many companies do not make continuous adaptation to gradual changes in product, in demand and external influences. Instead they suffer a major upheaval after a long period of apparent stability. In the worst cases, shipbuilding companies which do not adapt may go out of business.

Catastrophe theory provides a useful, symbolic model for this (see Figure 8). The change in circumstances is represented by a shift along the X axis. To maintain equilibrium, the company should make the corresponding change along the Y axis, so that the current situation is always represented by the point on the line. Instead of incremental change as the situation of a company changes the company makes no changes, leading to points on the curve. At some point, as the mismatch between the required status of the company and the actual status becomes critical, there is a sudden, violent swing, represented by the curve. If the status represents, as an

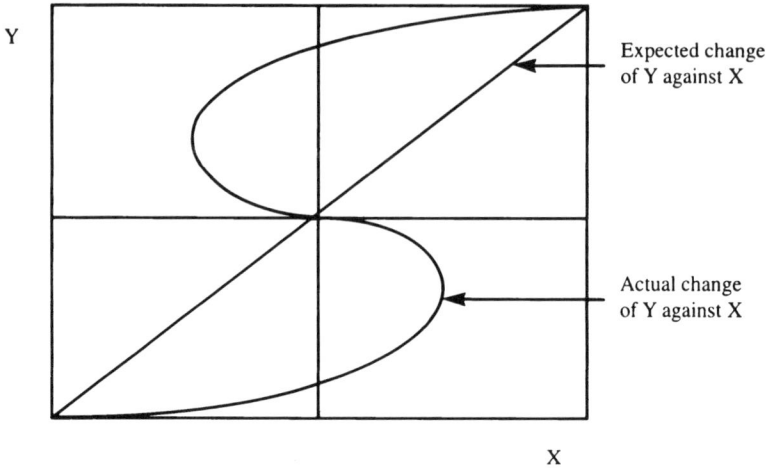

Figure 8.   Simplified catastrophe theory model

example, production costs against process, then the catastrophe may be in financial terms, leading to a company ceasing to be in the business at all.

As an example, if movement from left to right on the "X" axis is taken to represent a decreasing demand for a particular resource in a shipyard, then there should be a corresponding reduction in the provision of that resource, represented by moving up the "Y" axis. If the shipyard makes the necessary change, to keep supply and demand in balance, the position at any time is represented by the straight line. However, if no change in resource levels is made, the situation is represented by the curve. This shows that the provision of the resources is increasingly too large for the demand, and this would be reflected in excessive costs. Eventually, some action to reduce costs (resources) will be forced on the company, but this may result in overcorrection, so there is now little resource available. The curve represents this change. Eventually, the company may return to an equilibrium point on the straight line, but the way in which the correction is made can have serious—even catastrophic—consequences in terms of excess cost or programme delays.

PRODUCT LIFE CYCLES

The changes in products over time can be modelled using the product life cycle. Technological changes, varying demand for commodities and products, changes in economic activity all influence the types of marine vessels which are required. If the demand for a new product is studied, it typically follows the pattern shown in Figure 9, over a period which may vary from months to decades.

The product life cycle is a general model which represents the different stages in the life of any product. The figure shows these stages which are:

Product development, which is essentially the marketing stage in the shipbuilding business. Many products go through the early stages of development but are then

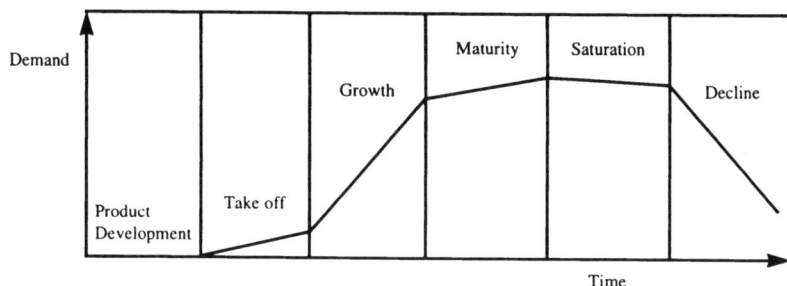

Figure 9.   Product life cycle

abandoned and fail to be sold. The product in shipbuilding will normally be a new or modified type of ship rather than a specific design, although there have been some successful standard types.

Take off, where the product makes an initial sale. Up to this point, the developer will have incurred costs, and if the product is unsuccessful, these costs are lost.

Growth, where further sales are made, and profits can be available, particularly where the developer is one of a small number or perhaps the only builder with the product.

Maturity, where the demand for the product reaches a peak, and other builders enter the market. The emphasis is now on cost control rather than innovation.

Saturation, as demand begins to drop and yet more competitors appear. At this stage, it may be prudent to leave the product and move onto a new one, unless the shipyard has a significant cost advantage.

Decline, where the demand is dropping as new advances make the product obsolescent, or simply all the vessels that trade demands have been completed.

In some areas, the cycle is lengthy, for example bulk carriers, where the market is saturated with numerous builders pursuing the market. There are incremental changes in the product, but it is continuing as broadly the same. In others, such as fast ferries, the cycle has been shorter.

The life of a company can be viewed as a series of product life cycles. For a company to survive in the long term continuous product updating and development of new products is needed. As the demand for a product grows, more producers appear. When most potential customers have been served, there is more supply than demand, causing the price to fall and/or some suppliers to leave the market. Developing new products is the means of remaining in business. This results in a series of life cycles, where the development of new products is financed by profitable existing products. Exit from a particular market can be as important and difficult as introducing a new product, particularly as the exit has to be managed without losses.

At any time, a company will have several products at different stages. The position can be modelled using the product life cycle as a basis (see Figure 10). Many products fail to reach the take off stage after development, and in the shipbuilding business this may represent a failed tender. The business of making

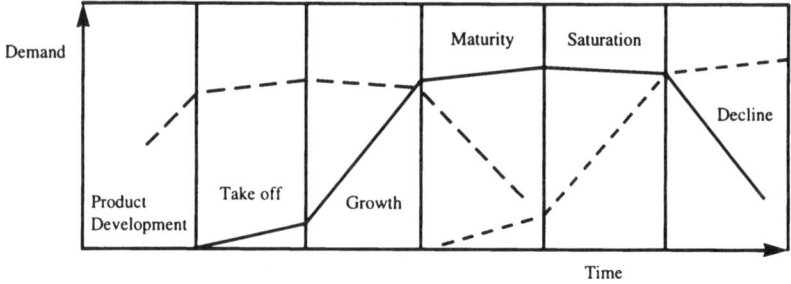

Figure 10. Overlapping product life cycles

large made-to-order products, like ships, is difficult, since the only alternatives are
to have an order, or not.

SECURING ORDERS

In order to be in a position to secure new orders for ships to build, a shipyard will
have to be competitive, making use of the most appropriate level of technology for
its labour cost, and then using that technology effectively to achieve a competitive
cost per CGT. With that as a supporting structure, it is the marketing and associated
sales functions in a shipyard which are required to secure the actual orders. In the
reports which have made assessments of competitiveness, the ability to market
effectively is one of the most important factors.

The marketing function covers a number of elements, including:

— primary market research;
— concept design;
— promotional activity;
— product development;
— enquiry screening and response.

At that point, the shipyard begins the process of securing a particular sale.

To secure an order from an enquiry, a number of additional functions are required.
These are:

— preliminary design;
— estimating;
— strategic planning;
— contract (project) management.

In addition to the market research prior to and leading to firm enquiries, other
activities which shape the shipyard's response to owners assist the marketing and
sales process. These are not always considered as part of these processes, but
research has demonstrated their importance. They are essentially after-sales service
and include:

— the guarantee period;
— collecting operational feedback;
— supplying guarantee engineers;
— publicising the ships.

The last of these completes a feedback loop back into sales and marketing.

Primary market research is important to the shipbuilder. The extent to which individual shipyards are able to conduct such research depends on the scale of their operation, and on the market sector in which they operate. Thus, a niche market builder may only need to maintain contact with a small group of shipowners or operators. The close relationship which is developed, the ability to respond to the owner's needs and such factors as technological barriers to market entry give the required competitive edge.

A small shipyard may have to depend on published market research reports. On the other hand, many small shipyards operate in a regional, or even national market, which again means that maintaining contact with a modestly sized owner group may be adequate.

The basis of the market research activity has been described in the first chapter, and also when dealing with supply and demand in the shipbuilding market. The pitfalls of mechanistic models, accepting that nothing more effective has yet been developed, have been identified. As a minimum, it is necessary to consider different views of the future and have some contingency plans if a market proves to be weaker than expected.

The timescale for such activity varies. In seeking new orders, a relatively short term view can be taken, identifying existing orders, the position of competitors and then focusing the sales effort on those owners who have yet to enter the immediate market. In seeking product development, a longer term view is needed, looking beyond the demand for current ships and taking into account new technologies and developments in the trade for which the shipyard's products are intended.

Whether through direct, original research, or by proxy using published work, the shipbuilder must be aware of the future shape of its particular market, including trade patterns, technological advances and owner requirements.

In non-niche markets, the over-supply of shipyards essentially results in a price-driven market. The opportunities to secure a competitive edge through any technological factors or special relationships are very limited.

Promotional activities are often regarded as of limited value to the shipbuilder. Advertising as such is limited to awareness advertising, and only serves to gain a position where enquiries are directed to the shipyard. This can allow a wider group of potential customers to be reached than is the case when direct contact is the only means. However, beyond alerting owners, or their agents, to the ability of a shipyard to produce particular types, advertising potential is limited.

The response to enquiries is of major importance. Prompt, effective responses help. Supplying the owner with information and maintaining contact can help, but ultimately, if there is a competitor with a lower cost base, obtaining orders becomes difficult. At this point, the use of after-sales service to try to ensure repeat business comes into the picture. While loyalties to particular shipyards are no longer a feature of many owners, and there is a problem of securing the initial order in a competitive market, good service can be a feature of successful sales campaigns.

The experience of marketing activity in many different industries leads to a number of generally accepted conclusions.

It is generally easier to secure a repeat order than to break into a new market or persuade a new customer to buy. So the level of service which an owner receives will influence to some extent his propensity to return. After-sales service has an important role to play in this area.

It is also noted that word of mouth is often far more powerful in the selection of industrial products, including ships, than any advertising. So a shipowner who has received a high level of service from a particular shipyard is likely to be a far more powerful help to marketing that shipyard's products than any advertising campaign.

The after-sales service, including:

— the guarantee period;
— collecting operational feedback;
— supplying guarantee engineers;
— publicising the ships;

is therefore of great potential importance in securing further orders.

Historically the period of 12 months after delivery sees a ship under guarantee. Where there is a strong relationship with an owner, the shipyard can exploit this period to develop that relationship further. When any country has a dominant market position, owners will return, but retaining the position depends on relationships. There is nothing sentimental about close ties between owner and builder. Where the two work together, the owner's needs are foreseen by the builder, the designs of ships are specific and the owner receives a reliable product for minimum effort.

However, that relationship is threatened when competition arises, particularly where the competition is based on ability to deliver a ship at a lower price. In the face of price competition, the shipyard has to rely on non-price factors in the short term. (In the longer term there may be opportunities to improve the technology in use and restore the competitive position.) One of the non-price factors is the ability to support the shipowner after delivery and the use of a guarantee engineer is one way. This requires not only correcting minor, hopefully not major, problems which occur (which is a negative view of the function), but also actively seeking operational feedback which can influence future design work.

In effect, the use of a guarantee engineer is one way of completing the feedback loop from ship operation to design. In the process, the relationship developed with the owner, and his employees may help to influence future purchase decisions. The collection of operational data also provides the product development team with direct information on the trades and use of the ships which the shipyard builds. The effect can be to supplement the market research requirements, and arguably replace them with more effective, direct feedback.

The use of guarantee engineers can be regarded as an investment, rather than a cost, and as a means of marketing the shipyard's products more directly.

A successful sale of a successful ship, once it is in operation, provides a good publicity vehicle for the shipyard. In particular if the design has some novel features, or is in some way differentiated from others in the same trade, then it can attract the attention of other owners. Having an existing, proven product, even if it does not precisely match a new enquiry specification, can be a powerful incentive to a shipowner.

A coherent strategy is an important basis for the marketing and sales effort. For shipyards which simply respond to enquiries, with little attempt to specialise or actively promote their specific expertise, each sale can effectively require breaking into a new market. This can take time, and if time implies a lack of work, then the shipyard is in serious trouble, with no, or reduced, income. A shipyard in this position, with no parent to provide any interim support, is extremely vulnerable.

Successful shipyards can generate a stream of orders for new ships. Discounting assistance, for example in the form of directed orders or subsidies, these shipyards must have appropriate technology, effectively deployed to achieve a cost competitive performance. They must then attract owners with a portfolio of well-researched designs, whether at concept or preliminary stage. Since repeat business is easier than new business, after-sales service for existing customers and a reputation to place before new customers are essential. It is easier to be successful for a shipyard which is already successful.

CHAPTER 6

THE SHIPBUILDING CONTRACT

INTRODUCTION

Legal framework

To establish the legal framework of a newbuilding project, the buyer and the builder will enter into a contract. The form of that contract will be influenced by a number of factors: the strength of the relationship between the buyer and the builder; the nature, extent and value of the works to be undertaken; and the general state of the market.

The buyer and the builder will assume significant risks over the course of a newbuilding project. It is, therefore, prudent for the builder and the buyer to obtain specialist legal advice on the terms of the contract, which will regulate and apportion such risks. The contract is likely to be preceded by detailed negotiations. Each party will normally wish to consider carefully the other's financial standing and prior experience of similar projects of the type in question and the buyer, in particular, will rely upon the experience and information provided by his shipbroker. Where the shipbuilder has previously developed a standard design for the vessel to be built, he will often be in a position to supply the buyer with a résumé of the specifications, "principal particulars", describing the vessel in outline, the standards to which she will be built and the major items of her machinery and equipment.

Invitation to tender

The buyer may be required, or simply wish, to invite shipbuilders to tender for the works and prepare an "invitation to tender" on the basis of his outline specifications and a summary of proposed contract terms. In such cases, unless the vessel is to be constructed to the builder's standard specification, the technical basis for the project will need to be finalised (including where necessary model tank tests and detailed consultation with the classification society and the regulatory authorities).

Letter of intent

Given that such matters and the pre-contract negotiations may involve significant expense on the buyer's part and a commitment on the builder's part to maintaining a "slot" for the works, it is usual for the parties at this stage to enter into a "letter of intent" or "LOI", setting out their mutual understanding of the basis of the proposed project. By the time they agree a letter of intent, the parties will typically have defined the key commercial terms underlying the project. These will usually encompass the price of the vessel, the currency and terms of payment, the date for delivery and the law which will govern the contract, as well as the options (if any) the builder is prepared to grant to the buyer should their discussions lead to a concluded agreement.

At this stage of the project the buyer's ability to conclude a firm contract is likely to depend upon his obtaining a satisfactory offer of financing in respect of the vessel's purchase price. Letters of intent are widely regarded as non-binding, imposing moral rather than legal obligations. They will usually expressly state that the project is conditional upon certain "subjects" (board approval, availability of financing, agreement on the terms of a detailed contract etc.). In such cases, under English law, until each of the subjects has been satisfied, neither party is legally bound to the project. The extent to which the LOI binds the parties will depend upon a number of factors, not least the law, if any, chosen by the parties to govern the LOI. Certain jurisdictions will be more ready to enforce obligations to negotiate, notwithstanding the inclusion of express "subjects".

Interim agreement

Where substantial work will be involved in developing the project to the point when a contract can be signed, either party may be unwilling to rely only upon a letter of intent and may insist that an interim contract be concluded. For example, the builder might be prepared only to provide design and other technical services to the buyer for the development of the project in return for a fee. This type of arrangement is particularly common in relation to the construction of highly specialised vessels and structures for use in the offshore industry.

In such cases it will normally be agreed that the interim arrangements should be subsumed within the main contract if and when this becomes effective. From the buyer's perspective, it is important that the builder's liability under any express or implied design warranties should not be discharged by termination of the interim contract and these should be restated in the main contract itself.

Contract form

Contract negotiations will often be undertaken by different teams of representatives of each party, one commercial/legal and the other technical. This necessarily involves the risk that, if the contract negotiations should fail to reach a conclusion, considerable time and expense may have been wasted in the parallel discussions relating to the technical specifications. Most negotiations will be based upon a standard contract form amended by the parties to meet their particular project requirements. The choice of form is likely to be significantly influenced by the builder's identity and domicile. Many shipbuilders and shipyards (especially those involved in repair works) are reluctant to contract other than upon standard (pre-printed) forms prepared or recommended by the trade associations to which they belong.

The principal form of contract in use in large-scale newbuilding projects is that published in January 1974 by The Shipbuilders' Association of Japan and collo-quially known as the "SAJ form". This wording is also the basis of various standard contracts used in South Korea, China and Taiwan.

Other standard contracts in use are those of the Association of West European Shipbuilders (the "AWES form"), the Maritime Subsidy Board of the US Depart-ment of Commerce, Maritime Administration (the "MARAD form") and the Asso-ciation of Norwegian Marine Yards.

The SAJ form is weighted in favour of the builder, as is evident from the provisions relating to sub-contracting (Article I.4), modifications (Article V) and *force majeure* (Article VII) and in the express exclusion of any liability of the builder for damages in the event of the buyer's rescission (Article X).

There are also a number of significant omissions in the standard wording, in particular the absence of terms relating to design liabilities, the effect of the builder's liquidation or other financial default and the provision of security for the repayment of the buyer's default. Depending upon the parties' previous relationship and the strength of their respective bargaining positions, these issues may, however, be specifically addressed through negotiation and amendments to the standard form.

Whichever form is in use or proposed, there are certain standard terms which will usually be set out in the contract.

OUTLINE OF STANDARD TERMS

The following list identifies those standard terms which any contract is likely to include. The later section below addresses some of the key points likely to arise in negotiating a contract for a newbuilding project.

Parties/Preamble

Identity of the buyer and the builder, their place of incorporation or principal place of business;

Description of the scope of the works to be undertaken, in particular whether the builder will be responsible for the design of the vessel and the shipyard at which the works will be undertaken.

Description and Class

Description of the vessel (hull number, dimensions and principal character-istics);

Scope of the buyer's requirements, including issues such as performance (speed, deadweight, fuel consumption), classification and other regulatory requirements;

Builder's authority (if any) to sub-contract all or part of the works;

Buyer's chosen place of registration and flag for the vessel;

List of detailed specifications, plans and drawings, usually exhibited to the contract and expressly incorporated in the contract.

Contract price and terms of payment

Contract price, usually expressed as a lump sum;

Method of payment of the contract price;

Terms of payment, usually by instalments upon completion of stages of the construction (milestones);

Responsibility for bank charges and currency of payment;

Right (if any) to make prepayments;

Prohibition (if any) against the exercise of rights of set-off and deduction.

Adjustment of the contract price

Liquidated damages payable upon delay in delivery of the vessel;

Buyer's right to rescind for excessive delay;

Builder's bonus (if any) for early delivery;

Liquidated damages as compensation for failure of the vessel to meet the Builder's guarantees in relation to performance (speed, fuel consumption, deadweight capacity).

Approval of plans and drawings and inspection during construction

Approval by the buyer of plans and drawings;

Buyer's representatives, their rights and obligations during the construction works.

Modifications (to the specifications for the vessel)

At the buyer's request;

"Class" or compulsory modifications;

At the builder's request;

Disputes about the consequences of modifications (adjustments to contract price and delivery date).

Trials

Notice of the tests and trials to be given by the builder to the buyer;

Conduct of the trials;

Location;
Effect of adverse weather conditions;
Responsibility for crewing and navigation during the trials;
Responsibility for provisioning;
Completion of the trials;
Method of acceptance or rejection by the buyer of the vessel;
Presentation of the trial results by the builder;
The buyer's election to accept or reject the vessel;
Consequence of acceptance of the vessel;
Consequence of rejection of the vessel.

Delivery

Time for delivery;
Documentation to be produced by the builder upon delivery, including the
protocol of delivery and acceptance, protocol of trials, protocol of inven-
tory of equipment, protocol of fuel oils, lube oils and consumable stores
on board, classification and trading certificates, declaration of warranty of
freedom from encumbrances, drawings and plans, commercial invoice
and bill of sale/builder's certificate;
Title to the vessel;
Builder's lien;
Risk of loss or damage;
When delivery is deemed to have taken place;
Removal of the vessel from the shipyard.

Delays and extension of time for delivery/force majeure

Delay caused by breach of contract or negligence;
Force majeure events;
Notice requirements upon the occurrence of *force majeure*;
Effect of *force majeure*;
Permissible delay;
Excessive delay/"drop dead date".

Builder's warranty

Scope and nature of builder's warranty;
Defects existing on delivery;
Time limits;
Loss of use of vessel;
Design liabilities;
Replaced parts;
Sub-contractors' warranties;

Notice requirements;
Builder's obligation to remedy;
Builder's right (if any) to appoint a "Guarantee Engineer".

Rescission by buyer

Buyer's right to rescind if delay or builder's default;
Total loss of the vessel;
Effect of buyer's rescission;
Builder's obligation to refund the instalments of contract price paid by the
　　buyer;
Buyer's supplies;
Rights (if any) to complete the contract works;
Disputes.

Buyer's default

Events of default by the buyer;
Effects of an event of default;
Effect of rescission by the builder;
Common law remedies.

Insurance

Builders' duty to insure;
Scope of coverage;
Latent defects;
Exclusions;
Buyer's supplies;
Assignment of insurances;
Consequence of partial losses;
Consequence of total loss.

Dispute resolution

Governing law;
Technical disputes, choice of expert/classification society;
Non-technical disputes, choice of forum (arbitration or the courts).

Right of assignment

Buyer's rights of assignment;
Builder's rights of assignment.

Taxes and duties

Responsibility for taxes and duties.

Patents, trade mark, copyrights, etc.

Ownership of, and indemnities against infringement of, intellectual property
rights in plans, drawings, etc.

Buyer's supplies

Buyer's obligations;
Effect of buyer's default;
Title and risk of buyer's supplies.

Notice

Notice requirements.

Effectiveness

Conditions precedent and subsequent;
Effect if not satisfied;
Waiver of conditions precedent.

KEY ASPECTS

Some of the key contract issues which are likely to arise in relation to the practical
aspects of a newbuilding project are briefly summarised below. It is usual for the
parties to retain their own legal advisors in relation to any negotiations concerning
the contract. This is a reflection of the significant risks to both parties in any
newbuilding project.

Parties/Preamble

Parties

The identity of the buyer may be determined by tax considerations and/or the place
of registration for the vessel's flag. As a consequence, there may be credit issues
about the buyer. Where the buyer is a single-purpose vehicle established solely for
the purpose of commissioning the newbuilding or for the purpose of owning the
vessel, the builder will usually require a parent or third party guarantee of the
buyer's obligations under the contract.

Where the shipyard at which the building works are to be undertaken is controlled by a third party, perhaps associated with the builder, it may be desirable to include such third party as a named party to the contract.

Location of works

Where the builder maintains a number of shipyards, the buyer may prefer that the contract specifically identifies the shipyard at which the works are to be undertaken. This may be especially important if the buyer has inspected one or more of the builder's yards and such inspection has formed the basis for its decision to proceed.

Design responsibility

The most material aspect of the preamble to the contract is that part which allocates responsibility for the vessel's design. This is fundamental because problems with design may not manifest themselves until the buyer has accepted the vessel after completion of the works and the vessel has commenced trading. Poor workmanship or materials will more frequently be detected during construction and, therefore, be capable of remedy before the buyer accepts the vessel. Neither the SAJ nor the AWES form attempts to legislate for design responsibility and, from the buyer's perspective, it is important to ensure that the contract makes specific provision for the same.

The vessel must normally be built in accordance with a design which is acceptable to the preferred classification society and regulatory authorities. The parties are, otherwise, free to allocate design risk and responsibility between them. Unless the builder accepts design responsibility, it is likely to refuse to provide any warranty that the vessel will be adequate to meet the buyer's intended operation.

Where design responsibility is expressly provided to be that of the builder under the contract, other provisions within the contract which permit the buyer a right to approve plans and drawings for the vessel will not usually transfer any design responsibility to the buyer, although it may be advisable to ensure that express provision is included in the contract to this effect.

Description and Class

Specifications

The contract will typically state that the vessel is to be built in accordance with specifications and certain principal plans and drawings, including a general arrangement plan (or guidance plan). These will usually be initialled by both parties prior to or upon signing the contract and will be incorporated within the contract by reference. The contract will also dictate an order of precedence, should there be any conflict or ambiguity between the terms of the contract and the specifications and plans or drawings. Care should be exercised if it is proposed that a copy of any quotation given by the builder should also be attached to the contract because this is likely to include less detail than the contract itself and/or the specifications and thereby create uncertainty.

Performance guarantees

Certain "guarantees", usually relating to the vessel's speed, deadweight and fuel consumption, will be given by the builder under the contract. If the vessel fails to meet these standards, the contract usually provides expressly that the buyer shall be entitled to liquidated damages and, in extreme cases beyond any reasonable tolerance, to reject the vessel and to rescind the contract. The type of the vessel will dictate whether any additional or alternative guarantees are required. For example, contracts for the newbuilding of cruise or passenger vessels may expressly provide guarantees in relation to maximum levels of noise and vibration in cabins and public areas.

"Class" status

The contract will provide that the vessel must meet the standards defined by a recognised classification society and a number of national and international bodies (which are usually known as the regulatory authorities) who will license the vessel's operations after the works have been completed.

The buyer will need to be certain that the vessel will achieve its classification status appropriate for her intended operations. The contract usually imposes an obligation on the builder to procure that the construction of the vessel will take place subject to a "special survey" by the classification society, which will require the classification society's surveyors to attend at the shipyard during the course of the vessel's construction to inspect and approve the works as they proceed. In keeping with this practice, the contract will usually expressly provide that, in the event of any dispute or issue as to whether the works comply, the classification society's decision shall be final and binding upon both parties.

The contract will also reflect the fact that the classification society is employed on behalf of the builder, who is usually responsible for the society's fees and charges.

Regulatory requirements

In addition to satisfying the requirements of the classification society, the vessel will need to comply with the rules for vessels of her type and size issued by the relevant regulatory authorities, whose permission or licence will be required for the intended operations of the vessel. For example, certain vessels will need to be equipped to the standards of the Panama and Suez Canal authorities and cruise vessels will need to be constructed to meet the rules of the United States Coast Guard, if they intend to operate within US waters or within the Caribbean cruise market. The regulatory requirements relevant to the works will normally be detailed in the specifications and/or within the contract.

Standard of works/QA

More generally, the contract will usually require that the builder undertakes the works in conformity with internationally recognised standards, whether U.S., Western European or Asian. This will be a matter of some negotiation, depending upon the location and nationality of the builder and the intended operation of the vessel.

The contract will also usually provide, either within the specifications and/or the contract, that the builder will comply with certain quality assurance standards. This again will be the matter of some negotiation with the builder, depending upon the extent of the builder's QA accreditation.

Sub-contracting of works

The contract will usually specify and limit the extent to which the builder may sub-contract or delegate all or certain parts of the works to be performed under the contract. It is customary for the buyer to permit the builder to sub-contract certain items (whether by reference to value or nature) provided that he will remain fully responsible to the buyer for performance of such works. The extent to which the builder is entitled to sub-contract works will also have an impact upon the buyer's costs of supervision. The contract will, therefore, usually provide that the builder may only sub-contract works with the buyer's prior approval in writing. It will be a matter of separate negotiation whether the buyer should provide such approval where it is reasonable to do so.

Where it has been agreed that certain aspects of the works will be sub-contracted, the contract may expressly refer to a "makers' list" which will identify certain manufacturers or suppliers which have been pre-approved by the buyer.

Where certain works have been sub-contracted by the builder, the contract may in advance provide that following completion of the works as a whole (for which the builder shall remain responsible at all times) the builder may be entitled to assign to the buyer the benefit of any guarantees provided to him by the sub-contractor(s) in lieu of the builder's own warranty.

Registration and flag

The contract will usually provide that the buyer shall register the vessel at a predetermined location, i.e. its chosen flag, and that the buyer will bear all costs associated with registration. The contract should, however, also expressly require the builder to provide on delivery of the vessel, if required, a bill of sale or builder's certificate, which will need to be notarised and legalised, upon which the buyer's application for registration will be based.

Contract price and terms of payment

Lump sum price

In keeping with most large scale, modern shipbuilding projects, the contract will state a fixed price for the works to be undertaken, on the basis of a quotation provided by the builder. Likewise, the contract will usually provide that the price is to be paid in a number of agreed instalments falling at various stages of the construction and with the balance payable upon delivery of the vessel.

The contract should define those elements of the overall project cost which are included within the fixed price, such as the cost of design, drawings, etc.

Adjustments

The contract will usually provide that the price will be adjusted in the event of any compulsory or agreed modifications to the specifications and to reflect any liquidated damages payable by the builder to the buyer as a result of delays in delivery or deficiencies in the vessel.

It is of paramount importance that the price, the terms for payment and the currency are clearly defined within the contract. These issues will significantly affect either party's ability to finance any element of the project.

Payment terms

It is often the case that the builder will rely upon the payment by the buyer of instalments of the contract price prior to delivery as his primary source of financing the works. Many factors will dictate the timing and size of the instalments. The extent to which the buyer is prepared to release a substantial proportion of the price in advance prior to completion of the works and delivery of the vessel will depend upon whether a satisfactory refund guarantee is offered by the builder, such that the buyer has a valuable, third-party security in the event that the buyer cancels the contract at any stage during the construction of the vessel and seeks a refund of the instalments he has paid. The contract will not otherwise usually include any provision in relation to the builder's financing arrangements. The buyer may, however, be asked to consent to an assignment of the benefits of the contract in favour of the builder's financiers, if the builder is dependent upon an external source of finance. The builder may seek to negotiate a right to assign the benefit of the contract, without the buyer's prior consent, in order to allow the builder to offer the same as security to any financier he may approach during the construction process, should the need arise.

The builder's financing arrangements may otherwise affect the buyer because in certain jurisdictions he may be able to register a mortgage over a partly built vessel, but this will not affect the terms of the contract itself, which will usually provide that the builder shall retain title to the vessel (unless otherwise provided) until delivery, and the contract will expressly provide that the builder will deliver the vessel free from all mortgages and encumbrances.

The contract will also need to reflect any credit extended by the builder in respect of which the builder may require a guarantee or promissory notes to secure the buyer's obligation to pay any instalments which fall due after the contract has been signed and become effective.

Bank charges, currency, etc.

The contract will usually deal with various other matters relating to payment of the contract price, in relation to responsibility for bank charges, the currency in which payment is to be made (which may be affected by foreign exchange issues), and, most importantly, the timing of such payments. The contract will normally provide that the instalments of the price have to be paid upon certain events constituting completion of a part of the construction process (i.e. milestones). The most common events are (i) upon signing the contract or upon the granting of all necessary consents, including export licences; (ii) upon keel laying; (iii) upon launching; and (iv) upon delivery and acceptance of the vessel. The contract may also provide that instalments are payable upon commencement of steel cutting or installation of the vessel's main engine. The events in question should be capable of being clearly determined. It is sometimes agreed that the builder's notification that the event in question has occurred is sufficient. The contract may, however, require that each of the events shall be certified by a surveyor or by a representative of the classification society, whose certificate shall be conclusive for the purposes of triggering instalments of the contract price.

No set-off

The contract will also usually provide that the contract price is to be paid without any deduction, set-off or counterclaim, thereby protecting the builder's right to receive an instalment of the contract price. The existence of a dispute which affects or delays the builder's ability to recover an instalment of the contract price may not only increase the builders' costs of financing the project but also put the project in jeopardy. The buyer may be content with a prohibition against set-off or deduction where he has the benefit of a refund guarantee, should he be entitled later to cancel the contract and recover the instalments he has paid from a third party bank.

Where the prohibition does not exist, the buyer will have various legal grounds upon which to seek to withhold payment of the contract price or a part thereof in relation to claims he may have against the builder arising out of the project, either for sums due by the builder to him or by reason of claims he has arising out of the works performed by the builder.

Method of payment

The contract will provide for the means by which payment is to be made and effected (i.e. telegraphic transfer etc.). The contract may specifically provide that the instalment of the contract price payable upon delivery of the vessel shall be deposited in advance of delivery with the builder's bank, on terms that the same should be released to the builder upon production by the builder of a protocol of delivery and acceptance signed by the buyer, indicating the buyer's acceptance of the vessel under the contract. The SAJ form requires the buyer to deposit a sum equal to the delivery instalment or to provide a letter of credit from a bank acceptable to the builder.

Buyer's allowance

Where subsidised finance is available to assist the buyer in his purchase of the vessel, the contract price may be increased to include a buyer's allowance, which is a fund constituted by the builder equivalent in value to the amount of the increase in price upon which the buyer is entitled to draw during the life of the contract to meet his own costs of the newbuilding project. These typically comprise supervision expenses and the costs of buyer's supplies. Careful provisions will need to be incorporated within the contract and/or a suitable side letter to ensure that these provisions operate in accordance with the parties' intentions. These arrangements will also need to be disclosed to and be approved by any third party providing finance for the project.

Adjustments to the contract price

Liquidated damages

The buyer may incur significant losses in terms of the operation and/or value of the vessel if the builder fails to comply with his guarantee as to the agreed minimum performance standards relating to speed, fuel consumption and deadweight. The builder's risks in failing to meet his guarantee can be substantial. The contract will normally, therefore, limit the builder's liability. The contract will normally expressly provide that the buyer's remedy in relation to such matters shall be limited to his entitlement to liquidated damages, subject to the buyer's right (which may arise more generally in relation to any delay in completion of the works and delivery of the vessel) to cancel the contract.

Liquidated damages provisions should represent a genuine and reasonable pre-estimate of the losses arising from the breach to which they relate, rather than being a "penalty" which will be void under English law. The contract will, therefore, usually contain a sliding scale of liquidated damages to reflect the seriousness of the breach.

The contract will normally expressly provide that liquidated damages shall also be payable for any delay in delivery of the vessel beyond the date agreed between the parties as the date by which the vessel shall be delivered, all works completed. The contract will normally provide that such damages are payable on a daily basis, on a sliding scale depending upon the length of the delay. It is also customary that the contract will allow the builder a grace period (as per the SAJ form) during which, notwithstanding the fact that the delivery date has passed, the builder should not be liable to pay liquidated damages.

Permissible delays

The provisions relating to liquidated damages would normally apply, under the terms of the contract, only where there is delay following the agreed delivery date. The delivery date will normally be capable of being extended for certain delays, referred to as "permissible delays", in accordance with terms of the contract and for which liquidated damages are not payable. Permissible delays usually relate to events of *force majeure* or delay due to the buyer's default (i.e. events outside the control of the builder).

"Drop dead date"

Invariably the inclusion of a "permissible delay" clause will mean that unless the contract expressly incorporates a "drop dead date" the buyer (and the buyer's financing bank) is faced with the prospect that the works may continue indefinitely if caused by events outside the builder's control. A "drop dead date" is, therefore, normally incorporated within the contract, such that the buyer has a right to terminate it irrespective of whether the delay is due to permissible delays or otherwise.

Additional damages

Where the delay is such that the buyer is entitled to cancel the contract, for reasons associated with the builder's default, the contract may provide that the buyer shall, in addition to recovering the instalment paid by him upon cancellation, be entitled to damages at law or by reference to an agreed formula enabling the buyer to claim compensation for the costs incurred by him in the project (see below).

Builder's bonus

The contract may entitle the builder to a premium or a bonus payable when the vessel is delivered earlier than the agreed delivery date, with the buyer's consent. The bonus normally mirrors the daily amount of liquidated damages payable for delay in delivery, with a corresponding grace period.

"Cap" on liquidated damages

The contract on larger projects will normally impose a limitation or cap upon the maximum amount of liquidated damages payable by the builder. The contract will usually express this as a proportion of the contract price. This limitation will normally only relate to delay in delivery of the vessel.

Approval of drawings and plans and rights of inspection and supervision

Buyer's approval required

Where the builder is exclusively obliged to construct and complete the vessel in accordance with the contract and the specifications, the contract will normally afford to the buyer certain rights to enable him to monitor the progress of the contract works, including the right to approve in advance the builder's detailed plans and drawings for the vessel. The contract will usually also entitle the buyer to be represented at the shipyard by resident supervisors who are entitled to inspect and approve the contract works. The relationship between the builder and the buyer's supervisors can be a difficult one and the contract will need to provide a balanced approach to the scope and extent of the rights afforded to the supervisors. The contract will usually provide that working drawings will be prepared by the builder and provided to the buyer for the buyer's approval and comment as and when produced during the construction process. Many of these will need to be approved by the classification society and the regulatory authorities.

The right afforded to the buyer to approve drawings is intended to minimise technical errors and the need for any costly alterations; but the inclusion of such a provision is not usually intended to oust the builder's obligations to construct and equip the vessel in accordance with the contract and the specifications. Where this is a particular issue between the builder and the buyer, the contract may expressly provide that the buyer's approval of such drawings shall be without prejudice to the builder's obligations under the contract. This is more likely to be an issue where the builder is contractually responsible for the vessel's design and the buyer will wish to ensure that its approval of the drawings and plans does not enable the builder to assert later that the buyer should bear joint responsibility for errors in the drawings and in the subsequent design of the vessel.

Timing

The contract will normally incorporate strict time limits within which the buyer's right to approve drawings must be exercised. Any delay is usually treated as permissible delay (see below) extending the delivery date. The SAJ form initially permits the buyer 14 days, but no provision is made dealing with the situation where the buyer disagrees with the drawings or provides comments which are unacceptable to the builder. In such cases, significant disputes can occur and this will inevitably delay the project. This is one aspect in which it is difficult to legislate within the contract for what should happen. In practice, it will be in both the buyer's and the builder's interests that the construction works proceed in accordance with the planned time scale.

Buyer's supervisors

The contract should specify the name of the buyer's supervisors and provide that all communication should take place between the builder and the supervisors to ensure best communication. The supervisors will be obliged by the contract to attend to certain matters, such as test and trials of the vessel and machinery and equipment. The SAJ form also envisages that the buyer's supervisors will be authorised to agree to modifications to the scope of the works and the consequent changes to the delivery date and contract price. Buyers wishing to exercise a close degree of control in relation to any extension to the delivery date, contract price or other commercial matters may wish to exclude such authority and limit the supervisors' rights and obligations under the contract to attendance and supervision.

The contract should in any event permit the supervisors free access to the works and to the vessel at any time within working hours and, in relation to their attendance at tests and trials, reasonable notice should be given in advance by the builder.

The contract will usually need to make a specific provision for any inspection which the supervisors are to be entitled to undertake themselves. The SAJ form envisages that the supervisors shall attend all tests and inspections undertaken by the classification society, other regulatory bodies and/or an inspection team of the builder. The buyer will normally wish to have the right to inspect the vessel with its own team, although the builder may require that any such inspection will not jeopardise the construction programme or otherwise interfere with the builder's works. The contract should also differentiate clearly between a right of inspection and a right of testing.

Supervisors' facilities

The contract should state those facilities which the buyer's supervisors will require in order to perform their functions at the shipyard (e.g. an air-conditioned office, telephone lines for equipment and other communication).

Defects, ongoing process of review

The contract will usually provide that the buyer's supervisors are to notify the builder as soon as they become aware of any defect in worksmanship or materials employed in the vessel's construction and the contract will provide that such defects are remedied by the builder, where the builder so agrees. The SAJ form is silent about the situation where the builder disagrees with the supervisors' assessment. In relation to technical matters of this nature, the contract will normally provide that the same be determined by a decision of the classification society, which shall be final and binding. The SAJ form contemplates that this procedure for dispute resolution of technical matters shall be optional, such that if the parties do not agree to refer the dispute to the classification society, the compulsory provisions relating to arbitration or court jurisdiction shall apply. The parties may decide that the contract ought to require the parties to refer technical matters to the classification society in the interests of ensuring effective dispute resolution.

Exclusion of liabilities

The contract will usually include an exclusion of any responsibility on the builder's part to the buyer for any personal injury, harm or death suffered by the buyer's supervisors, whether incurred at the shipyard or elsewhere. The builder may require an indemnity from the buyer in relation to the same. The contract may limit the application of the indemnity to all circumstances other than those where the builder is in wilful default or has committed gross negligence, as a result of which the buyer's supervisors have suffered injury or died.

Substitution

The contract will sometimes provide that the builder shall have a right to require the buyer to replace or substitute the supervisors in the event that there is any abuse by the supervisors of their rights and the performance by them of their duties under the contract.

Modifications to the works

The contract will expressly provide for modifications to be made to the scope of the works. The specifications for the vessel are likely to require amendment for a variety of reasons.

Buyer's modifications

The buyer will wish to retain as much flexibility as possible to make the modifications until delivery of the vessel; the builder will wish to ensure that his construction programme is not disrupted by any substantial or last minute changes. The builder will also wish to ensure that he has the right to extend the delivery date to deal with any modifications which require him to extend the construction programme and the right to recover the increased costs of any such modifications.

The contract will, therefore, usually provide the buyer with the flexibility to request modifications at any time, but that the builder's obligation to comply with that request will be subject to the parties reaching an agreement as to any extension to the delivery date and any amendment required to the contract price. The builder may also wish to retain the right to vary the guarantees given by him as to the vessel's performance criteria in light of any requests made by the buyer for modifications. The conditions attaching to the builder's right to refuse requests made by the buyer for modifications are likely, therefore, to be clearly defined within the scope of the contract.

The SAJ form limits the builder's right to reject the buyer's request for modifications in circumstances where in the builder's judgement these will adversely affect his planning or programme in relation to other commitments and subject to the condition that the parties have agreed adjustments to the contract terms necessitated by the modifications.

In certain circumstances, the contract ought to ensure that any modifications are the subject of an agreement in writing signed by both parties to avoid the potential for dispute. This will impact upon the rights and obligations afforded to the buyer's supervisors because there may be a tendency at a practical level for such matters to be dealt with orally between employees of the builder and the buyer's supervisors without the same being recorded in writing.

The contract will also need to prescribe when the buyer shall pay for any modifications. It is customary for the contract to stipulate that the final instalment payable upon delivery shall be adjusted to include any additional agreed cost in relation to modifications, although in certain circumstances the builder may require that payment for modifications be made 50 per cent when the modifications are agreed and 50 per cent upon delivery.

Compulsory modifications

The contract will need to prescribe for the eventuality that there is any amendment to the rules of the relevant classification society or the regulatory authorities during the construction of the vessel. Where there are changes, the buyer will inevitably wish that the works are modified to ensure that the vessel upon delivery will reflect the rules of the classification society and regulatory authorities then in force, if the value of the vessel is to be preserved.

The contract will normally impose an obligation upon both the builder and the buyer to advise each other of any known changes to the rules of the classification society or regulatory authorities. The builder will ensure, within the contract, that he is not under an obligation to perform such works, although in the case of "compulsory" modifications the buyer's negotiating position will be stronger, and it will be rare for a builder not to agree that the specification should be amended. Contracts sometimes provide that the builder shall be permitted unilaterally to amend specifications in order to ensure compliance with compulsory changes and the builder will be entitled to adjust the contract price to reflect the additional costs of compliance.

Builder's modifications

The contract may also permit the builder to propose modifications to the specifications, where he wishes to make minor changes to the specifications, if necessary, for improved production methods or otherwise (for example to correct technical errors or shortcomings identified in the plans and drawings). The buyer will, however, have the right to reject any request made by the builder to modify the specifications. The more important issue in relation to the builder's modifications is when the builder may wish to have the right to substitute materials in order to ensure that the vessel is delivered by the delivery date, in circumstances, for example, where materials are otherwise unavailable. The contract may make express provision for the eventuality that items or materials are in short supply but state that the builder's right to request such modifications is dependent upon his demonstrating that the delivery date will be delayed if he is not permitted to make the necessary modifications. The contract should provide that the buyer has an absolute discretion to withhold his agreement to the substitution of materials on this ground, although his right to do so may be subject to the test of what is reasonable, and there is a risk that if he does not consent the builder will seek to claim *force majeure* as soon as any delay in the construction of the vessel due to the short supply affects his ability to perform the contract and carry out the construction works in due time.

The practice has developed for labour and materials rates to be pre-agreed and appended to the contract to minimise the issues which have to be agreed between the parties at the time of any modification. Unless the contract otherwise provides expressly, the buyer's right to liquidated damages for delay shall not be prejudiced by any request he makes for modifications. Where the buyer has a unilateral right to demand variations to the contract, the exercise by him of that right may affect his ability to recover liquidated damages in the event of any delay in the delivery of the vessel due to his request.

Trials of the vessel

The contract will provide for a trial or series of tests and trials to determine whether the vessel complies with the condition and performance criteria set out in the contract and specifications. The contract will essentially require the builder to demonstrate to the buyer that the vessel meets these standards before the vessel is tendered for delivery. As is customary, the vessel will need to be classed and certificated and the classification society and the regulatory authorities will also wish to be fully satisfied that the vessel complies fully with their requirements before class and trading certificates are issued.

Sea trials

In complex projects, the builder may carry out his own trials or tests prior to the formal trials that are conducted as contemplated by the contract. The contract will usually provide for sea trials, during which the builder will be required to prove that the vessel meets the standards set out in the contract and specifications and conforms with the other requirements of the contract. The contract should detail the nature and extent of the tests to be conducted. The ramifications of the tests and trials will normally be contained within the contract itself while the detailed nature of the particular tests and trials will be defined in the specifications.

The contract will normally require the builder to give reasonable notice to the buyer in advance of any trials and the contract will normally prescribe that the buyer's supervisors will attend the trials. If the buyer's supervisors fail to attend in these circumstances, the contract may provide that the buyer will be taken to have waived his right of attendance and that, upon completion of the trials, the vessel will be deemed conclusively to comply with the requirements of the contract and the specifications. In this eventuality, the contract may determine that a certificate of compliance issued by the builder will need to be countersigned by the classification society. The SAJ form contains no such protection.

The contract will also deal with the location, weather conditions (adverse weather usually constituting permissible delay), crewing and navigation, and provisioning for trials.

Acceptance or rejection of the vessel

Due to its significance, the contract will contain detailed provisions as to the method by which the buyer will accept or reject the vessel. The contract will normally provide that the builder shall submit the results of the tests and trials to the buyer; the buyer will have a permitted time within which to evaluate the information and consult with the classification society, regulatory authorities and his supervisors, and either accept or reject the vessel. If the buyer makes no election, the contract will normally provide that the buyer will be deemed to have accepted the vessel. Once the buyer accepts the vessel, the construction process is concluded and the buyer is then obliged to take delivery of the vessel and to pay the contract price upon delivery.

Following acceptance, the buyer's rights are limited to claims under the warranty in relation to workmanship and materials. The contract may, if the builder so requires it, provide that the buyer's acceptance shall be conclusive evidence that the vessel complies with the contract. The SAJ form provides that acceptance shall be final and binding so far as conformity of the vessel to the contract and specifications are concerned.

The contract will usually provide that, where the buyer rejects the vessel, the buyer will be required to notify the builder of the deficiencies and defects identified by its evaluation and the builder will have the opportunity to remedy the same and re-tender the vessel for acceptance. The contract may prescribe that this process shall be repeated until the vessel is accepted by the buyer or the contract is cancelled by the buyer.

"Punch" list

The contract will need to reflect the fact that it is perhaps unlikely in a complex or large scale newbuilding project that the vessel will comply precisely with the contract and the specifications when she is first tendered for delivery by the builder. The contract will usually provide a formal method for ensuring that the buyer serves a notice, usually known as a punch list, detailing those respects in which the vessel fails to meet the requirements of the contract and the specifications, and giving the builder an opportunity to remedy the same. This will be less important where the buyer's supervisors have been closely involved with the builder's personnel throughout the construction process. Upon receipt of a punch list the builder has to decide whether to remedy the matters raised by the buyer or to challenge the buyer's rejection as unjustified. In the latter case the issues will need to be resolved, usually by the dispute resolution procedures agreed between the parties. Where the builder accepts the buyer's notice, or any part of it, the builder at his cost will be required to remedy the punch list items, following which the buyer has a further opportunity to re-inspect the vessel and to elect once more whether to accept or reject it. The contract may specifically limit the buyer on re-inspection to inspecting those matters raised in his punch list and to preclude him from raising new issues on the re-inspection. The contract usually provides for this "process of elimination" to continue until either the buyer accepts the vessel or either party cancels the contract in accordance with its terms or otherwise.

Conformity with the contract

Whether the vessel is in fact, by the time she is tendered for delivery by the builder, in conformity with the contract and the specifications is sometimes a difficult and technical area. If there are particular requirements or performance criteria for the vessel which the buyer regards as fundamental to the newbuilding project, the contract will need to ensure that the builder's right to tender the vessel for delivery is conditional upon their satisfaction. It is usually possible to discern from most newbuilding contracts that conformity with class and other regulatory requirements are conditions which have to be satisfied in order for the builder validly to tender the vessel for delivery, failing which the buyer may reject the vessel. The builder is likely, however, to resist any attempt by the buyer to introduce additional conditions into the contract and the matter is normally agreed to be left on the basis of the facts as they arise at the time of delivery. The position may be different where the buyer has intended employment for the vessel and there are conditions of the chartering arrangements that the vessel must comply absolutely with certain requirements of the charterers. In such cases, the buyer ought to make known to the builder prior to entering into the contract that this is the position and seek to include clear language to this effect within the shipbuilding contract.

Exclusion of implied terms

The contract will usually exclude any statutory implied terms, for example in English law under the Sale of Goods Act 1979 as amended by the Sale of Goods Act 1994. This reflects the customary practice by which the builder undertakes to meet the requirements of the contract and to rectify all defects discovered during the warranty period resulting from faulty workmanship or materials, but provides no general guarantee of quality and accepts no financial liability for the buyer's losses caused by deficiencies or faults in the vessel. The SAJ form provides that the buyer's acceptance shall be final and binding so far as conformity of the vessel to the contract is concerned and expressly excludes any implied terms relating to quality, statutory or otherwise. The AWES form provides that upon delivery of the vessel the builder shall be free from all responsibility or liability whatsoever except for the builder's warranty (see below).

Buyer's right to rescind

Where the vessel fails to meet the requirements of the contract, the contract will not usually afford the buyer an express right to rescind. The contract will usually provide for the process of elimination of defects until such time as the buyer is entitled by the express provisions of the contract to rescind the contract for delay. The buyer will need to consider whether he wishes to include an express right to rescind in certain circumstances where the vessel is tendered for delivery and the defects are clearly irremediable, or the position adopted by the builder is that the buyer must "take it or leave it". While it may be possible to argue under the structure of the SAJ form that the buyer has the right to rescind the contract in such circumstances, the contract ought to include express provision for this if the buyer is able to negotiate the same with the builder.

Delivery

Protocol

The contract will usually provide that delivery shall be effected by the tender of the vessel for delivery by the builder and the buyer's formal acceptance, and the signature by both parties of a protocol of delivery and acceptance and the assumption of physical possession and control of the vessel by the buyer's master and crew.

Location

From the buyer's point of view, the builder should provide that the vessel is delivered at a safe berth or anchorage at or near the shipyard or some alternative location if the buyer wishes to take delivery somewhere other than the shipyard.

Time for delivery

The time for delivery is normally agreed and specifically stated to be a calendar date on which the builder undertakes to deliver the vessel. This date is, however, capable of adjustment by reason of permissible delays arising, usually, by agreement under the contract due to *force majeure* and other delays which entitle the builder to claim that the delivery date is postponed by the amount of delay caused. The date for delivery is simply a target date. It is important from the buyer's point of view to ensure that the contract clearly defines the circumstances in which this date can be adjusted by the builder. Where the vessel is not delivered by the target date (as adjusted from time to time) the contract will provide for liquidated damages and ultimately entitle the buyer to cancel the contract.

Title to the vessel

Whoever owns the vessel during the construction process has an element of security against the risk of the other party's financial default, provided that such party's rights prevail against creditors of the other party. Depending upon local law and practice, ownership of the vessel may afford to either party the right to mortgage the vessel for the purpose of securing finance. The majority of contracts will usually provide that title to the vessel will remain with the builder throughout the construction period, on the basis that the buyer's credit risk is secured by a refund guarantee given by the builder that it will repay all instalments paid in the event of the builder's default. The contract ought to provide, in this case, that the buyer's obligation to pay the first instalment under the contract is conditional upon the delivery by the builder of a refund guarantee in terms acceptable to the buyer and given by a bank acceptable to the buyer. In such cases, where the builder retains title during the construction process, title will be transferred to the buyer concurrently with the execution of the protocol of delivery and acceptance and the contract will usually expressly provide for this.

Where, however, the builder is either unable or unwilling to provide a refund guarantee, the contract will usually expressly provide that title to the vessel will pass to the buyer, together with all equipment and materials intended for her, during the course of her construction.

Questions in relation to title cannot always be predetermined by reference to the contract terms alone and both parties will need to consider what the effect is of the governing law of the contract and local law (that is the law of the place of construction) in relation to title. For example, the local law may prescribe that certain formalities in relation to registration of title are observed, such that, if these are not observed, notwithstanding that the contract provides under English law for title to pass during the construction process, this may not be capable of enforcement.

The SAJ form and standard AWES form do not provide for a continuous transfer of title during the construction process but provide that title shall pass upon delivery and acceptance.

Builder's lien

The contract will usually provide that the builder has a contractual lien on the vessel to secure any unpaid proportion of the contract price, permitting him to retain the vessel pending payment. The contract may go further and provide that the builder also has a right to sell the vessel, although this is less common. This is an aspect of the contract which is likely to be unacceptable to the buyer because it may be used by the builder to exert considerable leverage in the event that there is any dispute about whether the vessel conforms with the contract upon its tender for delivery. In such circumstances, the buyer may be forced to pay the balance of the purchase price and accept the vessel, but under protest and under a reservation of rights.

Risk of loss, damage

Regardless of the time of transfer of title, the contract will normally provide that the risk of the vessel's loss or damage remains with the builder during the construction process until delivery and acceptance by the buyer, because she is likely to remain until such time at the builder's premises under the builder's insurance. The buyer and the builder will need to ensure that if the contract incorporates any exceptions (as the SAJ form) to the builder's assumption of risk until delivery and acceptance that additional insurances are obtained by the buyer.

Extension of time for delivery

The contract will usually provide that the target date for delivery of the vessel by the builder shall be extended by any time during which the performance by the builder of its obligations is impeded or prevented by circumstances beyond his control, the majority of which are typically listed as events of *force majeure* or delays due to the buyer's default.

Force majeure

The contract should define as accurately as possible those events which are to constitute *force majeure* and this will normally take the form of a list of events. If agreed, the parties may accept a general "catch all" in relation to any other circumstances beyond the control of the affected party which prevents or hinders its performance of its obligations under the contract.

Notice requirements

The contract should ensure that the affected party is required to give prompt notice upon the occurrence of any *force majeure* which prevents its performance and also gives notice upon the cessation of *force majeure*. The contract ought to state expressly that if the notice provisions are not adhered to by the affected party, the affected party cannot rely upon the event of *force majeure*. From the buyer's perspective, this is particularly important because any event of *force majeure* will have significant consequences if the delivery date is extended and the buyer will wish to have an opportunity to challenge any claim for *force majeure* by the builder at the time. Clear language will need to be used in the contract to describe the events of *force majeure* because the parties seeking to rely upon them will have the burden of demonstrating that the event has occurred and that it prevents or hinders their performance.

Effect on "critical path"

The buyer may also wish to restrict under the contract the builder's right to claim *force majeure* to events directly affecting the builder's critical path of the construction process and also to exclude any right to claim *force majeure* for any delay which is due directly or indirectly to the builder's negligence or default.

Excessive delay

The contract will usually incorporate an express provision that the buyer may rescind the contract in the event of excessive delay, even where that delay is caused by events of *force majeure* or other permissible delay under the contract (see below).

Builder's warranty

Scope of warranty

The contract will usually provide a warranty of the vessel, machinery and equipment for 12 months from the date of her delivery and acceptance. The contract will normally stipulate that in the event of a defect occurring within the warranty period the builder will rectify the same at his own cost, but on the basis that any incidental expenses, including in particular any loss of use of the vessel arising from either the defect or its repair, will be borne by the buyer. The contract will also usually provide that the builder's warranty is to operate to the exclusion of any other contractual or statutory warranties regarding the vessel's condition or performance, such that acceptance of the vessel will limit the buyer's future rights solely to the warranty under the contract (see above).

Nature and time of defects

Under the SAJ form, claims under the warranty arise only with defects identified after delivery and acceptance of the vessel. The warranty will not apply to defects identified prior to acceptance but which remained uncured or unrepaired. Rather than writing complex provisions into the contract to deal with this scenario, it is usually the practice for the buyer and the builder to agree any defects which are outstanding upon completion of the sea trials but which are insufficiently serious to justify the buyer's rejection of the vessel. They will then be treated at the time of delivery and acceptance to be specific warranty items and the protocol of delivery and acceptance will normally be "claused" accordingly to the effect that the buyer's acceptance of the vessel is subject to the builder's commitment to rectify the defects as soon as possible thereafter.

Drydocking

The buyer and the builder will often agree that the vessel should, at the buyer's option, be drydocked within a specified period from the date of delivery and that the warranty period should be extended in respect of her underwater parts to encompass faults discovered upon such inspection and notified by the buyer within a limited time thereafter.

Builder's liability extended

If the buyer is able to negotiate it, the contract might extend the warranty, such that the builder's obligation is not limited solely to the costs of repairing the defects but also to sharing any loss of income or revenue suffered by the buyer as a result of the vessel being unable to operate while the repairs are effected.

Design faults

If the builder is to assume responsibility for any design faults arising after delivery and acceptance of the vessel, the warranty should be extended to cover inadequate or erroneous design. The usual warranty language will limit the builder's liability for defective workmanship and materials.

Replacement parts

The SAJ form does not provide for a warranty either of machinery or parts replaced by the builder within the warranty or of repair works undertaken during such period. The warranty will normally be amended to state expressly that the builder will warrant the workmanship and materials of repair undertaken during the warranty period by the builder, but exclude any repairs undertaken by any third-party builder or yard. It is also usual that the contract be amended to provide that, in relation to any replaced parts, the warranty will be a separate warranty of six months from the date of installation or completion of the replacement, but that there will be an overall cut-off date for the warranty period of 18 months from the date of delivery and acceptance of the vessel.

Sub-contractors' items

The warranty may also be further amended in respect of items for which sub-contractors are responsible. In such cases, the buyer may either negotiate directly with the sub-contractor or manufacturer to obtain a direct contractual warranty or require that the builder should agree to assign to the buyer the benefit of any sub-contractor's or supplier's warranty issued in the builder's favour. An assignment of this nature may not be permitted and will depend upon the terms of the original contract concluded between the builder and the manufacturer or supplier. From the buyer's perspective, it is vital that he should assure himself, not only of the width of the warranty, but also the extent to which it is capable of assignment before he agrees to accept this in lieu of the builder's own warranty. For his part, the builder will wish to make clear that his own warranty does not extend to those parts of the vessel, her machinery and equipment which have been independently guaranteed to the buyer by a supplier or manufacturer.

Notice of claims

The contract will provide that the buyer must give notice as promptly as possible after the discovery of any defects to ensure that the builder's obligation to remedy the same is not prejudiced by any delay. The contract will normally make clear that this is not a condition to the buyer making any claim under the warranty and will result, where there is any failure on the part of the buyer, in a claim by the builder for damages to the extent that the builder's costs are increased. This is in contrast to the usual requirement that the buyer notify the builder of any claims no later than 30 days after the expiry of the relevant warranty period, which is usually expressed as a condition for any claim being made and therefore acts in effect as a time bar.

Manner of repairs

The contract will also prescribe the manner in which any repairs are to be effected. In recognition of the vessel's likely trading and operation, the contract will usually provide that, subject to the builder's right of prior inspection of alleged defects, the buyer shall be entitled to have repair or replacement works carried out at any other shipyard and to recover its costs on making the repair as if such repairs were undertaken at the shipyard. This may be unacceptable to the builder, who will therefore require an amendment to the usual contract that any such costs shall be subject to the requirement of reasonableness, precluding the buyer from recovering his actual costs which might be unreasonably high. The buyer may also wish the contract to state expressly the time frame within which the builder must comply with its obligations under the warranty.

Assignment of builder's warranty

The buyer may also require the right to assign the builder's warranty if the buyer knows or contemplates that the vessel upon delivery and acceptance will be sold or bareboat chartered or demise chartered to a third party.

Limitation on builder's liability

The contract will normally exclude the builder's liability for consequential or special losses, damages or expenses which arise out of the defects themselves or out of the works undertaken to remedy them.

Specific thought will need to be given to the extent to which this is acceptable, although an exclusion of consequential loss (without definition) will not limit the builder's liability for direct losses, which might in certain circumstances include loss of profit. This is a complex legal area and one which will require careful consideration by both the builder and the buyer.

Exclusions from warranty

The contract may also expressly state that the builder's liability will not extend to defects repaired by other contractors which have been caused or aggravated by misuse of the vessel or resulting from wear and tear or other circumstances beyond the control of the builder.

Rescission by the buyer

Recovery of instalments paid

In the event that the buyer has the right to cancel the contract, he will usually have an express right under the terms of the contract to recover from the builder those payments he has made by way of instalments of the contract price.

Value of buyer's supplies

In addition to recovering the advances he has made, the contract will also need to provide for the status of buyer's supplies and, in particular, whether these are to be recovered by the buyer or whether, if incorporated in the vessel, the builder is to pay the buyer the value of the supplies, including carriage, insurance and freight. The SAJ form makes no provision for owner's supplies in this respect and the contract ought to address this matter to avoid any dispute in the event of rescission of the contract by the buyer.

Refund guarantee

The buyer will normally require a guarantee from a third party bank, which the builder must produce prior to or as a condition either of the effective date (see below) or of the buyer making the first instalment. Where the contract provides for title to the vessel to pass to the buyer as it is constructed, the builder may reject any suggestion that he provide third party security and this will need to be a matter of negotiation between the buyer and the builder in the circumstances.

Builder's default

As described above, the buyer's right to rescind the contract will normally arise where there is delay in delivery, where the vessel fails to meet the guarantees in relation to its performance characteristics, where there may be financial defaults or insolvency of the builder, a total loss of the vessel or materials. It is not usual for the contract to incorporate a right that the buyer rescind in the event of a material breach of contract by the builder, other than in circumstances where there is delay in delivery or the builder is the subject of insolvency proceedings or is otherwise unable to pay its debts as they fall due. This may, however, be included where the buyer believes the same to be necessary and the builder agrees.

Insolvency of builder

The contract will need to describe the particular circumstances in which the insolvency of the builder shall be deemed to have occurred, taking into account any particular factors relevant to the jurisdiction of the builder.

Default interest

The contract will also usually incorporate a default rate of interest in the event that the builder fails promptly or immediately to repay advances made by the buyer and, if applicable, the CIF value of owner's supplies.

Where, however, the buyer's right to rescind arises following a total loss of the vessel, interest may often either not be payable at all or be payable at a lower rate, because it may be difficult for the builder to obtain insurance coverage for interest repayments.

Where title passes as the vessel is constructed

Where the contract expressly provides that title to the vessel shall pass as it is constructed, the remedies available to the buyer will be more extensive. Where the buyer has title to the vessel and the value of his instalments is reflected in the partly constructed vessel the contract might provide that upon rescission title shall re-vest in the builder following reimbursement of the pre-delivery instalments paid by the buyer, plus interest, or terminate the builder's contractual entitlement to undertake the contract works and permit the buyer to remove the vessel from the shipyard. These issues are likely to be significantly affected by the law of the jurisdiction of the builder or the shipyard where the works are being undertaken (if different), particularly where the builder may be the subject of insolvency proceedings and the contract will need to be amended to reflect the same when the buyer has advice about the local position to hand.

Right to complete the works

The contract may further expressly provide that the buyer has a right to enter the shipyard and to complete the contract works at his own risk and expense, using the facilities and materials available and that any costs incurred by him will be deducted from the contract price. Again, the enforceability of such a right will depend upon the law of the jurisdiction of the builder or the shipyard (if different) where the works are being undertaken.

Dispute as to rescission

Due to the stark consequences of a rescission by the buyer of the contract, the contract will often provide that if the buyer's claim to rescind the contract is challenged by the builder, the builder's obligation to refund the advances made will be suspended until the dispute has been determined by arbitration or litigation, depending upon the parties' chosen forum. If the builder acts in good faith such a provision within the contract will normally ensure that his refusal to make the refund will not expose him to further claims for damages for breach of contract. The SAJ form provides that the buyer's refund obligation is absolute unless the builder proceeds to arbitration under the contract, but does not prescribe any time limit within which the builder must take such a step. This may be an unacceptable risk to the buyer who, although he will be compensated for interest in the event that the arbitration tribunal determines that he was entitled to rescind the contract, will be left to recover any sums following the conclusion of the arbitration proceedings.

Limitation on builder's liability

The contract will usually expressly limit the buyer's recovery in the event of the builder's default upon rescission of the contract to the return of the instalments paid by the buyer. Both the SAJ and AWES forms include such a limitation. The buyer may, however, suffer additional loss as a result of rescission, such as the expenditure thrown away (reliance loss) and/or loss of profit or bargain, being the difference between the price and the market value of the vessel newly built. The builder will be very reluctant to accept any liability for market loss which might be open-ended and uncertain. The buyer may be able to negotiate a "capped" liability from the builder in such circumstances, failing which the buyer may take out insurance against such losses. In any event, unless the contract expressly excludes common law remedies, the buyer will have the right to sue for damages at law if the builder's default amounts to a "repudiatory" breach of the contract.

Buyer's default

Events of default

The contract will stipulate those events which will constitute a default by the buyer and their consequences. The factors and circumstances of each project will dictate what the parties agree will constitute events of default and the remedies available to the builder. Non-payment of an instalment by the buyer will usually allow the builder, if the default is not remedied after written notice within an agreed "cure" period of time thereafter, to rescind the contract. In addition, the SAJ form will entitle the builder (a) to claim interest at a default rate (usually agreed and stated in the contract) on any amount unpaid, (b) to recoup any additional expense incurred, and (c) to extend the delivery date for the period of any default. This latter right is usually restricted, such that the delivery date shall only be extended by reason of any delay caused to the construction of the vessel by the non-payment.

Rescission by the builder

The SAJ form states that upon rescission by the builder the contract will become "null and void". The contract will require amendment to reflect the fact that there will need to be an accounting between the parties following rescission which will be governed by certain terms of the contract, remaining in full force and effect post-rescission.

The contract will usually provide that upon rescission by the builder he shall be entitled to retain any instalments paid by the buyer (provided that he gives credit for the same in any final accounting). The contract will usually further provide that the builder will be entitled either to sell the vessel (in her then state of construction) or to complete the construction and then sell the vessel, in each case the buyer ensuring that the builder is required by the contract to take reasonable steps to achieve the true market value of the vessel. The builder will in principle under the contract usually be entitled to claim his actual costs of construction less the proceeds of sale. The builder is entitled to be placed in the position in which he would have been if the contract price had been paid in full. In this case the net sale proceeds are applied to meet the outstanding instalments of the contract price together with interest. This arrangement will work where the vessel is in a complete state. Where the vessel is sold in an incomplete state it is inappropriate that the contract price should be payable in full out of the sale proceeds. In this case the contract will normally state that the net sale proceeds will be applied to reimburse the builder's costs of construction to the extent that these have not already been recouped from instalments already paid by the buyer. The buyer should appreciate that in these circumstances the formula may confer a windfall benefit upon the builder because the builder's costs of construction are greater than the contract price.

Surplus/deficiency in sale proceeds

If there is any surplus available following the application of the sale proceeds the contract will normally provide for these to be shared between the builder and the buyer. Where there is a deficiency on the other hand, because the net sale proceeds are less than the contract price or the builder's costs of construction, the contract will normally oblige the buyer to pay the amount of the shortfall of the contract on demand.

Other remedies

In the absence of any provision excluding common law remedies the builder may, where the buyer is in "repudiatory" breach of the contract, elect either to affirm the contract, in which event he will normally sue the buyer in debt or for damages or to accept the breach as bringing an end to the parties' respective obligations and sue the buyer for damages for his loss of bargain. The builder will in any event be entitled to sue the buyer in debt for any instalment which is due but unpaid.

Insurance

Builders' risks

The contract will usually provide that the vessel is at the builder's risk until her delivery to the buyer. The contract will, therefore, require the builder to insure the vessel in respect of "builder's risks" for a sum which is not less than the total of the instalments of the contract price paid by the buyer from time to time. The contract may afford the right to the buyer to be a named assured on the policy to the extent of any supplies made by the buyer to the builder for incorporation in the construction of the vessel. The parties will need to agree and define the nature of the builder's risks coverage which the builder is required to take out and maintain, whether the Japanese Builder's Risks Insurance Clauses or the Institute of London Underwriters Builder's Risks Clauses. The buyer might also oblige the builder under the contract to provide satisfactory evidence that such insurances have been effected and/or are being maintained, from time to time.

Partial loss

In the event of any partial loss of the vessel the contract will normally state that the builder is entitled and obliged to apply the proceeds of the insurance claim towards her repair and that any delay in completion of the vessel caused by the casualty will automatically extend the delivery date.

Total loss

In the event of a total loss the entire project will be in jeopardy and the contract should afford the parties sufficient room to negotiate how best to proceed. For example, if the vessel is a total loss or a constructive total loss the contract may require that the parties agree that within a stated period of time thereafter either the builder shall reconstruct the vessel on the basis of mutually acceptable amendments to the contract terms or the contract shall terminate, in which event the buyer will be entitled to a refund of the instalments of the contract price he has paid, the builder recovering the proceeds of the insurance claim. The buyer may wish to amend the contract to provide that the builder is also obliged to refund the value of the buyers supplies if any are damaged or destroyed in the casualty giving rise to the total loss.

Dispute resolution

Generally

The dispute resolution procedures within the contract should be given careful thought. In any large construction project there is potential for disputes, whether technical or commercial in nature. The existence of any dispute may disrupt the project and involve additional management time and expense. It is vital therefore that the parties agree an effective mechanism by which disputes are to be determined promptly. Their choice of law and jurisdiction are important. These should be clearly defined within the contract.

Technical disputes

The contract will normally state that technical disputes shall be referred to either the classification society or another mutually agreed expert. The contract will further provide that such person shall act as an expert rather than an arbitrator and that his or her decision will be final and binding (as to the technical matters referred to them).

Arbitration

It is more common for the parties to agree arbitration as the main forum for determining disputes under the contract. London's pre-eminence as a place of arbitration for the resolution of international shipbuilding disputes has been endorsed by the introduction of the Arbitration Act 1996. There are, however, certain key distinctions between arbitration and court proceedings and careful thought should be given to these, bearing in mind the nature of the project.

The courts

Where the courts of any particular jurisdiction are chosen (in preference to arbitration) to determine disputes, the contract should, where the parties are not resident in that jurisdiction, provide the names and addresses of agents in the jurisdiction for service of process.

Assignment

Generally

By virtue of the nature of a newbuilding project the parties will be reluctant to permit any assignment by the other of their rights or obligations under the contract. This may, however, be necessary, particularly in the case where one party needs to secure financing. The contract should clearly state what will be permitted in order to avoid uncertainty.

Export licences/approvals

Special consideration will need to be given to the assignment provisions in the contract when it is intended that, for example, the buyer will assign the benefit of the contract to a third party in the context of any export licence or governmental approval which has or will be issued in favour of the buyer. In such cases, the right to assign may need to be subject to an amendment to such export licence or governmental approval.

Taxes and duties

Responsibility

The construction and sale of the vessel may involve the buyer or the builder in significant tax liabilities, in the form of either sales or value added taxes. There may also be customs or other duties levied on items imported in connection with the works. The contract will need to state clearly whose responsibility such taxes and/or dues will be. Normally the contract will state that the builder will meet all tax liabilities in his jurisdiction, or elsewhere, to the extent that these relate to the performance of the contract works and that the buyer will meet all other tax liabilities including those relating to buyer's supplies.

Patents, etc.

Builder's warranty

The construction of the vessel will involve the use of designs and construction methods over which third parties enjoy patent and other intellectual property rights. Consistent with the builder's role, the contract will normally include an express warranty by the builder that no infringement of third party intellectual property rights will take place in the construction of the vessel, and that the vessel will on delivery and thereafter be free from such claims. Claims in relation to buyer's supplies will usually be excluded from such warranty.

Indemnity

The warranty is normally supported by an indemnity given by the builder in respect of any losses suffered by the buyer as a result of any breach of this warranty. The SAJ form limits the indemnity to the consequences of patent infringements. From the buyer's perspective, this will need to be extended to cover intellectual property rights generally. The buyer may also require that the contract imposes an obligation on the builder to provide security to release the vessel from any actual or threatened arrest by a third party asserting intellectual property rights.

Builder's drawings, etc.

The contract will usually state that the builder shall retain title to all plans, drawings and other data relating to the design and construction of the vessel. The buyer may wish to include a right to such plans etc. and a right to disclose the same in certain circumstances (e.g. where necessary for the operation, repair and on-sale of the vessel).

Buyer's supplies

Responsibility

The contract will need to make provision for those supplies which are to be made by the buyer, usually for reasons of cost efficiency or where the items have long lead times for delivery. In such cases, the builder will be responsible for the safekeeping and storage of the buyer's supplies and their installation. The contract will usually provide that such supplies are to be delivered by the buyer in a condition ready and fit for installation in accordance with the builder's construction programme, failing which any delay caused will be treated as permissible delay and extend the delivery date.

Notices

Both parties should give careful consideration to the notice provisions of the contract to ensure that there is effective communication between them. It is now customary for parties to agree that any notice given by facsimile will be deemed to have been given upon transmission.

Effective date

The contract may incorporate terms which provide for the contract coming into effect at a time after signing of the contract, usually upon the occurrence of certain conditions precedent. This is customary where board approval or certain financing arrangements or export licences are still to be obtained. The contract usually states that upon satisfaction of the stated conditions the contract will become effective and the date of such satisfaction is known as the "Effective Date". The contract will, for certainty, usually state that if any of the conditions have not been satisfied by an agreed date then the contract shall become null and void and the parties shall be discharged from their obligations.

CHAPTER 7

SHIP DESIGN

THE SCOPE OF SHIP DESIGN

There are many works available which describe the design of ships, in all its aspects. These cover hydrodynamics, structures, arrangements at all stages from the preliminary work through to detail. The purpose here is not to consider these elements, but rather to overview the whole process of design, and particularly how it interfaces with the rest of the business.

The design process has a number of functions to perform. It is primarily concerned with the definition of the end-product—the ship which has to be built. Design is sometimes called product definition, which is intended to reflect the multiple functions which the design process has to perform. Design is carried out in several stages which have different outputs, although the complexity of the product and the process ensures that there is an overlap, and that there is inevitably some interaction between the stages.

The design process initially considers the ship as a whole, particularly from the point of view of the hydrodynamic performance, stability and seakeeping. It also considers the ship as a set of inter-connected systems, which deliver various mission requirements. These include propulsion systems, related auxiliary systems and cargo handling systems.

One aspect of the design process which is increasingly important is consideration of production—not only the final set of information which allows the parts, units and other elements of a ship to be produced, but also consideration of the work content and ease of production. At each stage of design, therefore, some attention is paid to the interim stages of construction as well as the complete ship. Where the ship is defined as the final product of the whole process of design and construction, the outputs from various stages of production are referred to as "interim products". That is, they represent the output of a particular stage of production, and are effectively complete. They may have been assembled in the shipyard which has the shipbuilding contract, or may be bought from a sub-contractor as an interim product that is completed to a pre-defined status.

The information developed at each stage of design reflects this increasing importance of production issues in design.

The stages of design are variously described, but the descriptions below are sufficient for the purpose of definition. The important aspect is the description of each stage, in particular the outputs, rather than the label which is attached. The stages are:

— conceptual;
— preliminary;
— functional;
— transitional;
— detail.

Each succeeding stage of design produces more detailed information. The outputs from each design stage are summarised in global terms.

CONCEPTUAL DESIGN

At this initial stage, the design process has the basic function of determining the features of the proposed ship which will satisfy the mission or owner requirements. The main output is a definition of the proposed ships which it is sufficient to promote in the market-place or to begin serious pre-contract discussions with a specific owner.

At the conceptual design stage, by selecting key dimensions and arrangements which correspond to shipyard-preferred material sizes and unit dimensions, the total steel joint length and the number of units can be reduced. In addition to a reduction in absolute work content, a potentially shorter build cycle time may be possible. The potential use of standard layouts can be identified.

PRELIMINARY DESIGN

This stage is in response to a serious enquiry for a ship, which has good prospects of leading to a firm order. It is therefore concerned with the features of the vessel which are sufficient to form a sound basis for a satisfactory shipbuilding contract. The level of definition will vary greatly, depending upon the relationship between the shipowner and shipbuilder. In some cases, only an outline may be the basis for the contract. Increasingly, given the greater complexity of modern ships, more definition is required so that the contractual basis is complete.

At the contract design stage engine room and other functional space layouts can be based on standards. The optimum location of equipment and auxiliaries, grouped by function, minimises the pipework and other connections which generate the bulk of on-board installation work content. A preliminary process analysis of the structure ensures that the design will be straightforward to build in the shipyard's facilities.

FUNCTIONAL DESIGN

Once the contract is agreed, then the focus of the design process is on completing sufficient detail of the features of the vessel to secure the formal approval of the design by the shipowner and also the appropriate classification society and other regulators, according to the ship type. The output includes the full set of classification drawings.

During the functional design, production process analysis is carried out for each planning unit to simplify connections and increase standardisation as the structural plans are developed. The work content reduction is small, but the necessary work content can be closely matched to the production processes which are available. The effect is on the productivity of the shipyard, rather than on absolute work content.

TRANSITIONAL DESIGN

The term "transition" indicates a change of emphasis from the function of the ship, which has been the primary goal of the design process through the product development, contract and approval procedures. This stage of the design process manages the translation of the design features from system to product orientation. Although usefully defined as a stage of the design process, it will be seen that transitional design is rightly part of the process through each stage. The outputs are information which is based on the interim products of production, rather than the systems which determine ship function.

One of the key outputs from transition design are arrangements of each of the areas or zones of the ship showing all systems and equipment. These are then used as a basis for the production of the work station drawings at the detail design stage.

Transition design develops the functional design into a format which suits production. Services and distributive systems are allocated to predefined functional spaces. Work is transferred to an earlier stage of the production process (via outfit assemblies, for example). Opportunities for standardisation are created. The emphasis is on increasing the potential productivity, rather than reducing work content, because of decisions taken at earlier stages.

DETAIL DESIGN

At this stage, the ship is fully defined as an operating entity and the primary outputs are the detailed definition of each of the parts which make up the ship. Further outputs are definitions of the features of each of the interim products which are sufficient to support their production.

This last stage of design has the primary function of developing production information, which includes:

— working drawings, which define each interim product;
— part production information, which includes plate and profile cutting, forming, pipe manufacturing;
— material lists, identifying all the parts associated with each interim product;
— material and equipment specifications (apart from major items which may have been defined earlier to secure delivery from suppliers);
— material requisitions.

The information which is developed through the various stages of the design process ultimately defines what is to be produced, at each stage of the production process. In addition to the arrangement and functioning of the complete ship, the information which is required also includes information to support the purchasing of all the materials and equipment. It also includes the detailed information required for part manufacturing.

At detail design, with the main features of the design fixed, only minor variations can be achieved. However, the maximum use can be made of standard details.

It must be emphasised that production should be a consideration at all design stages. Although transition design is defined as the stage at which production is considered, it is in reality an important consideration at all stages. Transition design translates information from systems to interim products. Although it is defined for convenience as a stage of design, in advanced organisations it starts at the earliest design stage.

In order for the design process to take production into account some variations from what might be regarded as traditional design processes are needed. The most important of these are:

— availability of detailed information about the production system. If the design function of a shipyard is required to take account of the requirements of production in the design information that is produced, it is essential to have an adequate definition of the production system, in a form which is accessible and useable by the design team;
— it is necessary to consider the design of an area or zone of the vehicle, as well as each individual system, primarily so that the installation of outfitting can be managed. Particularly in complex and congested areas, the complete set of systems is taken as a whole, which allows the locations of each to be decided and an optimum arrangement made;
— to be able to produce outfit assemblies, which have the benefit of moving much of the installation work from ship to workshop, it is important to look at the design of multiple systems rather than a single system. This allows, for example, all the pipes routed through a space to be designed together and combined onto a suitable structure as an assembly;

— as ships are produced using large units or blocks, and particularly where outfit assemblies or block outfitting is used, the definition of the interfaces between adjacent areas becomes very important. If pipes and other systems are simply installed after completion of the ship steelwork, their alignment is straightforward. If, on the other hand, to gain the benefits of working in better conditions, outfit units are assembled, the opportunities for adjustment to fit at the ship are very much reduced.

The different stage of design can best be defined in terms of their required inputs and their outputs, in the form of design information, and data for planning, purchasing and production.

Conceptual design establishes the overall features of a design to meet the requirements of a shipowner. The main inputs will be:

— service requirements;
— routes;
— market forecasts;
— technical change.

Production inputs will be the manufacturing strategy for the shipyard, including:

— a type plan for the ship;
— facility dimensions and other characteristics;

and the outputs will be

— preliminary general arrangement, midship section;
— preliminary specification;
— preliminary calculations (dimensions, capacities, etc.);
— preliminary body plan.

Production outputs will include a preliminary block breakdown and the identification of outfitting zones, along with any major assemblies.

Preliminary design is the stage at which it is required to establish the features of a design sufficient to provide the basis of a contractual arrangement. The main inputs at this stage are the outputs of the conceptual design stage, and:

— functional requirements;
— regulations;
— design standards.

Production inputs are once again the manufacturing strategy, along with company standards and industry standards, including:

— material sizes;
— modules;
— service runs;
— block sizes.

The design outputs include:

— general arrangement, midship section;
— specification;
— body plan;
— ship calculations;
— propulsion calculations;
— accommodation arrangements;
— machinery arrangements;
— piping diagrams;
— electrical-load analysis;
— plan list.

Production Outputs are contained in a preliminary build strategy, which includes:

— planning units;
— equipment identification, including especially long lead items;
— material requirements, with general quantities and again long lead items.

Functional design is to establish features of a design for the purposes of classification and other approval and material specification. Inputs are all the results of the preliminary design which has led to a contract being signed, plus functional requirements of the ship.

The production inputs are:

— the preliminary build strategy;
— standards;
— production processes;
— facilities.

The outputs are a detailed definition of the ship from an operational viewpoint;

— ship design:

  hull form;
  trim and stability;
  capacities, etc.

— structural design:

  approval drawings;
  scantling plans.

— machinery installation:

  arrangement;
  piping diagrams;
  electrical;
  fittings, etc.

— accommodation design;
— ship systems design;
— hull outfit.

Production outputs include:

— a contract build strategy, which formally defines how the ship will be built;
— plans and schedules for:

  erection on the berth or dock and for outfitting installation;
  steel and outfitting assembly;
  manufacture or procurement of all the parts;

— production information;
— purchasing information.

Transition design is the continuous process rather than design stage. It is used to translate the features of the design from the system orientation, necessary to establish functional performance, to a planning unit orientation, necessary to establish production requirements. The inputs as the design process progresses are from previous design stages:

— conceptual design;
— contract design;
— functional design.

The outputs include:

— process analysis;
— interim products;
— work package information;
— work station drawing information.

Detail design establishes the features or the design necessary to allow local purchasing, part manufacturing and subsequent assembly to be carried out. Detail design is carried out by planning unit, on those elements of the ship which have been developed to the stage where all functional and approval requirements have been satisfied.

The inputs to the detailed design are again all the previous stages:

— functional design;
— transition design;
— build strategy;
— standards;
— work station capacities;
— process analysis outputs.

The outputs are the:

— work instructions;

— work station drawings;
— material lists;
— dimensional requirements.

DESIGN FOR PRODUCTION

The need for a close match between facilities and products has led to the formal concept of design for production (design/production integration). This is intended to reduce production costs to a minimum, consistent with the vessel fulfilling operational requirements.

It is important to note that there is no inherent conflict between different design criteria. The basis of design, some would consider it the absolute definition of design, is design for operation; that is, the satisfying of all the operational requirements for the shipowner.

However, if the concept of through-life costing is adopted, there is a need also to consider design for maintenance. In addition to satisfying the operational requirements, this also involves the design function in ensuring that there is good access for maintenance workers. It also makes provision for routes for withdrawal of equipment for replacement. Provided the basis of the design is the use of routes and spaces with specified uses, taking maintenance into account does not pose any additional difficulties.

That leads on to design for production. Again, provided the basis of the design is the definition of spaces as functional or for distribution of services, then the definition of interim products can be made at a very early stage of design. The later stages, moving into greater detail, are then based on the development of these interim products, which by definition have taken into account the needs of production. In reality, production and maintenance are essential parts of the life of the ship, so taking care of these requirements is unavoidable.

Finally, some industries, notably the automotive industry, are beginning to consider the need to dispose of their products at the end of their useful life. So there is even a concept of design for disposal. The shipbuilding business is still in many cases coming to terms with the production and maintenance requirements. However, other branches of maritime industries are now grappling with disposal problems, notably the question of how to deal with the numerous oil and gas platforms in the North Sea and elsewhere. In time, disposal may become an issue for shipbuilders. Given the current problems of managing the scrapping of the ageing fleet, as referred to in Chapter 1, that time may be sooner rather than later.

The reality is that all the questions posed above are real, and have to be dealt with. A sound design process can satisfy all of them without sacrificing any aspect of operational performance.

Design for production is necessary primarily because of the need to keep the cost of producing a vessel to the minimum. The reduction of costs is achieved largely through two mechanisms. These are:

— reduction of inherent work content;

— making best use of available facilities.

It is a responsibility of the design function, but depends on adequate data from the production function. It must both support and respond to changes in production technology intended to reduce the costs or increase the output of production.

Standards

One of the key features of design for production is the use of standards, for example for steel. The standards which are used include:

— standard material sizes, which simplify the specification and procurement of the materials which are needed. Once the steel is available to the shipyard, the storage and handling requirements can be reduced. The actual stock levels may also be reduced, all of which provides a cost saving;

— standard properties, again making the specification and procurement process simpler;

— standard preparation requirements and standard process technology. These simplify the process flow in production. Less sorting is required, and there may be potential for interchangeability of parts and processes, simplifying the scheduling of production operations. Finally, standardisation in production reduces the training requirements;

— current standards for component characteristics, the adoption of which makes for improvements in performance and quality.

For smaller shipyards, examples of standards in materials and in component production would be:

• Standard material sizes, for example for a smaller shipyard;
    — all plates 8,000 mm or 6,000 mm in length;
    — all plates 2,000 mm or 2,500 mm in width;
    — thicknesses in 2 mm increments;
• standard bracket shapes, minimum number of bracket dimensions.

These will greatly simplify the material supply problem, with the sizes and thicknesses geared to the local market. The need to store large quantities of materials, for example large numbers of steel plates, each to a specific size for a specific purpose, is eliminated.

Standards can be applied at all stages of production. For example in the sub-assembly stage:

— use of standard components as far as possible allows their production to be scheduled more easily;

— the use of readily available welding processes in the down hand position reduces the man-hours required for production;

— making the assembly sizes similar, and compatible with handling equipment, increases efficiency;

— the design of assemblies which are suited to jigs and fixtures allows production to be more efficient.

At the unit assembly stage, as the products being designed are becoming larger, the design is such that it provides:

— self-supporting units, that is they can be positioned quickly and safely on the ship;
— minimum needs for staging and access equipment, because most of the production work can be completed before the unit leaves the workshop;
— ease of outfitting, so that the process of installation can begin early and be completed in good working conditions.

Prerequisites

There are a number of prerequisites for the application of design for production. The need to have adequate information about the production processes available to the designers has been mentioned. For the principles to be applied successfully, a number of specific features are needed. First, there must be a recognisable manufacturing strategy. This is a formal definition of the production operations, and will incorporate the standard processes. This manufacturing strategy is considered in Chapter 9. These must also be stable; that is, the standard methods and procedures are applied consistently, and also give consistent results. The need for standard and stable processes is considered in more detail under the heading of quality assurance in Chapter 13.

There must then be an effective feedback system from production to design. This will go beyond the simple description of the processes which are in the manufacturing strategy, and will provide specific information about how well the production processes are operating and what changes in design could allow improvements to be made. The feedback which is given to the design function includes information which makes it possible:

— to identify problems caused by design features;
— to identify opportunities to improve design features;
— to provide information in a suitable format;
— to provide non-confrontational feedback.

Once a manufacturing strategy is in place, and there is feedback from production, there must also be a ship definition strategy. This is designed to identify the specific outputs at each stage of design. The outputs have been referred to above, but the specific focus of attention is on the information which is generated for production purposes. It is also important that the production information is given in a suitable format, and this will also be part of the ship definition strategy.

In order to manage all of the interface requirements between the design and production functions in a shipyard, there must also be a production engineering function. This may be a separate department, or may be embedded in the design and production departments. In some cases, where multi-disciplinary teams are adopted, the teams include both design and production staff, and the production engineering is part of their brief.

The production engineering has a role in the design and development of facilities and processes in the shipyard. It also has a role in securing accurate estimating and scheduling, largely through the use of standardised processes and products for which accurate work measurement can be carried out.

The two key objectives which design for production is intended to help achieve are specifically directed at minimising the cost of construction. The objectives are:

— to reduce the work content in construction of a ship;
— to reduce the cycle time to construct a ship.

To achieve these two, and hence a lower cost, there are specific secondary objectives which are achieved directly from the changes in methods outlined previously. They include:

— an improved quality of construction—which is managed because design for production gives easier fit-up of parts, hence there is less re-work;
— an improved working environment through better access to workplaces. Where more of the work is completed at an earlier stage of production, and where good access is designed into the interim products, the conditions are better and this has a further impact on production quality;
— much improved material utilisation, by adoption of rational standards which results in less wastage;
— above all, there is improved productivity, primarily through the reduction in re-work.

The process as outlined does require the ship designer to consider production from the start of his process. Initially at least, the designer primarily considers the ship as a whole, or a collection of systems including hull structure, cargo handling and propulsion. It is also necessary to consider the ship in terms of work breakdown structures. Work breakdown structures are considered in the chapter on planning and scheduling.

The conventional design viewpoint results in a system work breakdown structure (SWBS). There is also a need to consider the way in which the ship will be divided into units and smaller elements for production purposes. This is generally called a product-oriented work breakdown structure (PWBS).

It is also important to consider other breakdowns, depending on the requirements being addressed. The purchasing of materials and equipment may require an alternative breakdown, grouping the elements of the ship not by system, nor by interim product, but in batches which best suit the needs of purchasing. Similar items from different products and systems may be purchased in batches to secure discounts.

The decisions taken at an early design stage often have a major influence production costs. By considering PWBS (using the manufacturing strategy) from the start of design, the impact on production costs can be minimised. The decisions that can be taken at an early stage, preferably pre-contract, include most significantly how the structure can be split into blocks or units for erection on the building berth or in the building dock. This has the biggest influence over the time it will take to construct the ship—the berth (or dock) cycle time—which effectively sets the level of production which can be achieved in a shipyard.

Application of design for production

The correct application of design for production can reduce the cycle time by reducing the number of blocks. Fewer, larger blocks ensure less work to be performed on the building berth. There are also opportunities to simplify the connections between the blocks, which also reduces the work content, and the possible need for re-work in the fairing and welding processes. The objective is to maximise the weight of blocks within the limitations of the capacity of the cranes which are available for erection.

Once the basic breakdown of the ship into blocks or units has been decided, an early decision can be made with respect to the assembly sizes and arrangements. This enables a shipyard to make the maximum use of specialised production systems, such as panel lines, web lines and curved unit assembly jigs.

Early decisions, based on the structural element sizes, allow the raw material sizes to be determined. The objective is to use the largest plate sizes which the facilities can handle, and also to make use of standard sizes as far as possible. To achieve the cost reductions, production information is needed which is accurate, up to date and in a form which the designer can use readily.

The information which the designers need about the capabilities of the production facilities includes:

— work station capabilities, primarily the size and other characteristics of the interim products which are produced. Also important is the level of accuracy which can be achieved, which dictates the sequence of assembly and largely determines the potential need for re-work;
— crane capacities, lift heights and outreach, so that the ability to lift and manipulate the interim products is known;
— the capacity of multiple crane lifts, for lifting special blocks (for example, deckhouses);
— size of doors and other transport restrictions.

Information is also needed on the production processes which are in use, for example the welding capabilities. In the outfitting area, standardisation of items including pipes is one means of reducing work content. To do so, the information required by the designers includes preferred pipe bending diameters and standard lengths.

For many ship types, the outfitting is as important as the steel structure, if not more so, and therefore outfitting also requires early consideration of production

Plate 1. High volume steelwork – cutting steel plate parts in Japan

Plate 2. The scale of large ship interim products – a 2000-tonne plate rolls

Plate 3. Frame bending of complex profile shapes

Plate 4. Mechanised assembly – flat panel production for large bulk cargo ships

Plate 5. Assembly jigs for complex hull shapes

Plate 6. Ship construction – accurate location of a structural unit

Plate 7. Installing ship's equipment as ready-assembled packaged units

Plate 8. Technology for positioning large structural blocks – saving cost and time

Plate 9. Final outfitting for a cruise ship remains labour intensive

Plate 10. Large-scale shipbuilding under cover – Meyerwerft

Plate 11. The finished product – a cruise ship

requirements. The key is to identify potential outfit assemblies (modules) from the earliest stage of design. In the same way as steel units are identified, and can then be designed for efficient production, outfit assemblies can be designed as independent structures which are then completed in a workshop and installed as a single item rather than as a large number of individual pieces.

The identification of service routes is also important, because much of the work content associated with outfitting of a ship is in the connections between items of equipment which then form the ship's systems. Installation of pipes and cables can be time-consuming, but if service routes are selected, then they can be pre-installed on foundations and again placed on the ship as a complete unit. By so doing, common foundations for services can be developed for a variety of ship systems in a particular space. Also, pipes and other services can be run in parallel, permitting lower production costs, reduced space requirements and inherently better access for production (and maintenance). A major benefit is that work can be moved from installation on ship to the workshop, and interference between systems which may occur if they are installed on the ship as individual pieces are eliminated.

The dimensional accuracy and stability of production are also important. The preferred production methods, and therefore the preferred design characteristics, are influenced by accuracy. If parts and then assemblies can be produced with accurate dimensions, then the ability to develop independent units is enhanced, because they can be reliably expected to fit when brought together at the ship.

Stable and accurate production therefore allows the use of large, complex three-dimensional blocks. It also permits large scale installation of outfitting on blocks, and contributes to minimum work at the final construction stage. On the other hand, if there is poor accuracy, then large units, and outfit assemblies would not be capable of being joined without substantial re-work to enable the units to fit. So a lack of reliable dimensional accuracy leads to simple panel units, with welding left unfinished to allow final adjustment when they are joined. The quantity of outfitting which can be completed early is limited and inevitably there are large quantities of work completed only at final construction.

The effects of changes in technology

In all of these decisions, and to enable the most effective production regime, the design function has to play the key role, basing design decisions on the known capabilities of the production system. There are some complicating factors which may be found in some cases. Historically, many shipowners had technical departments, which would be responsible for the preliminary design of their own ships. The shipyard would then be asked to tender against a fairly complete specification, and would basically then be responsible for the detailed design stages and the information for production. This arrangement would not take much account of production needs, unless the shipyard and owner had a long term and close relationship. In other cases, the owner would ask the shipyard to complete all stages of design, against a fairly basic specification. Most shipyards also had a large technical department, with capability for all the stages of design, and a large drawing office for the details. Gradual increases in ship complexity, and an increasing sophistication in the design processes, notably the use of digital computers, has had a major impact on the overall organisation and practice of ship design.

The design for production techniques described are made more practical and readily available through the use of CAD/CAM. It is CAD/CAM that simplifies the presentation of design data in the multiple formats required by this approach. The advantage which CAD/CAM was originally expected to confer was a simple increase in drawing speed. This ultimately proved to represent only a small proportion of the overall savings, although it was the most visible and was used for cost justification in early applications. The ability quickly to insert objects and to copy existing input was seen as a means of improving the productivity of detailed designers in particular.

There is some productivity gain, and this is important. In the present shipbuilding market, many shipyards are experiencing difficulty in attracting and retaining an adequate staff of properly qualified technical personnel. This problem is partly eased by increasing the productivity of available designers.

The early use of CAD, then a relatively new and unproved technique, was similar to the early use of many technologies. Although it was not immediately justified in cost terms, the long term benefits of the mature technology are now recognised.

More important than any localised increase in speed of drafting is the creation of a single or multiple interconnected design database. As the design develops through progressive stages, the level of detail increases and the focus of attention shifts from systems to areas and from the whole vessel to parts of the vessel. The database, the product model, maintains integrity and allows re-use of previously generated information.

Entire steps in the detailed design process have been eliminated, including pipe sketching, sheetmetal sketching, lofting and the production of NC data for piece part manufacturing and steel cutting. Design effort is reduced as preliminary models are used in engineering analysis including naval architecture and finite element analysis. Data stored in the system assists in the production of technical manuals and test procedures.

A major objective of design for production is to provide the worker with an information pack, including drawings that show only the information needed for the task at hand. Since many fewer data appear on each drawing, many more drawings must be generated. CAD systems provide powerful tools to achieve this goal. Through proper selection of parts, figures and layers, drawings may be produced of any desired portion of the database without any additional input effort.

Once a model of any area of a ship has been produced, working drawings may be produced using any desired views. Units may be shown in the orientation corresponding to the actual building position. Isometrics may be produced almost as easily as any other view. With solid modelling, shaded pictorial views are available for illustrative purposes and portions of the foreground may be eliminated, producing windows through which hidden structure may be seen.

Inherent in the CAD system is the ability to obtain dimensions across any plane with reference to any datum. If the designer is informed with respect to the dimensions and fitting data that are required on the shop floor, this information can be included on the drawings and significant hours can be saved in production.

Using standards is recognised as an important element of design for production. Standards reduce the diversity of parts, increasing the proportion of pieces which can be made in specialised work stations, even on transfer lines, and in family piece part manufacturing. Since standards are created only once and then re-used, it is economically feasible to invest the production engineering effort required to produce the most efficient design.

CAD contributes to the ease with which standards can be created and utilised. Libraries of standard piece parts can be placed in the database, then accessed and inserted into a model. For ease of manufacturing, families of standard parts can be created which vary only in a few critical dimensions.

The CAD system allows consideration of a greater number of design alternatives because of the system speed and the ease with which the input may be changed once the model has been built. By considering more alternatives the probability of achieving a time- and cost-effective design is increased. This capability is useful in detail design as well as in conceptual and contract design, where fast response to customers' needs may make the difference in obtaining a contract.

Although there is emphasis on standards, and on carrying out a task only once, the existence of a product model greatly increases the ability of a designer to respond to necessary change. With proper system integration, the speed with which changes may be transmitted to production is also dramatically increased.

. In the past, physical scale models were used extensively to generate production data for ship construction. The use of CAD-generated 3D models eliminates the need for such models, in effect replacing them with an electronic equivalent. The CAD model has all the benefits of a physical scale model, but with the added benefits of the ease with which specific production and design data can be extracted. It is also readily altered, and through the use of standards the reuse of previous models is greatly simplified.

The existence of a composite model, which effectively includes all the structure, equipment and systems for all or part of a ship, greatly reduces the difficulty of checking for interference between parts of different systems and between parts and structure. Many systems provide automatic mathematical interference checking. Reduction in interference reduces both design and production re-work.

The successful integration of CAD with material control systems has led to earlier and more accurate ordering of parts. CAD provides data directly to the material control system. As a result, the ability to reduce build cycle times is enhanced by the reduction in delays incurred waiting for material. More accurate material identification also gives a potential for a reduction in scrap material.

The increasing use of computer systems has had a major impact on both the design and manufacturing processes. The real goal of using computers is the full integration of CAD, CAM, CAE, material control, planning, production control and other design, manufacturing and management information systems. This integration results in what is referred to as computer integrated manufacturing (CIM). For all the benefits which can be achieved in terms of productivity improvement from individual elements, the real productivity gains are only achieved when this complete level of integration is achieved. To achieve the level of integration which is sought, CAD/CAM cannot be implemented alone, but has to be one element of an overall shipyard development plan. This includes both the physical facilities and the supporting "soft" technologies. The interconnection of different information systems must be given a high priority. This will avoid the development of islands of automation unable to communicate with each other.

The increasing complexity of design analysis has resulted in the ship design staff being required to master more and more complex techniques. At the same time, there has been pressure on their numbers to reduce costs. The use of CAD and other computer-based systems has been one approach to cost reduction and improvement of performance.

However, as in many other areas of the shipbuilding business, the tendency has been towards reducing the permanent in-house capability of the shipyard and using external suppliers. These may be technical specialists, with expertise in particular design areas, or the wholesale use of sub-contractors for detailed work.

This book emphasises, among other aspects of the business of shipbuilding, the need for a consistent approach to the various activities associated with the design and production of a ship. A standard approach to construction, through a build strategy, a well-defined hierarchy of interim products and a structured design process are all essential to the overall goal of improved ship production performance.

Consequences of not designing for production

A formalised approach to the design process has been outlined. This approach is based on identifying the form and content of the information which is input to and output from a series of stages which take the design from concept to detail. It is desirable that this structured approach should be adopted in all cases, and it would ideally be the basis for an agreement with an external design agency, whether as a sub-contractor or as the representative of a shipowner.

The shipbuilder can determine, through his manufacturing strategy, how a given ship type should be built. The processes are predetermined, as is the level of advanced outfitting and all other elements of the production system. For each standard ship contract only timescales need to be added. Management can then concentrate on the small number of unusual features which inevitably occur.

Following a clear strategy allows the builder to develop precise information requirements from the design function, in terms of form, content and timing. The results of achieving or not achieving these requirements can be determined.

For the structured process as described above to operate, the designer must respond to the requirements of the shipbuilder, as much as the builder works to produce the design. Failure to achieve this co-operation can generate a series of problems. Some are clear and well understood. Others are obscured by being accepted as part of a normal situation, and are only identifiable by reference to the activities and performance of more productive shipbuilders.

If the requirements of both builder and designer and the specific information to be provided are not clear, consequences can be:

— required information is not available to production and either a delay will occur or re-work will be necessary later;
— information is not provided and additional cost is incurred in developing it;
— revisions to the design are introduced at a late stage, causing delay and introducing additional cost;
— different interpretations of the design information are made, causing delay during their resolution.

All of these, and other consequences, will result in a cost increase and delay. The allocation of cost and responsibility between the design and production functions is a potential further cause of problems. The timing of information is also critical, which requires the designer to be part of the planning and scheduling of the whole project, not taking design in isolation. If this is not done, again problems can occur:

— late delivery of information to production, with consequent schedule problems;
— late delivery of equipment from suppliers;
— late delivery by sub-contractors;
— late revisions to elements of the design, where no date for finalisation has been agreed;
— areas of the design which present difficulties remaining unresolved, despite their critical importance to the production schedule.

The design and production of a ship is too large and complex a project to be controlled other than by a comprehensive and detailed planning system. The system can be responsive and largely decentralised, but must be effective. It must include the supply of design information, which is a major input to production.

CHAPTER 8

MATERIALS AND SERVICES FOR SHIPBUILDING

DEVELOPMENT

Shipbuilding is, as has been emphasised previously, an industry with a very long tradition. In many aspects, what may appear to be an entirely new method is in fact a logical approach to a problem, which has been used before. This is particularly true if the timescale considered is long enough.

Purchasing, and the whole business of materials management, is one such aspect of the industry. Initially, consider only the modern era, by which is meant the period since the steel ship became the standard—something over 100 years. As the shipbuilders developed steel construction, the relative quantities of steel they required made producing their own steel in some cases an economic proposition. Shipbuilding therefore migrated to areas where iron ore and coal were available—in the UK from the south coast to the north of the country.

The outcome, with the shipyards representing the major industrial units in their areas, was largely self-contained organisations, capable of producing from raw materials to finished products, and making many of the parts and equipment items needed for their ships within those organisations. At a time when organisations were generally small by late twentieth century standards, and when specialised production and the use of flow production for large quantities were in their infancy, the self-contained shipyard was a rational organisation.

As industry in general developed, opportunities arose for shipyards to purchase, rather than make, items they required. The largely self-contained shipyard gradually began to seek suppliers for more and more of its product requirements, always driven by the need to reduce costs.

Early steel shipyards were usually associated with a marine engine works. This arrangement gradually changed as engine design became more sophisticated and specialist. The shipyard moved to producing other specialists' designs, then began in many cases to buy the engine as well. Other equipment items also became the province of specialist manufacturers, taking advantage of economies of scale in production and offering competitive prices for their products.

In the last decade of the twentieth century, the use of suppliers—outsourcing —has increased at a more rapid rate. The development of supply chains, often in

145

association with a group of shipyards, is a feature of Dutch shipbuilding in particular. In some cases, not only the materials and equipment are outsourced, but the
labour required for their assembly and installation is also a sub-contracted item.

The century has thus seen a move from shipyards which accounted for 90 per cent
or more of the cost of their products within the organisation, to a more typical 30
or 40 per cent, and in some cases a reversal with 90 per cent of the cost accounted
for by outside suppliers.

PURCHASING SERVICES AND MATERIALS

From the above outline of the more recent development of the cost structure of the
shipbuilding industry, it will be apparent that there has been a massive increase in
the importance of purchasing. This represents, in some cases, a return to a situation
which obtained in the days of wooden ship construction. However, since the ship of
today is massively more complex, the requirements placed on the purchasing
function are far greater.

There has to be a close link between purchasing and other functions. The ability
to obtain a keen price is still important, but the ability to secure certain delivery on
time may outweigh price. The need to receive items of adequate quality, in good
condition, can, in some circumstances, outweigh both of the others.

The need to obtain reliable quality and delivery of items, still at a low price, has
led to the need to co-operate with suppliers. The current and developing trend is to
regard suppliers, at least of the large and more valuable items supplied (and major
suppliers of labour sub-contracts), as partners.

The increasing cost of all materials and labour and low prices have been the driver
for the changes. The need for reliable delivery is partly a function of the need to
minimise inventory. While just-in-time delivery is not the usual case in the industry,
in part because of the large variety of equipment and materials required to build a
ship, minimising the time items are in stock accumulating costs is an important
aspect of managing materials.

In order to manage these diverse requirements, the purchasing function in any
shipyard now has to have a close liaison with other shipyard functions. The
breakdown of the complete ship into the necessary interim products can influence
the purchasing requirements. The production engineering function therefore has an
influence on purchasing. The timing of assembly and installation work is now far
more critical, as will be explained in the next chapter, so there must be close liaison
with planning, to ensure that all dates for delivery are consistent with production
requirements. Finally, the technical (engineering) function continues to be the
source of specification for the materials and equipment which are required.

Once the material has been obtained, preferably at a price which is acceptable, on
time and in good condition, the materials management role is not complete. The
needs of production should have been taken into account, both in terms of the

breakdown into interim products, and therefore the sequence of work, and the production schedules, and so timing of work. However, the purchasing function may well have arranged to buy some materials in batches to secure better prices, and to support supplier schedules. In other words, the materials will arrive in the shipyard in packaging and in a sequence that does not necessarily correspond to the requirements of production.

There is a need to package materials to suit production requirements. Some stockholding is inevitable, the quantity depending on both external factors and the internal organisation of the shipyard. In a compact, industrially developed region, with a high density of suitable suppliers, the shipyard can keep very low levels of stock. There are inevitably some items which are influenced by supplier schedules and other considerations, but in general shipyards in such regions can rely on rapid supplier response.

On the other hand, in remote, newly developing regions, the lack of local suppliers and the distance from the suppliers in other areas will dictate a different policy. Large stocks will be held, both against the possibility of late deliveries causing production delays, but also because the economics of transport may require relatively few deliveries of large quantities of materials. Even the inability to visit suppliers will be a handicap. In these circumstances a policy of holding large stocks will be entirely rational, both to minimise transport costs and to provide assurance of continuous production.

Supplier relations

As the industry has developed over the last 50 years, the importance of good relationships with suppliers to the shipbuilding industry has increased. This is for the reasons discussed earlier, including in particular the increase in the proportion of bought-in materials and services which are used in the construction of ships. There is also the increasing product complexity, resulting in a greater volume of specialised equipment on which the performance of the ship, for which the builder is ultimately responsible, may depend. Finally, the reduction in production cycle times has made reliance on timely supply much more critical to shipbuilders.

The proportion of costs represented by bought-in materials and services is now typically between 60 per cent and 80 per cent of the total cost of the product. Both internal and external factors affect purchasing, Internally the organisation of purchasing and material control, and its integration with other functions to focus on effective production have been considered. The external factors are primarily how the shipyard deals with its supply chain to achieve its main objectives. These are to obtain materials and services at an acceptably low cost which are of adequate quality, delivered on time, with supplier support. The level of support varies. For consumables the support is modest, limited in many cases to the supplier keeping the shipyard up to date with new developments and product changes, which are generally small. For large equipment items of a specialist nature, the support starts with the initial specification and continues through installation into commissioning and trials.

There are a number of important issues in supplier selection. Historically, purchasing was largely based on obtaining the best, in general the lowest, price. Delivery had some importance, although the cost of stockholding was less of an issue and buffer stocks could avoid many of the problems which would be caused by late delivery. Quality of supplies was measured by inspection at delivery.

Leading shipbuilders now have to take a much more critical view of these issues. In addition, they now also consider the ability to build solid supplier relationships to ensure reliability of supply. There is also increasing interest in co-operative purchasing, where several shipbuilders work together to secure bulk price discounts, but also to assist the supplier to plan more effectively. There is also much more emphasis on the need for good quality assurance.

Price considerations are still a major preoccupation of any purchasing function. One of the primary objectives must always be to acquire the materials and equipment needed for a ship at a low price.

The low price can be achieved in two ways. The traditional way is simply by hard negotiation, ideally with the ability to choose one of several suppliers, so that the purchase price can be forced down. The threat, or actuality, of changing suppliers can also be used as a means of reducing prices. Finally, there is the possibility of seeking the lowest possible specification which will just meet the owner's requirements. Although these are well-tried methods, they depend on the shipbuilder having sufficient financial influence, through size and level of production, to achieve the desired result.

The alternative means of securing a low price is by building relationships with suppliers and treating them as partners. This has a number of potential benefits. First, it is possible jointly to forecast future production levels, which may allow the supplier greater stability in his business with better utilisation of resources. In this situation, production costs can be lowered, and hence prices may be reduced. There can also be joint reviews of material and equipment specifications, rather than unilateral action by either the shipbuilder, as mentioned above, or the supplier, who may choose reducing the specification as a means of recouping a lower price forced on him by negotiations. All of the positive steps to work with, rather than against, suppliers may lead to more trust and to agreeing long term contracts with one or a few suppliers.

Quality assurance is another important issue. Inspection on delivery of items to the shipyard can identify whether an item or batch is acceptable. However, this is a late stage at which to make the discovery that there is a defect, and although compensation can be sought for the defective item, there are likely to be consequential losses to the shipbuilder. Relatively minor items can cause delays to shipbuilding programmes with possible contractual implications.

Once again, it is increasingly common to use the building of good relationships with suppliers as a means of managing quality issues. At the start there can be detailed discussion of the product requirements and specification, so that requests from the shipyard which are difficult to fulfil can be identified and possible alternatives can be sought. Building on this, it may be possible to take joint measures to improve production methods for the supplier. Rationalisation of the items, without loss of any important characteristics, can lead to improved quality as well as cost savings. There can also be joint inspection of items during production, or at some time prior to delivery, so that action is taken before anything reaches the shipyard.

On the other hand, the shipyard retains ultimate responsibility for the complete operation of the finished ship, and it is important to carry out comprehensive supplier evaluation before one is selected. If there are problems of quality which cannot be improved by any joint measures, then it may be necessary to decide on a change of supplier if quality fails to improve.

Delivery on time is the third key requirement from any supplier. For the ship-building business, in almost any case, late delivery is a serious problem. The consequences go beyond the immediate item concerned. In the worst cases, the whole contract may be delayed. Steps can, and must, be taken to reduce the potential for late delivery. These include accurate and realistic scheduling, with purchasing fully integrated with other departments, and with the capability of the supplier taken into consideration. There should also be absolutely no engineering changes after an agreed point in time, so that these are not going to cause schedule delays or possibly quality problems. There should also be joint progress reviews, in greater or lesser detail according to the value of the items to be purchased and their importance to the ship construction schedule.

It remains important to carry out an initial supplier appraisal, on a formal basis, and make some on-site inspections of quality and progress of the items during their production at the supplier's premises.

Many of the problems associated with purchasing have been caused by factors which are internal to the shipbuilder. Some examples of these are listed. Very detailed technical specifications, based on previous knowledge, may actually limit the potential choice of suppliers, by including features which are specific to a particular product. Features of the specification which are perhaps not necessary, or are over-complex, may give rise to problems in production for the supplier, which in turn also cause quality or delivery problems. The purchasing function may be working to unrealistic schedules, or there may be late changes to the schedule which may affect delivery. A culture within the shipbuilding company which is dominated by a focus on minimum price may result in reduced quality of the items supplied. A shipyard with a track record of late payments to suppliers may find difficulties in the future. If there is insufficient internal discussion in the shipyard, and a lack of information interchange between different departments or functions, this may limit the level of service which the suppliers are able to offer. The purchasing require-ments are built into work breakdown and scheduling. The production schedule determines when delivery of materials and equipment is required. The purchasing lead time determines when an order must be placed. The technical information is required in time to place an order. The organisation of the functions, and the work breakdown, must take these factors into account.

Inventory management

Inventory is the material and equipment, purchased for contracts, which has not yet been used in production. Inventory costs money, so that minimising inventory is a reasonable objective for any company, and particularly for a shipbuilder, with a high proportion of bought-in items. There are very good reasons for maintaining some level of inventory. These include the need to allow the various production processes to operate independently of each other. The inventory in this case provides a buffer stock between successive processes, so that any unexpected delays or production problems, possibly a machine breakdown, will not stop the entire sequence of operations. In this it is different from, for example, an automotive production line.

The use of buffer stocks also makes it possible to permit some flexibility in local scheduling. So the internal operation of a particular process can be scheduled for maximum efficiency, even if that schedule does not match completely the demand for the interim products which are being made. In the case, for example, of pipe production, where there is a necessary set-up time for each different type and size of pipe, the use of buffer stocks allows the process to cater for variations in product demand.

Considering the interface with external, rather than internal, suppliers, the inventory which is maintained in the shipyard provides some measure of insurance against late delivery from those suppliers. This may be for reasons beyond the control of either shipyard or supplier, for example a transport delay. There is also some benefit in inventory if it allows purchasing of economic batch sizes. An economic batch size is one which minimises the total costs, by giving lower unit costs for purchasing and transport, balanced against the cost of holding larger inventory stocks. Although the concept of just in time purchasing is fashionable, there are many difficulties in applying it in practical terms to shipbuilding, where there is a wide variety of materials, of which a high proportion are made to order, as is the ship itself.

So some inventory is essential, although in an industrially developed area, with suppliers close by, inventory can be very low. Even in the 1970s, many observers in Japanese shipyards remarked on the low level of steel stocks. This was possible because the shipyards and steel mills were close, and there was a degree of standardisation. More and more shipyards are reducing their steel inventory by using steel stockholding companies as a buffer between themselves and the steel mills. While there is a cost for the service, it is outweighed by the savings from having virtually no inventory in the shipyard itself.

There are a number of costs associated with inventory, and these must be taken into account when deciding the correct inventory levels. The typical costs of inventory are first, *holding* costs. These include the costs of handling materials into and out of storage and any interim movements which may be needed. Also included are the actual costs of the storage facilities. Buildings and compounds are required, and their construction and running costs are all part of the inventory costs. It may be necessary to provide some special conditions for some materials to preserve them, or for delicate equipment, including maintaining a suitable temperature and humidity. Also included are insurance costs, in case of fire or damage. There is also a possibility of materials or equipment becoming obsolescent.

There are also *shortage* costs. If inventory is not maintained, because of the costs which have been referred to as direct inventory costs, or if a low level of inventory is maintained to reduce those costs, then other problems may occur. In the event of a delayed delivery, or some accident, the company may run out of an item. In such a case, there will be a cost associated with lost or delayed production. In the shipbuilding business, with its large complex products, delays even to relatively minor items can cause major project delays, giving rise to large costs.

Other costs are associated with the actual purchasing process, and are known as *ordering* costs. The mere placing of an order for materials results in costs, and as the volume of materials and equipment bought into a shipyard increases, so do the ordering costs. The placing of an order with a supplier requires a precise definition of what is required. While this may seem obvious, the situation when an item is produced within an organisation may be different. If there is a question of clarification about an internally produced item, it can be resolved quickly between departments. However, if the same question arises when an external supplier is involved, there may be costs, of communications, of meetings, perhaps for extra work to be paid for or later delivery. As a result, the placing of an external order requires a requisition, to provide a precise and adequately detailed definition of the item. There are then costs associated with order processing, and often with expediting the item to ensure delivery.

Reduction of the costs associated with ordering can be achieved by reducing the number of orders or by placing orders for materials in large batches. However, that may simply increase the inventory holding costs referred to above.

In the production processes there are often machine or other *production* set-up costs. The pipe production shop is a good example. The cost of changing production from one to another product may also need to be considered. If a small inventory is maintained, then there may be frequent changes of product, or interim product. Each time a production change is made, there will be a cost incurred. This may be in re-setting a machine, in changing the jigging arrangements at a work station or in other reorganisation of the production system. More frequent changes result in more costs.

Management of the appropriate inventory level is therefore essentially a question of balancing conflicting requirements to try to minimise the costs. The balance is between ensuring that production is not delayed by shortage of materials and keeping the inventory cost to a minimum. In the past, shipbuilders generally erred, if at all, on the side of caution. Early ordering, relatively large stocks and a safety-first policy were adopted, because the consequences of delays to production, possibly resulting in a delayed delivery, were seen to be the worst consequence.

However, with the drive to minimise costs which is now paramount in the business, and often with reduced lead times enforced by shorter contract to ship delivery times, managing with a lower inventory is becoming a necessity.

The key to successful management of more or less any human endeavour is the planning of the work to be done. Purchasing and management of materials are now firmly within the planning system.

For large items of equipment and specialist materials bought to order, the overall planning system for the ship contract will determine when they are required. This will be at the optimum point in the production cycle, and may well be relatively early to facilitate installation in good workshop conditions. The same planning for the contract also determines the timing of technical information, so that requisitions can be fully prepared in good time. The timing of ordering is also determined for the major items.

In some cases, the ordering of major equipment may be done at a very early stage of the contract, or even before the contract is formally signed. In these cases, there is a need for management intervention to deal with what are exceptions. If there is a well-organised plan, then most of the materials procurement will be based on routine procedures, which allows management effort to be focused on the exceptions.

In the management of inventory for bulk items, various models can be used. Of these the two most common are:

— fixed quantity ordering;
— fixed time ordering.

These can be used whether future demand is certain or uncertain, and the general principles are shown in Figure 11.

The level of inventory is determined by the size of the orders placed. These will be determined by the level of confidence in the supplier and the relationship which will perhaps allow for frequent small deliveries, as a trade-off against regular ordering. Ideally, there will be a more or less continuous supply which will allow the

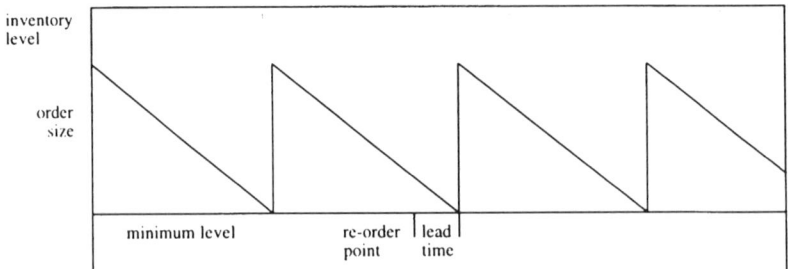

Figure 11. Model for managing inventory levels

inventory level to be minimised, but this is a counsel of perfection which cannot be realised in many practical situations.

The timing of a new order is set by the minimum stock level. This is a level of inventory below which it is dangerous to allow stocks to fall. In effect the minimum inventory level is the amount of stock which is necessary to keep production flowing while some disruption of the supply chain is fixed. If the shipyard is remote from the supplier, or if a new supplier is being used, then the level may be relatively high. As confidence in the reliability of a supplier is gained, the level may be reduced, and for a supplier which is very close to a shipyard, and which maintains its own stocks, inventory may be virtually zero.

An important feature of the entire business of buying and managing the materials and equipment for ship construction is the need to match *production requirements.* Mention has been made of the differing work breakdown structures which may be used in the industry. The material may have been purchased in batches which do not entirely match the production sequence. The delivery from the supplier may also be to a schedule which is not the same as the production needs. The result will be the inventory to ensure that no delays will ensue to production.

So, once the material has been received in the shipyard, it has to be delivered to the production location. The entire production work for a ship is split, initially into interim products, then into small work packages. The information for each work package includes a bill of materials (BOM) or materials list, which details all the items needed for that particular sequence of work.

The sequence of work will have been determined by means of the work study applied to the ship contract. The planning system has then identified when materials are required in production, and this has been used as the start point for the planning of the materials purchasing. The actual materials information has been prepared by the technical department as part of the complete information package for the work package in the work station.

The role of the materials department, operating one or more stores within the shipyard, is now to marshall the items which are required into the sets which correspond to the bills of materials for each package. At the same time, there is a final opportunity to ensure that all the items are available, that no defects are present and that no breakages have occurred.

Many different arrangements are used for storage. In some cases a single central store is used, which manages all the materials for the shipyard. This can be a cumbersome arrangement and generate excessive handling as materials are transferred into the various production processes. Typically, steel materials and pipes are stored separately, and adjacent to the appropriate workshops for ease of access and reduction of materials handling.

In the past, it was common for some of the workshops, which were trade based, to purchase and manage their own material supplies. This has generally been abandoned in favour of more centralised systems which give opportunities for improved cost control. In conjunction with improved information technology, using distributed systems, a mix of centralised management with a degree of local control is possible.

Procurement as a topic is of increasing importance as industry conditions change. Successful procurement is dependent on *internal factors*, in particular the integration of procurement with design, planning and other functions. It also depends on effective organisation using information technology. The process covers all aspects of materials management from the initial requirement to place an order with a supplier to the final delivery of the correct materials to the production site in the shipyard.

The management of many *external factors* is also important. This begins with the identification of good suppliers through some formal appraisal procedure. It may proceed in some cases to the establishment of effective partnerships to secure the best price, delivery and quality. Once a supply chain is established, there is a need to establish a system for monitoring levels of service, and to take some action if problems are found.

CHAPTER 9

SHIP PRODUCTION PLANNING AND PRODUCTION ENGINEERING

PRODUCTION ENGINEERING AND PLANNING HIERARCHY

Shipbuilding projects are generally large—even a small ship is a large undertaking by most industrial standards—and the design and production may be spread over several years. The production engineering and planning of these projects is therefore also a major task. The construction of a ship is also a very diverse operation, and covers a wide range of activities.

The information which is available for planning during the pursuit of an enquiry, and perhaps even at the beginning of a contract, is often sparse, based only on key dates. Similarly, the information available for engineering, to determine the methods of construction and the integration of design and production, is also often sparse. The initial planning and engineering is often limited to the overall breakdown and a high-level master plan.

As the project develops, so does the information available, and the planning of the work can also be developed in more detail. At the senior management level, only the overall status of the project is considered, primarily to monitor that the key dates are, and will continue to be, met. Also, the satisfactory completion of each of the major planning units is an important measure of progress.

This leaves the more detailed planning to lower levels in the organisation. As more and more information is made available through the design process, the more detailed definition of production and the accompanying schedules can be developed. At the most detailed level, the local scheduling of work stations is often performed by the supervisor. The supervisor may also be responsible for the determination of how the work will be completed, although this may be predetermined by shipyard standards.

As a result of this steady increase in detail and in information availability, several levels of planning and engineering can be identified in most shipbuilding companies. These are often designated as follows, although the terminology may vary from company to company.

Corporate planning looks at the long term future of the whole company. This is like corporate planning in any company, and is primarily about the long term direction of the company and the achievement of some mission statement. As such it sets overall guidelines in terms of preferred product mix, marketing and long term development. It provides a framework within which the rest of the company operates. The production engineering element in this is primarily about the long term development of the facilities and methods in use, and ensuring that these match the product mix requirements through a long term facilities plan. This process effectively determines the manufacturing strategy of the shipbuilding company. Facilities development is reviewed in Chapter 12.

Strategic planning looks forward for the duration of a project, and serves to co-ordinate the different projects a company may have in hand, allocate and manage overall resources and provide a basis for senior management to monitor progress. The production engineering element is the breakdown of the project—the ship —into logical planning units as the basis for the plan and also as a basis for the more detailed design work, bearing in mind that this is increasingly geared to the requirements of production as well as function.

Tactical Planning covers the next few months in a department. The requirements of all the projects which the shipyard has in hand are aggregated, to provide a demand schedule for a department. Production engineering identifies the resource requirements and matches the interim products to be made in the department, in accordance with the demand schedule, with the facilities and equipment.

Detailed Planning covers the next few weeks for a work station, and is the lowest level of planning. It optimises the use of the work station resources, while meeting the overall schedule requirements. Production engineering is about work station design at this level, to assist the work station supervisor to achieve the optimum production.

More or fewer levels may be found, depending on circumstances. In particular, a small shipyard, with generally shorter contract durations, may well have only two levels, with a long term plan effectively only for a year or so. This is dependent on the duration of the typical shipbuilding contract. The lower level plan will then deal with the (relatively) small number of work stations in the small shipyard.

On the other hand a very large shipyard, or one constructing complex, particularly military, ships, may have four levels of planning and engineering below the corporate level. The key is that the complete set of products—the ships to be built—and the production processes are broken down into manageable elements, with logical links between the levels.

As well as finding differences in the structure of planning, according to product complexity and the other factors referred to, the organisation of planning varies from company to company.

In some cases, all planning is in a centralised department. This is usually not the best arrangement, except perhaps in a small shipyard, where maintaining control is simplified by the relatively small number of people and processes to control. A centralised system tries to manage all the detailed activities of the shipyard from a single source. The variety inherent in a complex product and production system is such that the usual outcome of a centralised approach is that the planning function is spending time catching up with what actually happens in the workshops and on the berths, rather than helping to manage these activities.

Generally, though, planning at the detailed level, and sometimes at the tactical level, is localised. This allows the local management and supervision in each work area to schedule its work to gain maximum efficiency, within the constraints of completing all its interim products to meet the overall, strategic planning targets. The local autonomy effectively increases the number of people involved in planning and engineering, which makes it easier to manage the variety. Thus, if a problem occurs in a specific area, the local management can often solve it without reference to higher management. Provided the solution is achieved and the ability to meet the demands of the overall schedule is maintained, this is ideal. Only if additional resources are required, or particularly if the higher level schedule may be affected, does higher management need to know. This approach limits the need for senior management to have involvement in day to day operations, except when really necessary.

The ideal approach does depend on an open approach to management, effectively trust between different levels in the company.

Although tactical and detailed planning may be de-centralised, the strategic planning, however, is generally centralised, typically reporting to the chief executive, but maybe also reporting to a project manager in a large organisation. There may then be a further, corporate planning level which co-ordinates several projects.

HOW PLANNING AND PRODUCTION ENGINEERING WORK

Historically, the production of a ship was essentially a craft operation. From the development of a limited number of drawings of the proposed vessel and a specification, the work was handed over to the craftsmen. Before the development of drawings, the ship was generally defined by a series of rules, which related most scantlings and other product information to key ship dimensions. The craftsmen were organised into squads, according to the trade or specialisation. Each squad was under the control of a foreman, who reported to a head foreman, and under his direction the craftsmen expanded the basic information, typically full-scale. Only a minimum set of information was prepared, due to the relative simplicity of the ships. Many aspects of production could be decided as work progressed, with information, for example dimensions, taken directly from the ship under construction.

A number of factors have caused this to change over several decades. Some of these have been identified earlier, when dealing with supply and demand. The need to produce ships much more rapidly is a key factor, along with the increase in labour costs which characterises expanding and developing economies. The much greater complexity and size of modern ships has also been a factor which has forced a change in production technology. This change will be reviewed in the next chapter, but first it is appropriate to look at the preparation for production, and to describe how the work is planned and organised.

In order for a ship to be produced, a number of key questions need to be answered. These can be summarised relatively simply as:

— What is to be produced?
— How will it be produced?
— When is it to be produced?
— Where is it to be produced?
— With what resources?

The production of a marine vessel depends on the generation of a large amount of information. Historically, technical departments were concerned primarily with ship function, and other information was developed within the production departments, as outlined above. However, this approach has largely been superseded by the more efficient builders of ships, as described in the chapter on ship design. There is much better integration of design and production, so that the whole development of the design in increasing detail is guided by production needs. The question of what is to be produced is no longer a case of a complete (or sometimes incomplete) design definition being handed to the production management. This is reflected in the way ship design is now organised, which is recapitulated here. In answering the "what?" question, the other four questions become the province of planning and production engineering.

WHAT IS TO BE PRODUCED?

This is determined by the design activities. The changes in design which have occurred, and indeed are still occurring, have been described earlier. Here the concern is primarily with the design information which is intended for the production department, or, increasingly, the sub-contractor.

Design is concerned with the definition of the end-product—the marine vehicle. It can also be called product definition, and is carried out in several stages. Production is now an important factor in the information developed at each stage of design. These stages are often referred to as:

— conceptual, dealing with the features of the vehicle which meet mission or owner requirements;
— preliminary, creating the features of the vehicle which are sufficient to form a contract;
— functional, defining the features of the vehicle sufficient for owner and classification approval;
— transition, translating the design features from system to product orientation;
— detail, expanding the information on the characteristics of the interim products sufficiently to support production.

Each succeeding stage of design produces more detailed information.

Production should be a consideration at all design stages. Although transition design is generally identified as a stage at which production is considered, it is really an important consideration at all stages of design, right from the initial concept. The later stages of design are primarily to develop production information. In terms of design effort and resources, the detailed design stage, preparing the production information, is the most intensive.

The information which is developed to support the production departments includes:

— working drawings, which define each interim product;
— material lists, associated with each interim product;
— material and equipment specifications;
— material requisitions.

The information may well be destined for a sub-contractor, and this will often require to be more detailed and complete than is the case for production within the same shipyard.

The design information essentially identifies what is to be produced, which includes the requirements for:

— purchasing materials and equipment;
— part manufacturing;
— compartment arrangements;
— installation drawings;
— testing and trials.

The information is used at the detail design stage to produce work station information packages, including drawings, which are, from a production viewpoint, the ultimate output of the design process.

HOW WILL THE SHIP BE PRODUCED?

Once the question of "what?" has been resolved, at least at the strategic level, the next question is "how is the product to be made?". This is a question for the *production* or *industrial engineers*. The strategic solutions to how the ship is to be produced will then be input into the next level of design, so that the more detailed arrangements of the ship reflect the preferred production methods. The more detailed design information is then analysed by the production engineers to identify how the interim products will be made. This then influences the design of individual parts, so that they are specifically developed to suit the production equipment and proposed methods. In many cases, the outcome of many years of development of the shipbuilding process as a whole has resulted in these decisions being captured in shipyard standards. These may be in the form of libraries of standards, included in the computer aided design system, so that the designer merely selects the appropriate standard.

In this case, the functions described are there to seek and implement improvements. These may be the use of new processes, in which case revisions to the design standards will be needed to take full advantage of some new production capability.

Except in the case of new or substantial re-development, production engineering is often not a distinct function. It may be left to production management or supervisors, or be part of the planning function. However, it is important that the personnel who do carry out the function of production engineering are suitably trained. As with other aspects of shipbuilding, the complexity of the product and the need to achieve 100 per cent conformity to specification requires attention to detail. If these activities are not formalised and managed in a controlled manner, they will still be performed, since without them the ship will not be built. However, they will be performed in an unco-ordinated manner, and instead of contributing to effective production they will detract from it.

The activity described as production engineering includes:

— breakdown of the final product into interim products;
— decisions on the processes to be used;
— decisions on the design detail to support production.

It can be regarded as modelling the production process prior to production. For standard interim products, the process may lead to highly specialised production facilities such as a transfer line for the production of flat, stiffened panels, jigs for the production of curved panels, facilities for the production of outfit assemblies.

Over a period of time, the various definitions of how to produce ships evolve into a Manufacturing Strategy for a company. This is a description of how that company currently carries out its ship production activities. As such, it generally takes as a start point a definition of the optimum organisation and methods within the framework of the company's shipbuilding ambitions. The optimum is modified by the realities of the existing shipbuilding market, by limitations in facilities, labour force or finance, to provide a strategy which defines current best practice within the company.

Accepting both the need to improve performance over time, and that the current strategy does not represent the ideal, the manufacturing strategy will also include a plan for improvement. This may be a plan for re-developed or new facilities, new equipment, changes in methods or for personnel training, so that the strategy in a year's time will be an improvement on that which is current.

The corporate objectives of the company are a significant input to the development of its manufacturing strategy, and typically include:

— To be competitive in terms of total cost, combining labour cost and performance.
— To meet all contract delivery dates.
— To be competitive in terms of project duration.
— To build ships of a quality which makes them "fit for purpose".

— To be profitable.

A shipbuilding company will have an overall set of business objectives, designed to achieve some mission statement. Meeting these objectives will require a set of strategies covering the whole range of company activities, including for example:

— corporate strategy;
— marketing strategy and product development;
— materials management;
— shipbuilding planning and production;
— human resources;
— administration and finance.

The manufacturing strategy is the response of the technical and production part of the company to the overall business objectives. It therefore forms, along with similar responses from all the other departments, part of the overall business strategy. This sets a series of targets for the technical and production part of the organisation. To meet these targets, a set of decisions are required on aspects of the business including:

— facilities development;
— productivity targets;
— make, buy or sub-contract?;
— engineering and production organisation.

These form the core of the manufacturing strategy. The various elements of a clearly defined strategy are an important input into the design process, at various stages from conceptual to detail. The development of such a policy is therefore essential both for definitive and procedural purposes.

The manufacturing strategy is in effect a set of standards that can be applied to contracts. The standards are at different levels of detail, which correspond to the development of planning and design:

— strategic level, related to contract plans, interim product types, overall facility dimensions and so on applied at the Conceptual and Preliminary Design stages;
— tactical level, related to analysis of planning units, process analysis, standard products and practices and so on, applied at the Contract and Detailed Definition stages;
— detail, related to work station operations, accuracy tolerances and applied at the Detailed Definition stage;
— productivity targets.

PRODUCT WORK BREAKDOWN STRUCTURE

The complexity of the product has been referred to a number of times. This complexity and sheer scale make the construction of a ship potentially also a complex process. If the process is not carefully managed, then complexity in production will cause major problems. The first objective in answering the question "how to produce the ship?" is to make the complexity more manageable.

Any large project, including a ship or an offshore structure, or perhaps a chemical plant, creates a complex management and control problem. In order to be able to control such a project, it is necessary to divide the project into smaller elements. In effect, this is reducing something of huge complexity to a human scale, creating smaller elements can be grasped, understood and managed by an individual. The smaller elements can be controlled more readily than the large project.

One error which is sometimes made is to assume that the project management capabilities of a computer system can give an individual control of a large project, by the ability to process and present large volumes of information. The problem is that this simply transfers the complexity of the project to complexity in a plan. Although the computer may process the information, the human operator can hardly be said to be in control of a large and complex planning network.

The division of a major project into elements is called a work breakdown structure (WBS). For very large projects, the division, or breakdown, may be into several levels, creating a hierarchy of elements. This obviously parallels the breakdown of planning into several levels, of increasing detail, and the stages of ship design.

By breaking the work down into manageable elements, it is simpler to carry out the tasks which the project requires, including:

— setting up an appropriate management structure. Where the tasks are clearly defined, responsibilities for their completion can also be defined, and the management of an appropriate set of tasks provides a basis for the management structure of a project;

— estimating the work content, which for a complete project can only be done using a relatively crude, high-level measure of performance. For small, well-defined tasks, a more detailed performance measure can be developed and a more accurate estimate provided;

— planning the work. Using the estimate as a start point, it is simpler to plan a small task than a large one. The larger task can be determined by aggregating the smaller tasks;

— managing risk. By reviewing each element of the work breakdown, the risk can be assessed, and the total project risk then determined by considering the combinations of risks which have been found;

— giving all the personnel involved clear roles and responsibilities. The work breakdown should provide clear task boundaries, and also identify the interfaces between them.

Any work breakdown structure must be based on the idea of "deliverables". A deliverable is something which is tangible, usable and complete. So the completion of a task in a work breakdown represents something which is deliverable. This deals with the interface problem between tasks, and determination of responsibilities, since the output from one task represents the input to another. Completeness of the first task is essential to effective performance of the second, and represents something which can be measured.

Some examples of deliverables which would be appropriate to a marine project include:

— a design package for a zone of the ship, i.e. a complete definition of the zone, with all the information specified which will allow installation to take place. Any shortcomings in the information are failures to deliver, and thus complete, the task;

— an outfitted and painted structural block, again with the completeness carefully specified, so that the block is complete and ready for incorporation on the ship;

— a tested and fully operational ship system;

— an outfit assembly, ready to be installed;

— a package of bought-in materials, of sufficient quality and ready for production use.

It can be seen that the tasks cover a wide range of different processes and activities. This reflects the complexity of the ship as a project, but also the need for a work breakdown for a ship project to cover all the processes which are necessary. The definition of how the ship is to be produced includes all the design, purchasing, testing, quality assurance and other requirements.

The work breakdown is arranged as a hierarchy of such deliverables. At the highest level is the complete product definition for the ship and the complete ship itself. At intermediate levels, examples of deliverables are ship systems, structural blocks and information packages. At lower levels are structural units, sub-assemblies, and piece parts. Also included will be the relevant information packages for the production of these deliverables.

The "best practice" approach to work breakdown for the production of ships is based on deliverables called "interim products", and is known as a product-oriented work breakdown structure (PWBS). The ship is the final product, and the interim products are the stages on the way to its completion. The interim product concept is intended to reinforce the idea that the output from one stage of production is something sent to an internal "customer", and should therefore be complete and ready for use. It is entirely opposed to the idea of making adjustments later in the shipbuilding process, which is a major source of low performance in the shipbuilding business.

An interim product is one in a state which would be required from a subcontractor, where a payment is involved and a contractual arrangement is in place.

Although the PWBS is appropriate for production purposes, and a lot of emphasis is, rightly, placed on the need for efficient and effective production, there are other work breakdowns in use. These are equally valid, and are absolutely necessary for some functions.

A system-oriented work breakdown (SWBS) is needed for functional design. The finished ship is a set of interrelated systems, which combine in operation to fulfil the ship's mission. Therefore the ship has to be designed as such, and the systems have to be considered as a whole, to ensure that they will function adequately.

Other breakdowns include a division of the ship partly by time period, for purchasing requirements. The need successfully to procure a large number of items of equipment and a large volume of materials has been considered earlier. To achieve this, the elements of a ship have to be broken down in terms of the material and equipment characteristics and the time when the items are required.

To see how the different work breakdowns are interrelated, it is helpful to consider an individual item or part. Any part to be fitted onto a ship belongs to more than one hierarchical structure. For example, a pipe piece will belong to:

— a system, where it is part of the operating function. The pipe is one of many which connect together and form the system;

— an outfit assembly, on which it is assembled. Rather than being installed as a single piece, the pipe will be located on an assembly, and the whole assembly installed as a single item, which will reduce the man-hours and time required. The pipe is now part of a batch from several different ship systems, which are required for the assembly;

— a hull unit where it is installed. Either as a single pipe, or on an assembly, the pipe will be installed on a structural unit of the ship;

— a zone, where it is tested. The testing programme may call for all the part systems in a particular zone of the ship to be completed and tested;

— a work package of similar pipes, for fabrication. To allow efficient pipe production, it will be necessary to batch pipes of similar size and specification, to use the pipe bending machines efficiently. The pipes may be from different ship systems, and for different zones or assemblies;

— a material package, with which it is purchased. Batching of materials for purchasing will require items from the same supplier, and of the same material or specification to be grouped into packages.

There is therefore no single, absolute, correct work breakdown. It has to be a function of the particular project, its schedule and of the organisation and facilities where the project will be carried out.

The principles of a PWBS are based on the ideas of group technology and deliverables. The ship is divided first into zones, which are broadly geographic, but also separate types of work. A typical division for a cargo ship would be into:

— machinery space, dominated by the main engine and its auxiliaries;

— cargo spaces, generally dominated by steelwork;

— fore and aft ends, again steelwork but of much more complex shape;

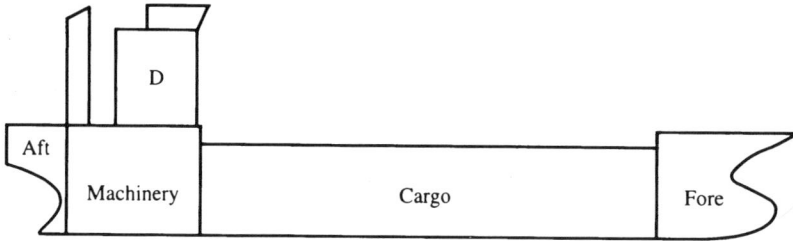

D - deckhouse

Figure 12. Typical ship breakdown into zones

— deckhouse, lighter steelwork and domestic and electrical requirements;
— hull, deck equipment and painting being major elements.

Electrical work is often kept separate, as an integrated system.

The zones are then divided by stage, that is into different stages of the production process. The stages are simply the sequence of activities, each ending in interim products, which have to take place before the zone is complete. Both geography (zone) and stage are sub-divided, primarily by class of work (or problem).

The PWBS is used as a basis for planning the project. The PWBS is hierarchical, and is developed into progressively more detail as the design phase of the project progresses. The planning of the project is also hierarchical, and follows a similar development path.

The highest level of planning shows contract milestones, typically payment dates. Each milestone requires the completion of a number of "planning units", which correspond to the main interim products. The breakdown into these planning units is done at an early stage of the project, and includes:

— hull structure breakdown into major blocks (or units);
— ship breakdown into installation zones;
— identification of outfit assemblies built separately;
— system completions.

By adding timings to the completion of each of these planning units (typically 100 per project), the information for a master network is produced. For each planning unit, a sub-network can then be developed, which divides the work to achieve its completion in stages. For an installation zone, these would typically be:

— installation of equipment on hull sub-assemblies;
— installation onto units or blocks (prior to turning);
— installation on a complete block, as an assembly, or a single item.

Separate networks can then be developed for design development and purchasing, using the appropriate WBS but planned to provide support to the agreed production programme.

BUILD STRATEGY

The interim products for a ship are the basis for the *build strategy* for that ship. Each new or potential ship contract received by the shipyard requires the formulation of a build strategy. The build strategy is the application of the manufacturing strategy to a particular contract. It may be drawn up formally, as a document, although where a shipyard has been working to a relatively uniform construction method over a period of years a more informal approach may be acceptable. In that case much of the work to be done in completing the build strategy would be produced quickly, with most attention being given to those areas identified as being unusual.

A well organised shipbuilder will have production facilities which are designed to suit a chosen product mix. The production methods in use will meet the needs of that product range. The production system as a whole will be supported by the various technical and administrative functions. This coherent set of facilities and systems will be documented to provide a well defined manufacturing strategy.

When a new order is obtained, only those parts of the design which differ from the usual products will require detailed analysis by production engineering. If the ship is part of the normal product mix, most of the production requirements will be standard. There will be a need, as the products change over a period of years, and as the production facilities and methods are developed, to update the strategy. If this is not done, the vessel designs may not be updated to match new facilities and the production methods may not be optimised for new design requirements. A formal method is therefore needed which will enable changing requirements to be identified and met in a controlled manner.

It is essential that each new vessel should undergo a systematic analysis to determine the proposed construction method, listing key events and their timing with respect to the overall project duration and identifying possible problem areas and bottlenecks with a view to their timely elimination.

The output from this evaluation of the vessel and the definition of the means of producing it is known as the contract build strategy. This has a number of objectives:

— to ensure that the company manufacturing strategy applies to each contract, and that standard methods are used, as far as possible;

— to ensure that every department make a full contribution to the planned construction of the vessel;

— to ensure that design development takes full account of production requirements;

— to production engineer the design to reduce vessel work content and construction time;

— to identify rational interim products and to create a product-oriented approach to designing and planning of the vessel;

— to identify the requirements for resources and the overall loading on the shipyard's facilities;

— to identify any shortfalls in the shipyard production capacity in terms of facilities, manpower and skills;

— to provide a basis for planning of production, including procurement dates for "long lead" material items;

— to communicate consistent information between the various technical and production departments of the shipyard and, where appropriate, the sub-contractors.

Typical contents for a build strategy are as follows.

Introduction

— details of vessel;
— details of special features/requirements.

It is not uncommon for managers and supervisors in a shipbuilding company to be unaware of details of the ships to be constructed. If only to keep people in the picture, it is desirable to provide a note of the main features of the vessel. Particularly where supervisors work in remote work areas, away from the berth where the finished vessel takes shape, providing more information can be good for morale. The build strategy, which should have wide circulation, is a good medium for this.

Of greater significance is the need to identify special or unusual features of the vessel and to draw attention to these. The second part of the introductory chapter of the build strategy carries out this function. The manufacturing strategy documents and the ship specification provide essential inputs.

The features so identified may be unusual or novel aspects of the design, parts of a vessel requiring particularly high accuracy or elements of the ship beyond the normal capabilities of the shipyard. For each feature, the impact on the shipyard facilities must be assessed and an action proposed. At the build strategy stage, the action may not be finalised because some further evaluation or design is needed. What the build strategy is able to do is list the requirements for action, identify who should take action and, through planning, determine when action must be taken. The fact that the need for action is noted in the build strategy does assist in ensuring that action is taken.

Main production parameters

— key dates/planned production rate;
— build location/launch condition;
— productivity targets;
— labour resource requirements;
— potential bottlenecks;
— sub-contract requirements.

The second part of the contract build strategy document defines the main production parameters which affect the vessel. The necessary inputs to this definition process are the manufacturing strategy documentation covering facilities and production rates, the ship specification and general arrangement drawings, and strategic planning information.

Planned production rate

From historical data, and any planned improvements in methods or facilities, the capacity of the various elements of the production system will be shown. At a minimum the capacity of the shipyard in man hours or tonnes will be known. Ideally, the production rates for various assemblies and installation activities will be available in some detail. In either case, the requirements imposed on the system can be calculated and compared with capacity. Any bottlenecks can be identified.

Build location

It is, of course, necessary to check that the vessel can be built on the proposed berth (or dock). The berth information should include any obstructions, water depth limitations or other restrictions. Available crane capacity and outreach data are also essential. Once the vessel location has been decided, in conjunction with strategic planning information for other vessels, any special requirements or restrictions can be identified and noted as requiring action.

Launch conditions

Initial calculations should be made to ensure that no problems will arise. The calculations should take into account the shipyard's standard strategy for installation of outfitting items prior to launch.

Key dates

A master programme will be prepared, having around 30 to 40 key activities, and will cover events from contract signing to delivery. Examples of items included will be in the order of long lead, high cost materials, design drawing approval by zone, approval of building programme, production start, keel laying, launch and sea trials. The programme will also be resourced, at least with those trades likely to show an overload. Sub-contractors should also be shown.

Labour resource requirements

The assessment of productivity targets, planned production rates and the key date programme will give an indication of labour resource requirements. These must be compared with available resources and decisions made about varying resources or dates, if possible, to ensure that the overall contract programme is achievable. Requirements for sub-contractors, which are increasingly commonly used in the shipbuilding business, will be generated from this analysis.

Potential bottlenecks

These will have been identified during the assessment of production rates. It may be necessary to upgrade facilities, vary resource levels or take other action. The most likely action is once again the use of a sub-contractor if at all possible. In any case, each bottleneck must be listed with the intended remedial action.

Sub-contract requirements

When the assessment of contract requirements and the evaluation of the shipyard's ability to meet those requirements have been completed, some adjustments may be made to balance the two. There will be some unavoidable mismatches between requirements and capabilities, and these need to be met by sub-contract.

The requirements for sub-contract must be clearly stated and both the timing and potential sources identified. Any outstanding problems must be noted, with action for their resolution.

Build strategy—hull

- — hull sub-division;
- — erection sequence;
- — outline methods descriptions.

In the third part of the build strategy document, the method for production of the ship's hull is considered. The first task is to make preliminary weight calculations to assist with establishing the best subdivision of the hull. The cargo-carrying part of the hull is ideally divided so as to give clean vertical breaks, with self-supporting blocks. If such blocks cannot be made using a block length approaching the maximum plate length that can be handled, then there is a shortfall in crane capacity for building the ship being analysed. This will not stop the project going ahead but will limit the overall performance potential, and may point to a need for long term facilities development.

Erection sequence

The next task is to determine the most appropriate erection sequence. Since the machinery spaces are usually the critical areas of high work content, it is usually found that shipyards achieving high productivity and short building cycles start erection at the forward end of the machinery space.

Initial process analysis—steel and outfit

When the hull blocks have been defined, a series of sketches or isometric drawings may be made of each block type which show how each erection block is further subdivided into sub-blocks and sub-assemblies. The sketches will be supported by outline method descriptions, covering both steel and outfit activities. Information given will include the block or sub-block weight, overall dimensions, location of build and orientation during building.

Build strategy—machinery spaces

- identification of installation zones;
- installation sequence;
- identification of outfit assemblies;
- outline method description.

For a conventional cargo vessel, the primary zones breakdown into hull, machinery and accommodation will be sufficient. For more complex vessels, more primary zones may be identified which have sufficient specialised features to require separate consideration in the build strategy. In all cases, the process will be similar.

Within the hull envelope, installation zones are identified, the installation sequence considered and potential outfit assemblies identified. Given a detailed manufacturing strategy, much of the analysis will be based on standard procedures. The preliminary arrangement drawings will be a major input.

Identification of outfit zones

In parallel with the block sub-division, the division of the hull into spaces will be completed in order that post erection outfitting may be organised into definable zones. The machinery space breakdown must take account of the proposed outfitting method and the engine room arrangement. It will be necessary to discuss this with the designers in order to find the best solution. The eventual breakdown will again be influenced by crane capacity, but the main aims should be to design the machinery arrangement and block boundaries such that a substantial amount of outfitting may be completed on blocks prior to erection.

Installation sequence

Analysis of each zone is needed to decide which elements of the outfit content can be installed at various stages of steel assembly and ship construction. The guiding principle is that installation work should be completed as early as possible, in the most convenient location to reduce the work content and in the elapsed time required to complete the work.

Identification of outfit assemblies

The outfitting work will be examined with a view to drawing up a list of outfit assemblies which may be installed on to a steel structural block or installed after the erection of the relevant steelwork. Outfit assemblies will be identified and a list made of the main components included in each. They will then be either linked with a steel block (pre-erection) or a defined post-erection zone.

Build strategy—accommodation

- accommodation structure sub-division;
- erection sequence;
- identification of installation zones;
- installation sequence.

As with machinery spaces, more than one primary zone may be defined. The preliminary arrangement will be essential input. This arrangement should be in accordance with the manufacturing strategy of the company.

Subdivision

The subdivision into steel assemblies or blocks should facilitate the early installation of equipment and fittings and make the best use of available cranage.

Erection sequence

The building of the accommodation block, or the assembly of hull blocks with a high outfit content, must be related to the overall erection sequence. It may be necessary to accept less than optimal sequences in some steelwork areas to allow more outfit installation.

Identification of installation zones

As with machinery spaces, the accommodation area will be divided into zones for installation. The zones will be co-ordinated with the steel assemblies and blocks to ensure that maximum work content can be completed early.

Installation sequence

Each zone will be analysed to identify work to be completed at each stage of assembly and construction.

Planning framework

- list of planning units;
- building programme;

— interim product groups and work stations;
— work station load analyses.

From the analysis of the various zones of the vessel a list of planning units can be developed. In conjunction with the key date plan, and a type plan for the vessel type if available, an overall building programme can be developed. From the previous analysis, a list of all steel blocks, zones and major item installation activities can be developed. These are the planning units, which represent significant events in the building programme. They also provide the basis for all subsequent planning activities.

Building programme

If a type plan is available, it will form the basis for the building programme. If not, then the sequence of erection and installation will be determined from the analysis of the vessel characteristics by primary zone and from shipyard practice. The master plan will determine the overall timescale. The building programme shows the start and finish date for each planning unit.

Interim product groups and work stations

The numbers of the various interim products will have been estimated from earlier analysis. For larger products, such as flat panels, accurate numbers will be known. Each product group will be linked to specific work stations.

Work station load analysis

Using the estimates of numbers of interim products and the dates from the building programme, the loading on work stations can be calculated. This gives an indication of resource and facility imbalances and work station utilisation.

Main purchasing dates

— high tensile steel;
— mild steel plate;
— steel profiles;
— high cost/long lead time equipment;
— pipe and fittings;
— electrical cables.

The build programme shows the dates on which the planning units must be completed. Using standard lead times for the various manufacturing assembly and installation activities, the delivery dates for bought-in items and raw materials can be established. From these, ordering dates can be determined. Which items may cause problems will depend on the ship type and building programme. Typical areas to be highlighted in the build strategy document are listed below.

High tensile steel

If the vessel requires high tensile or other special steel, the order date must be established, and the ability to secure delivery made certain. Some materials may not be readily available in the sizes or quantities required.

Mild steel

For mild steel and other materials the overall purchasing programme must be established.

Profiles

Any unusual profiles must be identified, potential delivery problems highlighted and solutions proposed. Some profiles may be difficult to obtain, unless special orders are placed with the suppliers to match rolling programmes.

High cost and long lead time equipment

The number and value of these items will depend, of course, on the vessel specification. Whatever the case, the purchasing programme must be integrated with the build programme. It must also conform to any changes in practice, for example, to decisions regarding the extent of advanced outfitting to be applied to the vessel.

The build strategy will always apply to a particular contract, and will be produced immediately after the contract is awarded. It will then be in sufficient detail to serve as a basis for subsequent planning, design and procurement activities. However, there is value in having at least some elements available at an earlier time. A preliminary version of the build strategy may therefore be produced at any time during the preliminary design stage. Typically, the preliminary build strategy would accompany a bid, to demonstrate how targets can be met and to show, for example, how a major new design feature would be undertaken in production. In its preliminary form, the build strategy is an important input to the preliminary design. In its final form it guides the development of functional design into transition design.

Inputs to the contract build strategy, whether pre- or post-contract, include the following:

— design information, such as general arrangement plan, preliminary midship section, preliminary lines plan, bulkhead plans, preliminary machinery arrangement, outline specification;
— proposed construction rates;
— proposed productivity targets for shipyard activities;
— details of shipyard production facilities in documentary form;

— assembly analysis information for typical units.

The formal preparation of the build strategy ensures that all significant features of the contract are considered early enough for problem areas and bottlenecks are identified and effectively overcome. It ensures that the company manufacturing strategy is applied to the contract and that all relevant departments contribute to the planning of the construction of the vessel. The distribution of the document ensures both the communication of key decisions throughout the shipyard and that everyone is working to a common plan.

The build strategy becomes the basis for all decision-making related to the timely completion of the contract from basic design through production to commissioning and delivery. A formal approach to build strategy (and the production of build strategy documentation) provides a means of planning for change from contract to contract within the framework of the manufacturing strategy.

A major element of the build strategy for any ship is the breakdown of that ship, through application of PWBS, into interim products.

Hull block breakdown is carried out by the production engineering function in a shipyard. As part of the production engineering at a strategic level, a routine approach to hull block breakdown should be defined for each ship type in the company product mix. The standards should then be incorporated into the company manufacturing strategy.

The principles of hull block breakdown incorporated in the company manufacturing strategy must be known by the designer and be taken into account at the earliest design stage. The hull block breakdown should therefore be incorporated in the build strategy. Unless the ship is of a type totally new to the shipyard, it can be included even in a preliminary build strategy prepared before contract signing. If the ship type is new to the yard, then a preliminary block breakdown can be included in the preliminary build strategy and the final details can be worked out as the build strategy is developed and the design progresses through contract and functional stages.

The breakdown into blocks and units is necessary to allow the ship to be built. Both the limits to the size of raw materials and the limits to the size of assembly that can be handled in the shipyard impose restrictions on how the ship can be constructed. Within those limits, the objective is to make the maximum use of the capacity which is available. The assemblies are then as large as feasible, which has the benefit of moving work to an earlier stage of production, at lower cost.

Other objectives are to simplify the erection process, reducing the time during which a crane is required and reducing the complexity of fairing one unit to another, to minimise erection and construction time and to achieve high labour utilisation.

For a basic cargo vessel, some basic principles can be used to guide the breakdown procedure. The more complex ship types, with additional outfitting requirements, present a different case, and it may be necessary to give more weight to the outfitting requirements. The structural breakdown will then be modified to suit.

Fore and aft ends should include the fore and aft peak bulkheads, with the shell butts close to bulkheads. The remainder of the hull should ideally be cleanly cut into a number of even-length slices across the ship. The position of the shell butt should be a regular dimension from a frame line, close enough to retain a "hard edge" but allowing sufficient space for easy welding access. The hard edge is created when the butt is located close to the bulkhead or other transverse structure. Since the butt is close to transverse structure, the edge will remain firm when the edge of the adjoining block is brought to it and the butt is faired. Fairing is more difficult when the butt is positioned an equal distance from the transverse structure on both blocks. In that case both edges are "soft" and will probably distort under fairing.

The length of each slice should be a whole number of frame spaces and be as near as possible to the maximum plate length which can be processed at the shipyard. The slices should be subdivided into a minimum number of self-supporting blocks. Erection breaks should be clean, in line, and should avoid cutting through structural members if at all possible. When subdividing the hull, every attempt should be made to design blocks which have the same work content. The use of fillet, downhand and automatic welding should be maximised.

It may be seen that the basic block breakdown rules apply equally to a wide range of ship types, but with the proviso that large outfitting work content may dictate some modification. Blocks should be as large as possible (according to shipyard facilities) and designed as 3-dimensional right-angled structures. Blocks should be designed to allow a maximum degree of pre-outfit, whether for the simpler ship types or not. All hot work, except that in way of block breaks, should be completed before erection to facilitate painting. The superstructure and engine casings, preferably separated, should be subdivided such that they may be built as outfit assemblies and erected pre-outfitted, in as few pieces as possible. Blocks should be designed so that the volume and work content of each is clearly defined and similar at each stage of assembly. Avoid the need for staging by subdividing in such a way that the structure itself provides a work platform. Stringers, horizontal girders, flats or purpose-designed structural arrangements may all be used to reduce staging requirements. Restricted space working should be kept to a minimum. In some cases, however, a restricted space may offer a significant advantage. For example, a superstructure joint may be designed in a cofferdam to enable hot work to proceed without damage to outfitting and painting work in adjacent areas.

WHEN IS THE PRODUCT TO BE MADE?

The next question to be asked is "when is the product to be made?". This is the essential function of the planning activities. Planning determines the overall timetable for the production of a ship. It includes more than simply production activities, encompassing also the design process, including the preparation of information for production and purchasing, as well as production of interim and final products.

The several stages of planning have been referred to already. They run in parallel with key design stages:

— strategic planning: the whole product;
— tactical planning: planning units;
— detailed planning: individual interim product.

Planning models the time dimension for production of a marine vehicle.

Strategic planning is the first stage for a ship project. It is developed along with the design, and will provide as an output the basic project plan which can be used as part of the shipbuilding contract. This key output from strategic planning is a key event network for the ship project. The network will typically have around 100 planning units. It will also be used to determine the overall resource loadings, and to ensure that these are adequate, using shipyard resources or sub-contractors as required.

The starting point for the network is the critical dates for the project. These include the delivery, which is paramount, also the keel laying (when the building dock or berth is available), and the launch or float-out. The period to be spent on the berth is planned, with a network produced which demonstrates how the ship can be built from blocks or units to meet the required dates. Again, this may involve the use of sub-contractors for some work. The network which is developed will be based on the idea of planning units.

A *Planning Unit* is a major event in the project, typically:

— the erection of a major structural unit;
— the completion of outfitting of a major zone of the vehicle;
— the installation of a major equipment module;
— the completion of connection and testing for a major system.

The network is developed to give the most effective construction sequence, taking into account the needs of both the steel structure and the installation of the outfitting for the ship. A standard network analysis technique is used to identify the critical path and find the optimum sequence. In many cases, where a standard type of ship is to be built, the sequence will be pre-determined, and the network will be developed directly from this (often termed a "type plan").

The strategic network is frequently drawn in a hybrid format, with characteristics of both network and gantt chart formats. Having determined the sequence for the construction of the ship on the berth, driven by key dates in the contract, additional key events can be added. These cover the pre-production activities, and also post-launch activities, primarily final outfitting installation and the various necessary tests and trials for the completed ship. See Figure 13.

Each major activity, which ends in the completion of a planning unit, is listed. The starting point is the set of linked activities which represent the erection of major structural units at the construction site (berth or dock). These are shown as the due

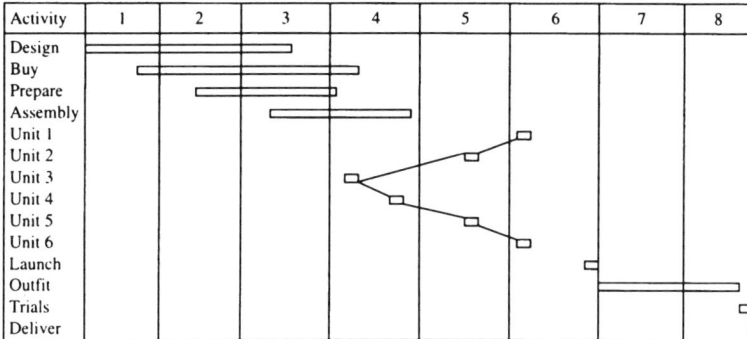

Activity	1	2	3	4	5	6	7	8
Design								
Buy								
Prepare								
Assembly								
Unit 1								
Unit 2								
Unit 3								
Unit 4								
Unit 5								
Unit 6								
Launch								
Outfit								
Trials								
Deliver								

Figure 13. Outline structure of a strategic network

date for each of the units (blocks) to be erected on the berth, that is the end of the block assembly, outfitting and painting activities.

On the outline above, the first set of activities, shown as bars, represent pre-production work. This indicates the time over which the various activities, design stages, purchasing activities and so on will take place. (The precise timing of these activities for each individual block is determined at the next stage; here the objective is to determine overall timescales and resource requirements.)

The final set of activities represents post-launch outfitting and testing/trials. Again, these initially show only the overall time, and are used to make a preliminary estimate of times and resources, using past data as a basis.

Each of the sets of activities which lead to the completion of a planning unit can then be represented by a sub-network, which includes all the work tasks which are required to complete that planning unit. Resources are assessed from estimates. The use of the, usually standard, sub-network for each planning unit allows the timing of resources to be determined. The overall resource loading is determined by taking a single stage of the sub-network, representing for example the steel cutting process, and identifying when the work has to be done. This can be measured in terms of the work content, or more usually applying some productivity factor to the work content to measure resources.

An example would be the man-hours required to complete a piece of work. For steel assembly, the man-hours per tonne for a given stage of assembly will be known, and there is also available a weight estimate for each unit. So the man-hours required for that particular stage of assembly for each block, and the timing of that stage, can both be determined. This then provides a picture of the resource loading over time.

Historically, where overloads in resource demand were demonstrated by a network, the response was to re-schedule to provide as level a resource loading as possible. Current practice is more usually to increase the resources by either temporary employment or sub-contracting part of the work to be done.

For a single department, all the tasks to be carried out for all the planning units are used as the basis for the departmental plan. The demand from the network has to be met, in terms of the completion of the activities in the correct order and by the correct dates. The internal organisation of the work to achieve the targets is determined locally in most cases.

Within the departments, the work packages which make up the tasks are then assigned to work stations as the final, detailed stage of planning and scheduling the work to be done.

WHERE IS THE PRODUCT TO BE MADE?

This is a function of *Facilities Engineering*.

The level of definition varies considerably. This function may be left to production management or supervision to carry out at a late stage. It may be part of the planning function in a more progressive company. Where a company builds using relatively standard interim products, the work stations where they are to be produced will be engineered to give a close fit between the two.

This may lead to very specialised production areas, for example:

— panel assembly workshops;
— block assembly shops.

At the corporate planning level, long term decisions will be made about facilities, based on the product mix which is anticipated. The whole question of shipyard development is discussed in a later chapter.

At strategic level, the decisions are related to the planning and production engineering decisions, and lead to determining whether existing facilities are sufficient for the ship production programme. If not, then a development and upgrading plan may be required, or a decision may be taken to utilise the services of subcontractors.

WITH WHAT IS THE PRODUCT TO BE MADE?

Resource Planning answers this question. The resources which must be allocated include:

— workers;
— equipment;
— portable tools;
— time.

The determination of resources in the short term (for a single contract) is a function of estimating and then planning. Specific needs for individual work stations are determined by the local management assisted by the production engineers. The requirements are determined initially from the build strategy for the ship, which highlights variances from normal practice in the shipyard. The final requirements are worked out on the basis of the more detailed design information as it becomes available.

The activity in the longer term may be carried out by specialist departments, for example facilities development and personnel, as part of manufacturing strategy.

Materials procurement. The technical information includes a definition of all the materials, equipment and services needed to produce the finished product. This information, along with a schedule defining when each item will be required in production, is the basis for procurement of all these items.

The need for appropriate timing of procurement is set by the interim product approach to production. The procurement dates are based on a preliminary identification of the products.

The activities which are carried out before the start of ship production are intended to answer five basic questions about the production of the vessel.

— what will be produced?
— how will it be produced?
— when will it be produced?
— where will it be produced?
— with what will it be produced?

It can be regarded as modelling the production process in advance. The vehicle is broken down through an interim product hierarchy to individual piece parts. Production is then the process of reassembling these into the vessel.

PROGRESS MONITORING

Having planned and scheduled the complex business of producing a ship, it is essential to monitor progress, to review whether the schedules are being maintained (and hence whether delivery on time is expected), and as a basis for taking remedial action if the schedule is not being maintained. Progress monitoring is therefore an important element of project management.

The timescale for a ship or offshore project is generally measured in months and years. It is essential that progress is monitored, so that any possible deviation from the plan is detected early enough for corrective action to be taken. The project is planned with several levels of detail:

— corporate;
— strategic;
— tactical;
— detailed.

Monitoring is carried out at each level. At the corporate level, monitoring is based on major events, and looks ahead typically five years. Monitoring is on the basis of the key indicators of performance for the company. At the top of the list must be financial achievement—basically, is the company making money?

Other key indicators of successful performance are the ability to adhere to the overall targets set for production, including ship delivery dates, and other key events such as stage payment dates. These link directly to the financial measures. All the lower level planning is tied back to the key dates, so that measures of progress can be directly translated into the probability of financial success.

The strategic plan is typically a 100 event network. Progress is monitored by:

— the completion of planning units in accordance with the schedule;
— the expenditure of man-hours in accordance with resource loading.

At the tactical level, progress on a project is measured at department level. The tactical plan is the three month plan for a department and progress is monitored by:

— completion of interim products in correct sequence;
— departmental man-hour expenditure.

Detailed planning is based on work packages in work stations. The timescale is up to one month and progress is monitored largely by completion of each work package within time constraints. Man-hours are monitored through the numbers fixed by the staffing of the work station.

The levels of planning and progress monitoring are linked, so that the completion of a work package is traceable to its impact on the potential payment schedule. As an example, at the corporate level, the key event is keel laying for the next ship to be produced. If all goes according to plan, then the due date is met and, most importantly, the company is paid on time. To achieve that keel laying, the output to be monitored is completion of the first planning unit, and the measure of success is that the unit is ready on time. This is still not predictive in any way, in that if the unit is late, the keel laying date will not be met and it is too late to take much remedial action.

At the tactical level, the assembly of the unit depends on the timely completion of all the required sub-assemblies, so this provides a measure that all the elements of the unit are ready.

Finally, at the detailed, work station level, the ability to complete those sub-assemblies will depend on, among other items, the cutting of all components. So the measure at this level is that a cutting work package is finished.

The success (or failure) in meeting dates at a lower level is an early warning of probable success in meeting higher level dates. If all the parts are available, then there is a good probability that the sub-assemblies will be complete, therefore the unit, and thus the keel laying—and payment—date will be met.

Progress monitoring thus compares the reality of production with the plan. Progress is monitored by completion of work, for example:

— material availability;
— key date achievement;
— work package completions;

and also by expenditure, which includes the numbers of:

— man-hours spent; and
— other costs associated with production.

Both the work completed and the expenditure must be monitored and both must be compared with the plan. The first element is the monitoring of work completion. It is common to use percentage completion as a measure but this has dangers, for a number of reasons.

First, the initial estimates of work completed always tend to be over-optimistic. Then as time passes, a high rate of completion is recorded, and eventually, work is recorded as "90 per cent complete" for long periods. If any problems occur, or the work is actually late, there may be re-work required, in which case the result is that the state of completion actually appears to be reduced.

It is therefore safer to monitor simply the completion of work packages at the detailed level. The work packages all have short timescales, typically only one or two weeks in duration. The status recorded for the work packages is that they are:

— not started, in which case progress is 0 per cent;
— in progress, in which case they can be recorded at 50 per cent;
— complete, and resulting in a deliverable interim product, so 100 per cent.

Aggregating the completion status of all the work packages for a ship gives first the tactical and then the strategic completion status. Provided the work packages are of short duration and have a small number of man-hours, the recording of progress is realistic.

Work packages ideally have enough work for:

— two to four workers;
— for one to two weeks;
— about 200 man-hours.

Around 20 work packages go into a planning unit and around 100 planning units make up the ship, for a typical medium-sized cargo ship.

Progress recording as described will tend to under-record the progress that has been made, but incomplete interim products cannot be used at the next stage of production, so the under-recording is realistic. The existence of a large number of open but unfinished work packages is a sign of potential or actual problems. Recording percentage completion is less likely to identify such problems. To take an extreme example, if 90 per cent of the work packages are 90 per cent complete, apparent progress would be 81 per cent, but this would not be a true reflection of actual progress on the ship.

The second element of monitoring is the recording of expenditure of man-hours. The man-hours for a project are the sum of hours for all the work packages. Ideally, the man-hours will be spent at a constant level. This can be achieved in a factory using flow lines, but is not practical for a large, made-to-order product such as a marine vessel. The man-hour expenditure follows a pattern:

— a build up from zero to a peak level at the start of the project;
— a steady peak level for most of the time;
— a run down to zero towards the end of the project.

Figure 14 shows the numbers employed on a particular contract at any time (as a percentage of the maximum number).

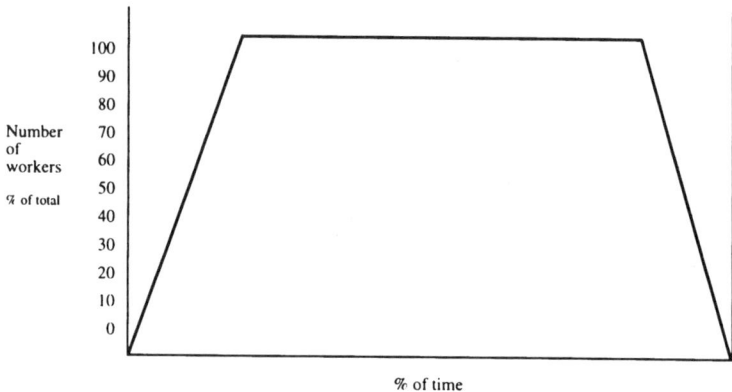

Figure 14. Simplified graph showing numbers employed on a ship over the contract period

Man-hour expenditure over the duration of the project can also be shown cumulatively. The cumulative expenditure is in the form of an "S" curve. See Figure 15.

The S curve shows the total hours to date at any time during the project. It can be represented as the percentage of total planned hours, against percentage time expended. The actual man-hours can be plotted against the planned hours, to show whether the expenditure is higher or lower than expected. See Figure 16.

The question is then how to interpret the information. Spending fewer man-hours than planned can have several causes. The alternatives are:

— the number of workers is fewer than expected;
— there have been late deliveries of materials;
— there has been unexpected work on the previous ship;
— there have been production problems, causing delay;
— the performance has been better than was expected and planned.

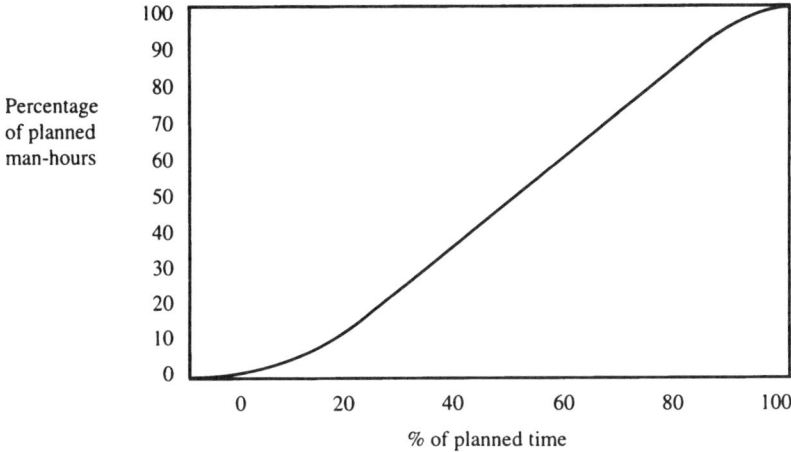

Figure 15.   Cumulative man-hours for a shipbuilding contract

The effect on the project, and the possible outcomes, can vary:

— the project will finish on time, and at less cost than planned;
— the project will be late, because there are too few workers;
— the project will be very late, because of serious production problems.

So in order to make a realistic assessment of the status of a project, both work progress and man-hours must be considered. The expected progress against planned man-hours can be plotted. Both actual man-hours and actual progress can be plotted, as percentages of planned man-hours and progress, against the percentage of time planned for the contract. See Figure 17.

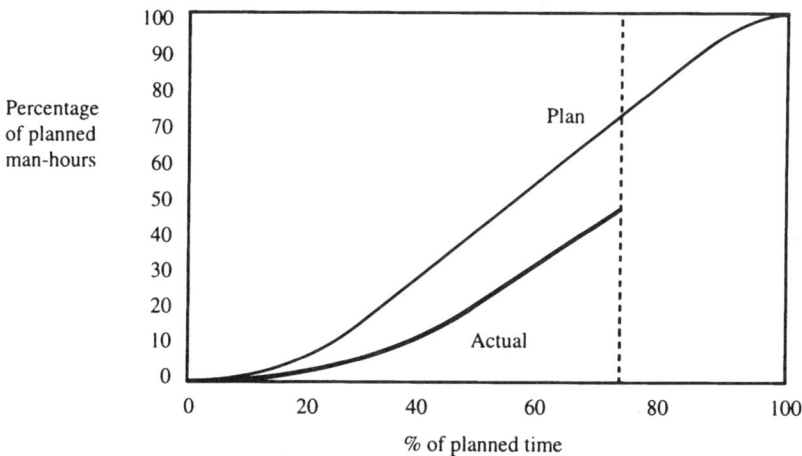

Figure 16.   Plotting actual man-hours against plan

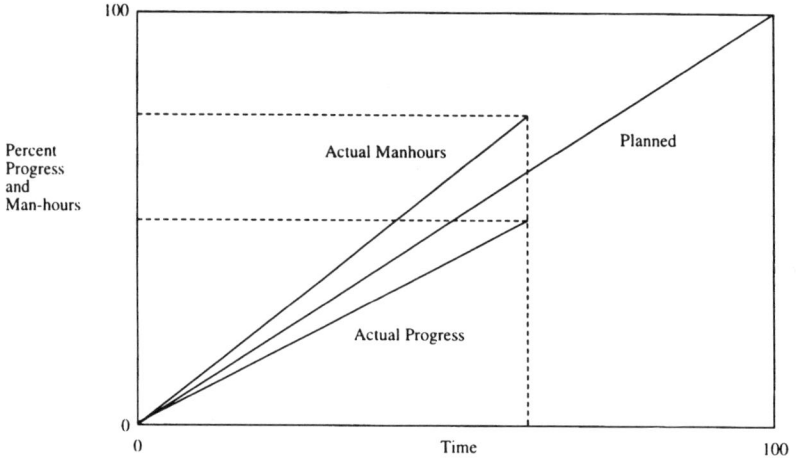

Figure 17. Plotting progress and man-hours against plan

To highlight variations from plan, the variance from plan over time can plotted, rather than the actual progress, or man-hours (Figure 18).

PRODUCTIVITY

An important aspect of the estimating, planning and monitoring process in any shipyard is the measurement of productivity. This is often looked at simply as labour productivity, but the productivity of machines, workshop floor area and other resources can also be measured. Productivity provides a non-financial measure of the performance of a particular resource in the shipyard.

Productivity is simply the measure of the ratio of output produced to input resources. Such measures as tonnes of steel per man-hour, or pipes per man-hour, are commonly used. It is sometimes more convenient to invert the measure, and

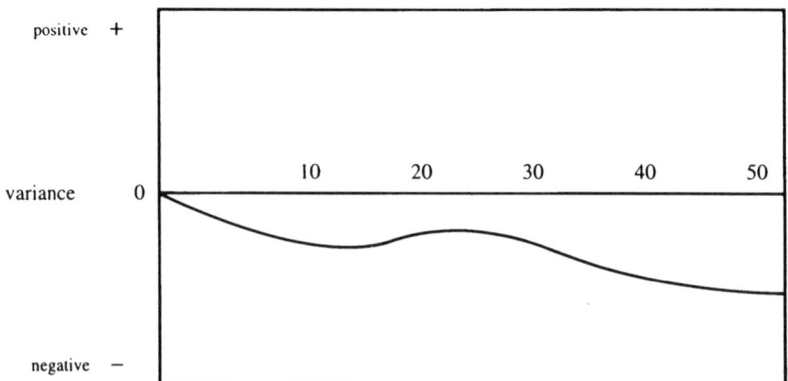

Figure 18. Highlighting variance from planned progress

man-hours per tonne is a measure favoured for many shipyards as an initial estimating parameter for steelwork. Man-hours per CGT is also used as a high level measure for comparison with other shipyards.

Over time, the productivity of most shipyards has increased. Most of those which did not increase productivity have ceased to be in the business of shipbuilding. Increasing productivity requires a change in output or input. However, the level of output is effectively set by market demand. This is obvious for such products as consumer goods or public transport, and it is also the case for the interim products in marine production. Increasing the number of output items for a process is not always an available option.

The inputs are determined by the company. They include both the inputs to the process, such as the number of machines or the workforce which is available, and the materials or other items which are processed.

If a shipyard needs to, or wishes to, increase its productivity, the requirement is either to increase production or to reduce input costs. For a work station producing 10 interim products daily where demand increases to 20 interim products daily, the options for the company include increasing the resources used. They could do one of a number of things, including:

— the setting up of a second, identical work station;
— working a second shift;
— increasing the numbers of men and machines.

Any of these options will satisfy the demand, but the ratio of input to output will be the same. The cost of each interim product in reality is likely to be greater, because the additional resources will not be as effective. Night shifts may well have lower productivity, and have less direct access to technical and other support information. New equipment and people will take time to reach their potential performance level through training.

Productivity can be increased by changing inputs to a process. For the same case, the additional demand might be met by a combination of:

— improving the quality of the inputs, to reduce work content;
— improving the training of the workers;
— altering the process to increase its capacity. This can be done in a number of different ways, including improved machine set-up times, automation, having more productive equipment, or by improved materials handling, so that work is more readily available.

Where the inputs are changed, the output:input ratio is increased, and the productivity is increased. This presupposes that there is an opportunity or need to produce more. A more likely scenario is that the same production is required, but the costs of production must be reduced.

For a constant demand for the interim products from the process under consideration, the same measures as above can also be used to reduce costs. If the demand for the products remains at 10 daily, the inputs required can then (in theory) be halved, or at least reduced significantly.

The ratio of output to input is again increased and the productivity is also increased in proportion to the change, and possibly even doubled.

Various measures of productivity can be used in the shipbuilding business. Ultimately, the measure applied to any company is its financial performance. There are a number of financial ratios which in one form or another measure how much money is output for the money which is input. However, the objective of management is to be in control of the company, and for this purpose any financial information has very severe limitations. For a start, it is generally available only after the event, and although it is important to know how well or badly a company has performed over a period, it does not help to anticipate and then avoid a bad performance.

Any financial information is not necessarily in a suitable format for management control. It is frequently sensitive, and whereas summary information might be generally available, detailed financial information is very private. Such information is also very expensive to calculate at a detail level. As a result, for management purposes, a number of alternative measures are used.

In general the development of suitable measures for steelwork productivity is a much easier task than their development for outfitting. For steelwork, the most common is man-hours per tonne, the inverse of a genuine productivity measure, but one which leads to easy comparisons and which is well recognised. There is an argument that this measure is now less appropriate than when the business was more labour intensive. This change has been remarked on earlier, and is a continuing trend. The argument therefore is that man-hours are no longer a totally realistic measurement, because, particularly in very high cost countries, the labour is now supported by a large investment in equipment.

However, man-hours were historically the major input to shipbuilding, and steel was historically the major output from the business. The measure provides some historical continuity and is readily used to make comparisons. Like CGT in the wider context, it is not a very good measure, but it is probably the best there is.

Alternatives can be used, including:

Tonnes of steel per square metre of workshop. This is useful, although the level of investment in equipment is again a factor which is not taken into account. It is a useful internal measure, and could be used for external comparisons, since the basic data are reasonably available.

Subdivision of the steelwork produced into different types, notably flat panel based, curved panel based, thin plate work (for deckhouses and decks, typically), complex shapes (such as bulbous bows) and miscellaneous or outfit steel. Each of these will have a different productivity. In general the more complex shapes and thinner materials will have lower productivity, measured in terms of tonnage.

The area of steelwork also provides a measure of productivity, since there is a direct relationship between the area of plating and the work content, in terms of butt welding and fillet welding of the stiffeners onto the plate. Other parameters to be taken into account are the spacing of stiffeners and the sizes of plates and stiffeners which a particular shipyard can use for production. It is relatively simple to develop a measure which give man-hours per square metre of steelwork, modified, if required, by type, as above. This is a potentially useful measure for early estimates, where surface area is generally the first parameter which is available from a preliminary general arrangement.

The use of computer aided design, which makes the production of the basic productivity information much simpler, and the basic data can be generated automatically along with the preliminary, and subsequently more detailed, design information.

For items of equipment and individual work stations, measures include the *numbers of items produced,* or *lengths* (of weld completed, for example), which provide adequate measures. These are valuable for internal comparisons, for reviewing the outcomes of investment or training programmes and for future target setting.

The outfitting of a ship is more complex. It requires a number of different trades, involves different types of work and lacks the reasonably homogeneous nature of steelwork. Therefore for outfitting, each major trade or function needs its own measure of productivity. Once again, the ratios are often inverted to give measures which include:

— man-hours per pipe;
— man-hours per metre of cable;
— man-hours per square metre of painting.

None of the measures is entirely satisfactory, because the definition of a pipe, for example, can vary dramatically. If it is a straight pipe, with flanges and no bends or branches, that is one thing. On the other hand, a pipe with one or more bends, possibly a branch, is much more complex. The choice in many cases is either to use the pipe as the measure, which is then really only useful as a high level estimate, or to make a more detailed analysis to identify different pipe families. The latter approach is very valuable for the larger shipyard, where the numbers of pipes is measured in tens of thousands annually. For a smaller shipyard, the more basic measure is the practical alternative.

Measuring man-hours is relatively straightforward, but does not give a complete picture. It is useful as a means of identifying trends in productivity and the outcomes of planned, or even unplanned, changes. But the output achieved in one man-hour will depend to a large extent on a number of factors, including:

— the level of investment in production equipment, whether labour intensive or partly automated;

— the technology used, in terms of planning and production engineering;
— full scale automation may be used in particular areas of the facility.

The output of interim products will also depend on the type of product. Output will be lower, given equivalent technology and facilities, for smaller ships, for thinner plate, for more complex shapes and so on.

If a comparison is made, then the range of productivity levels for steelwork is remarkably large. This is paralleled by the wide variations in performance as measured by CGT. Some comparisons can be made.

The productivity for other marine sectors is generally lower. For example, shiprepair generally deals in small quantities of steel. Typical work in shiprepair yards includes hull damage repairs, additional structure and conversions. The range of work and the way it is performed provides a model for the way in which steelwork in shipbuilding has changed. The way in which a small repair is made, with information taken directly from the ship under repair and labour intensive production methods, is not dissimilar to ship construction in the early twentieth century. Larger scale repairs become less labour intensive and make more use of conventional shipbuilding. At the other end of the scale, a major ship conversion, which may require hundreds or even thousands of tonnes of steel, is very close to new construction.

For most small scale repairs, high productivity is difficult, for reasons which include the fact that the low volume of production precludes any large scale investment. There is also the need to lift dimensions from existing structure. As a result, the steelwork productivity for shiprepair is typically 10–20 times lower than for new construction.

BENCHMARKING

Productivity measures are one element of benchmarking, which is increasingly used by many organisations, in many sectors of industry and services, to identify good practice as a basis for improvement. There are various definitions of benchmarking, but the most useful is "the objective measure of relative performance against relevant organisations in key business areas". The key elements of benchmarking are:

— use a measure which is meaningful and reasonably reliable;
— comparison of relative performance is more important than absolute accuracy;
— compare with organisations that are in the same market, with the same technology, or are using the same processes;
— select appropriate and important areas for comparison.

Why is benchmarking important, and what are the main objectives of a benchmarking programme? The measurement of performance or other factors is only a means to an end. Benchmarking has a number of functions, of which the most important are:

— to improve absolute performance of the company;
— to improve relative performance compared with competitors;
— to identify the best practice in the industry sector, or for a given process;
— to adopt best practice;
— to measure the resulting change in performance.

Various types of comparison can be made, depending on the information which is available and the specific requirements of the organisation. Comparisons can be made with others which are internal, that is in the same organisation. This is:

— to measure change in performance over time within the company;
— to compare different work stations or operating units;
— to identify performance levels.

Comparisons can also be made with external organisations, which may be:

— functional: to compare the performance of specific units with other companies;
— competitive: to compare performance in key areas with competitors;
— generic: to compare performance in generic areas of operation with a range of companies using best practice.

The benchmarking process generally follows a standard sequence of actions. These are as follows:

First, identify what is important:
— key performance areas;
— standards and variables;
— companies for comparisons.
Secondly, measure the appropriate parameters:
— regularly (not a one-off exercise).
Thirdly, analyse:
— use the information which has been gathered.
Fourthly, take some action:
— do something to make an improvement.
Finally, monitor the changes:
— measure what improvement has been made.

The approach to benchmarking is to keep it simple, since the cost of measuring can be high. Then look for differences, because absolute accuracy is less important than relative differences. Finally, remember that benchmarking is a means, not an end.

The measure used in shipbuilding for performance comparisons is compensated gross tonnes per man-year, which allows reasonable comparisons to be made. There is a need for care in using the measure. The output in gross tonnes is usually measured as a moving average over three years. This removes any distorting effects from delivery dates near year ends and is easier than measuring percentage completion for work in progress.

The inputs are based on the total workforce. This avoids difficulties in defining direct labour; the numbers are readily obtained from annual reports; and it is still necessary to identify and compensate for use of sub-contractors.

Where reliable data using steel man-hours per tonne is available, there is reasonable correlation with CGT per man-year.

The ultimate measure for a production unit is profitability. High performance is no guarantee of financial performance. Although money has been rejected as a usable measure for operational management purposes, it is still important.

CHAPTER 10

ORGANISATION OF SHIPBUILDING

SHIPYARD ACTIVITIES

There are many different ways of organising the work of constructing a ship. Although the basic set of processes is similar in all cases, the details will vary, and also the extent to which the processes are carried out in the shipyard or are sub-contracted. This chapter will therefore discuss the reasons for particular organisational structures in shipyards and review some examples of different structures. It will also attempt to develop and describe a logical model for a shipyard organisational structure.

The first question to consider is "why are shipyards organised in the way they are?". The simple answer is that the organisation is designed to manage the many activities and processes which need to be carried out. The organisation is intended to ensure that the flows of work, and also the information flows, are managed effectively. The starting point for the organisation of any shipyard is therefore some analysis of the necessary information and work flows, for all the activities which are undertaken in the company. As has been stated, shipyard activities are universal, although not all of them may be carried out in the shipyard, and some, particularly in smaller shipyards, may not be carried out formally. Thus, for example, in a small company detailed planning may be left to the shop floor supervisors, who will not necessarily be specifically trained in planning.

The relative importance of the different activities varies from company to company, and the organisational structure should reflect that importance. There is no unique, "correct" shipyard organisational structure, which can be universally applied. However, there are key requirements which all shipyards must fulfil. These can be summarised into a few main headings, and these are listed below:

— securing contracts;
— designing the products;
— completing the products;
— obtaining payments;
— maintaining the company.

These are requirements which any company would need to fulfil to stay in business and a more shipbuilding-specific view is needed. To satisfy these requirements for a shipbuilding company, a number of key production activities can be identified, and these form the basis for analysis of the work flow. The activities to be carried out can be grouped into main headings.

— Product development and marketing (securing contracts).
— Contract development (securing contracts).
— Product design (product design).
— Material procurement (completing products).
— Production preparation (completing products).
— Production (completing products).
— Testing and commissioning.
— Post delivery support (back to securing contracts).

There are also essentially maintenance activities, and included in these are the activities which are designed to secure payments. These activities are:

— Accounting.
— Payroll.
— Treasury.
— Personnel.
— Training.
— Facilities maintenance.
— Quality assurance.
— Security.

All of the activities can be represented on activity maps, of which an example is shown. The activity map lists the major activities, and then identifies what further activities are carried out as part of these. The maps can have several levels, moving

Product development and Marketing	Primary Market Research	Product Development	Promotional Activity	Shipowner Contacts	Screening Enquiries	Firm Enquiry
Contract Development	Enquiry Response	Developing Specifications	Cost & Price Estimating	Prepare Bid Documents	Contract Negotiations	Contract
Product Design	Functional Design	Design Approval Certification	Layout Design	Tactical Planning	Purchase Specifications	Approved Design
Material Procurement	Supplier Qualification	Supplier Negotiation	Order Placement	Progress Monitoring	Accounts Payable	Material Availability
Production Design	Design Schedule	Work Breakdown	Preparation Information	Assembly Information	Material Lists	Schedules	Production Documents
Production	Hull Production	Outfit Production	Assembly Activities	Vehicle Construction	Final Outfitting	Vehicle
Testing and Commissioning	Test Scheduling	Pre-assembly Testing	Installation Testing	Shipyard Trials	Owner's Trials	Ship Delivery
Post delivery Support	Guarantee Period	Feedback Collection	Guarantee Engineer	Shipowner Contacts	Repeat Business
Maintenance	Strategy Development	Facilities	Security	Quality Assurance	Personnel Training	Accounts	Working Company

Figure 19. Activity map for shipbuilding

from the overall activities of the company to the detailed activities in different work areas.

There are some current trends in corporate organisation, leading to organisations which are project-based rather than function-based, have fewer levels of hierarchy, have sub-contracting of non-core activities and flexibility of labour. This is also the case in the shipbuilding business, where the project-based approach is logical, given the size and complexity of the made-to-order product.

The project approach tends to produce some form of matrix organisation, where the activities are grouped, not only into departments (which are process or activity-based), but also into project teams. This can result in complex structures and multiple reporting, which is a potential source of problems.

The use of sub-contracting results in an organisation which may appear incomplete, as some of the activities are replaced by sub-contract management activities. This may be part of a related department, a sub-activity of purchasing, or part of a project management team. The way in which the activities are grouped into departments can vary widely.

INFORMATION FLOWS

In addition to the activities which can be represented on an activity map, as a basis for analysis the information flows within the shipyard, and to and from external organisations, can also be modelled. The information which flows through the organisation is developed in scope and detail as a ship project develops from initial concept through design to production and testing. The major flows of information are for design information, materials information, planning and production information (or work preparation), all of which have been considered in other chapters. These direct flows are supported by others, primarily *production engineering information*. There is also an important element in all cases, which is *feedback*. This reports on the actual outcomes of production operations, for comparison with plans. The subject of planning feedback as a means of monitoring progress of a particular ship contract was discussed in the previous chapter. There are other aspects of the production outcomes which can be monitored, as a basis for rectifying any problems, or, more optimistically, as a means for starting an improvement programme to increase performance. The other aspects on which feedback is required include adherence to quality standards and actual resource utilisation.

The flows of information can all be represented by simple diagrams (Figures 20 to 23). These show the general nature of the flows of information, but not the detail, which is much more complex. Also omitted is the interaction between the different flows, as information from one stage of design is additional input to the next stages of planning, materials and production engineering, as well as design itself.

The similarity of the flows is apparent, indicating that the general principle of increasing volumes of detail applies to all the functions. The flow of information provides one basis for the organisation of the work. The flow of work can also be

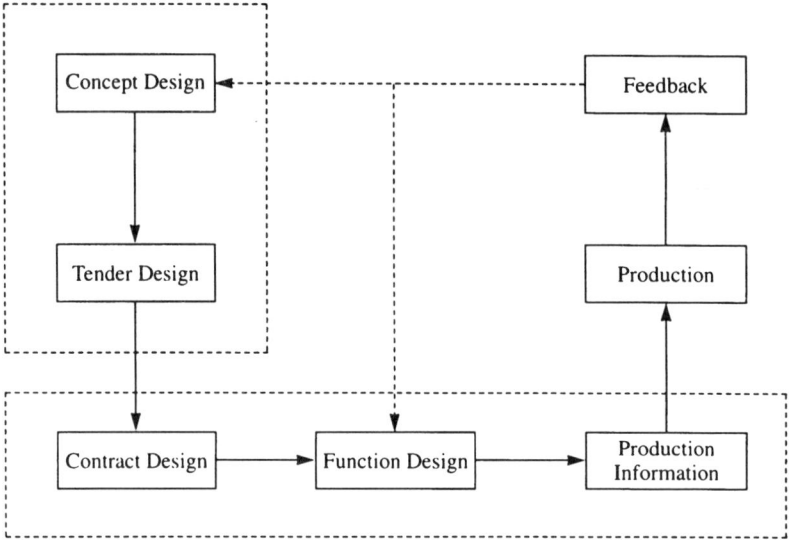

Figure 20.   Flow of design information

modelled (see Figure 24). This represents the actual, physical flow of materials and
interim products through a shipbuilding facility. The information and work flows
identify parallel activities. At each stage of the flow of work for a contract, there is
information of various types. This includes design information, planning informa-
tion, materials information, and production engineering information. The informa-
tion is then used for the processes at that stage and further information is produced

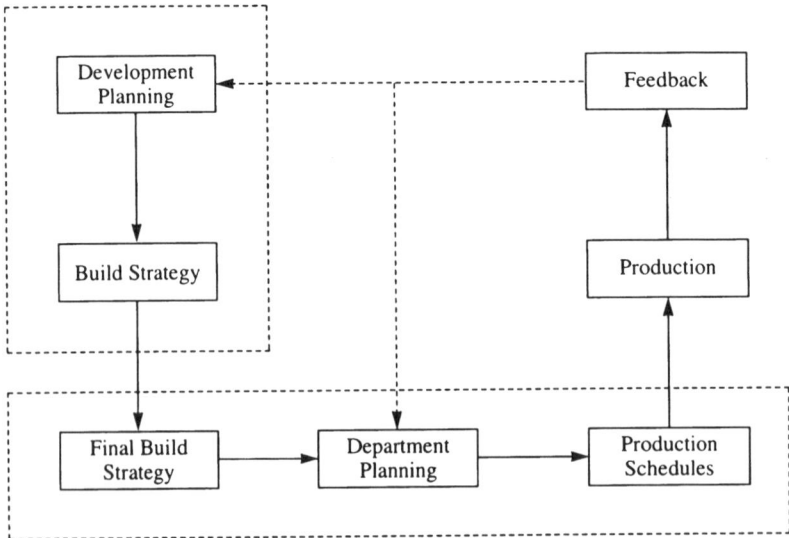

Figure 21.   Flow of planning information

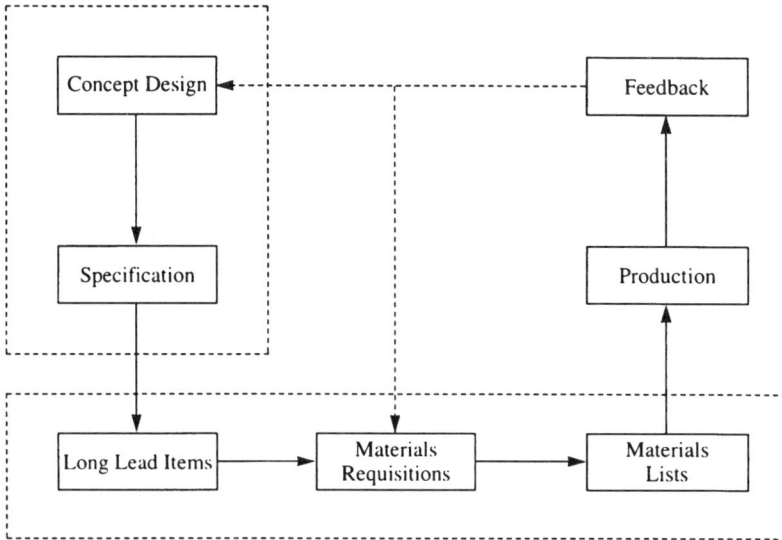

Figure 22. Flow of materials information

which is used both at the next stage and as feedback to the previous stages of work.

The organisation of shipbuilding requires sets of activities which must be performed in order to produce a ship to be managed. These activities can be logically grouped into departments, which are the basis of the organisation. Historically, departments were organised on the basis of the processes that were carried out. The

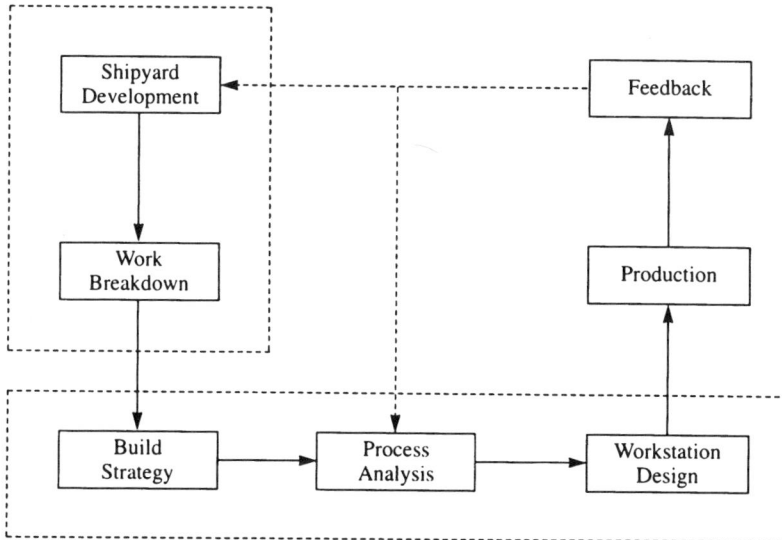

Figure 23. Flow of production engineering information

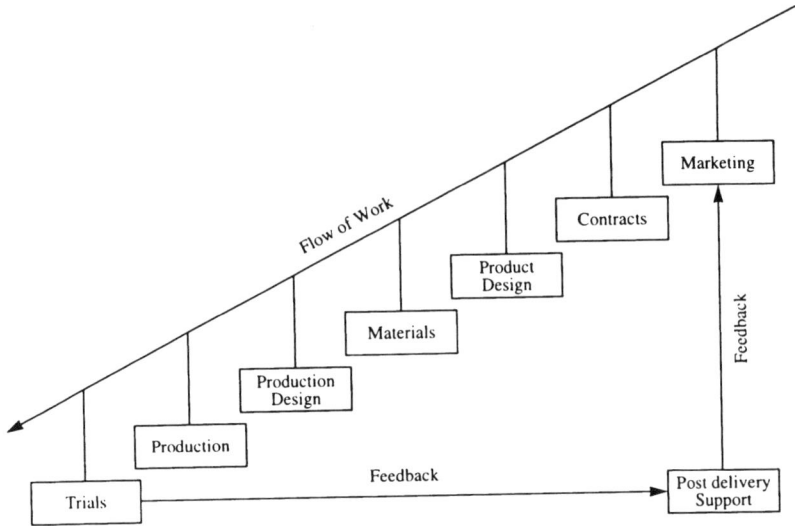

Figure 24. Work flow in shipbuilding

technical department, for example, was responsible for all the design and production definition. When it had completed all the work, and had defined a ship, the information could be passed to production, to procurement and to others who needed to use it. Within the technical department, the division into sections was based on the division of the ship into systems. The steel drawing office dealt with the hull and other structure. The pipe drawing office dealt with pipework, often with a further sub-division into hull pipes (running within the cargo areas) and machinery pipes (in the engine room). The machinery and electrical drawing offices were also separate.

The production department was similarly divided by trades, with the steel work and outfitting separated and the outfitting divided into the various different trades, including plumbers, joiners, electricians, sheet metal workers and so on. This arrangement was reasonably effective in circumstances where the ships were relatively standard in design, and also relatively simple. In addition, the timescale for building a ship was relatively long, with the outfitting being completed afloat, after the construction and launching of the ship's hull. There was relatively little interaction between the different trades, with work being carried out sequentially. The volume of information produced by the technical offices was also relatively limited, and production departments had groups within them, notably the mould loft responsible for steel part definition, who prepared the detailed production information.

The changes in shipbuilding that have been described elsewhere have also altered the organisational needs. The flow of information has increased, and the need to complete ships in much shorter timescales has made integration of the different trades and functions most important.

ORGANISATION

The organisation is now more often based on the revised flows of work and information, which are in turn determined by the short timescales and integration of shipbuilding. The splits between different technical functions are no longer applicable. The systems for the ships still have to be designed from a functional perspective by specialist groups, but the arrangements and layouts are determined by multi-disciplinary teams, who incorporate specialists for all the different systems —steel as well as outfitting—that occur in a specific zone or sub-zone on the ship.

While these multi-discipline teams may be convened for a specific project, bringing together people who work in the separate (traditional) system based drawing offices, they may also be a permanent feature of the shipyard organisation. In some cases, the shipyards also include production staff in the teams, so that a small team is effectively responsible for a specific zone of the ship. In effect, the team, which is an internal team, is acting as a design and build contractor for the shipyard management.

In designing the organisation, the objective is to map the organisational structure as closely as possible onto the information and work flow. The benefit of so doing is that the lines of communication are simpler and shorter. Decisions on priorities or use of space, which previously had to be resolved between departments at management level, can now be made within the work teams.

There is still a sequential flow, and there are logical points at which department boundaries occur. For example, the business development function is concerned with promoting the company, marketing, developing products and securing work. It therefore has a logical cut off point, where a contract is close to being secured, and the responsibility passes to a contract management team and the technical offices.

Within the business development function, there are commercial and technical roles, and to provide an effective operation, it is logical to blend the different roles into another multi-discipline team.

Business development therefore includes staff engaged in market research, concept design, marketing, enquiry management, tender design, estimating and preliminary build strategy.

Any organisation structure will be a compromise, in that wherever work is divided and allocated to different groups, there will be some cases where the structure has the potential to cause problems. However, the flow of work and information can be carefully monitored, and the organisation then designed to minimise the information flowing between departmental interfaces. In that case, an effective organisation, which meets the primary requirements of the shipbuilding company, can be developed.

CHAPTER 11

THE PRODUCTION TECHNOLOGY

INTRODUCTION

Organisations have many different roles. In very broad terms, they can be divided into two major groupings. The first of these is *manufacturing*, that is the production of tangible products for sale. These vary in scale from large companies, often engaged in mass production of consumer goods, to (often) smaller companies, engaged in customised production. These latter produce made-to-order products. Shipbuilders occupy an unusual position, which they share with relatively few other large manufacturing organisations. The products—ships—are large and made to order.

Because of the size and complexity of the product, shipyards exhibit some characteristics of most other industries. There are examples of flow production, typically at the early stages of production when relatively standard pieces are being processed. As the production process continues, the larger and larger interim products become more customised, until the final product—the ship—is constructed in a fixed position, and, even in the case of nominally identical sister ships, may have unique characteristics.

The second major category of organisations are providers of *services*. These include such activities as marketing, accounting, maintenance and distribution of products. Shipyards often include some of these activities within their own organisation. The complexity of shipbuilding also ensures that the shipyard is a major user of services provided by others.

In common with any other organisation which has a product to produce, shipbuilders need to manage their operations efficiently. This entails effective use of resources, in particular materials and equipment from suppliers, use of equipment and facilities, and, perhaps of greatest importance, use of people.

SCOPE OF PRODUCTION TECHNOLOGY

Production technology includes many activities:

— product design and development;

— facilities location;
— acquiring capital equipment;
— facilities layout;
— work design and measurement;
— production forecasting;
— production planning and scheduling;
— materials management;
— inventory management;
— quality management.

All of these are of sufficient importance to be considered separately in their own chapters.

Concentrating on the specifically production activities (although keeping in mind that the organisation may also have service activities), the objective is to provide a broad overview of the production process for ship construction.

Before production, there are a number of essential pre-production activities:

— market analysis, product mix selection;
— design development, specification, strategic planning;
— estimating, tendering, contract negotiation;
— detailed design, product work breakdown;
— tactical planning, purchasing;
— detailed planning, scheduling, production information.

Again, many of these are considered separately in other chapters.

The facilities which are found in a shipyard depend on the manufacturing strategy which is adopted. It may in some cases be more cost-effective to sub-contract certain activities. A comprehensive list of facilities for shipbuilding would be as outlined in the lists which follow.

Shipyard facilities for hull production are often seen as the most important. This is because the hull is often seen as the defining product—in effect the hull "is" the ship. The facilities required would be:

— steel stockyard;
— steel treatment (levelling, shotblasting, painting);
— plate and profile cutting;
— plate and profile forming;
— workshops for sub-assembly, assembly and unit assembly;
— block assembly, outfitting, painting workshops and storage area.

Shipyard facilities for outfitting are also needed. It is more common to sub-contract outfitting than hull work, but some shipyards retain a full range of facilities:

— pipe storage, cutting and welding;
— machine shop;
— accommodation work (woodwork, metal furniture, linings);

— electrical and electronic workshop;
— sheet metal workshop (ventilation trunks, metal fittings);
— riggers workshop;
— outfit unit assembly;
— material and equipment storage.

Some ship repair operations also retain such facilities as a blacksmith's workshop.

Shipyard facilities for ship construction are the major part in most cases. There are a number of methods for transfer of the completed ship to the water:

— inclined slipway (for dynamic launch—traditional);
— side launch slipway;
— graving dock;
— shiplift;
— load-out (to floating dock).

There are other methods used occasionally. All the alternatives can be enclosed in a building for environmental protection. All require large capacity cranes for lifting and manipulating blocks.

Shipyard support facilities are also required. These can form a substantial part of the cost of a new facility and include:

— electrical sub-stations;
— bulk gas storage facilities and compressed air plant;
— water storage tanks;
— associated services distribution systems;
— offices, amenities (changing rooms, canteens, etc.);
— training facilities;
— car and bus parking.

There have been many changes in shipyards since 1950, and the development of the industry over the last 50 years has been discussed in an earlier chapter.

New production processes are being developed, which will eventually lead to a new generation of shipyards. Some companies are pioneering the new approaches, and these include automation, new coatings and application methods. Other new processes are being developed to manage some of the external influences on the shipbuilding business which were noted earlier, in particular environmental problems.

The complete set of activities required in a shipyard includes many which effectively are required to maintain the organisation. These include maintenance of facilities, but also such activities as personnel (to deliver the necessary supply of qualified and trained personnel), accounting and development. These are also considered in other chapters.

HULL PRODUCTION

Taking the stages of hull production in turn, the first of the main activities is in part manufacturing, including material receipt, material storage and preparation, cutting and forming. The function is the conversion of semi-finished materials into products and delivery of these to a customer, which is the assembly workshop. In general in the industry this is an internal customer, but where the process is sub-contracted, there may be transaction with an external supplier.

Product assembly is second, including the various stages of assembly (minor assembly, sub-assembly, unit assembly and up to block assembly, which encompasses all outfitting and painting carried out during these stages). This entails building larger, interim products from the manufactured parts, and, once again, the delivery of these to a customer. The customer is more usually another department or function within the organisation, but there may still be an external supplier in some cases.

The first stage in production, in most shipyards, is to obtain the steel plates and profiles required to assemble the hull. The importance of this is apparent in all cases; without the materials the shipyard simply cannot operate. The scale of this first stage of the production process depends on a number of factors.

It depends partly on the proximity and reliability of steel suppliers. If there is a local supplier, whether a mill or stockholder, then the shipyard can limit the stock it holds and place orders with a relatively short lead time for steel as required in production. If the mill or other supplier is distant, then higher stock levels may be required, depending on the security and reliability of the supply. This in turn will depend on the degree of standardisation of the materials, and the size of the orders which are placed. A major user of steel products will be in a better bargaining position than a small shipyard.

The design of the shipyard's products also plays a role, in that the ability to make use of standard plate and profile sizes can minimise the requirement to maintain a stock of steel. Finally, the scale of the shipyard operation is important. Where a supplier is close, and a shipyard uses modest quantities of steel, the supply problem is a simple one. The shipyard can maintain a small safety stock, but in general will expect regular deliveries as steel is required. However, "just-in-time" supply, as practised increasingly in other industries, is not an option for the shipyard, unless a stockholder is available to manage the fluctuations in supply and demand. In that case, a price premium will be demanded.

Receipt requires the steel to be checked, for quantity and conformity to specification. If standard plates and profiles can be used, this process is much simpler. Where custom sizes are in use, to minimise the potential wastage at the cutting stage, each plate may require to be checked for dimensional accuracy, which can be time-consuming.

The use of electronic data interchange (EDI) can greatly simplify the process, by establishing direct communication between supplier and customer, allowing interrogation of databases and improvement of information accuracy.

The steel stockyard is required to a greater or lesser extent. For a large shipyard, dealing in many thousands of tonnes annually, a large stockyard is the norm. This provides a series of identified locations in which the steel is stored between its delivery and the date it is required in production. The stockyard is usually served by one or more overhead travelling cranes, and the cranes are equipped with magnet beams which allow safe and efficient handling of the materials. In most cases, the plates are of different sizes, and must be sorted by size and by the date required in production. The use of magnetic handling allows the plates to be stored horizontally, and sorted quickly.

Where the volume of production is smaller, the stockyard may be smaller, and in some cases, particularly where the shipyard makes use of standard sizes, only a small storage area is required. This can be located within the workshop used for steel preparation and cutting, which saves space and investment in handling equipment.

STEEL TREATMENT (LEVELLING, SHOTBLASTING, PAINTING)

In the days of building ships piece by piece, steel treatment was unknown. The plates were received as rolled, with millscale intact. The storage, followed by a lengthy building period, allowed the steel to "weather", and the scale was lost. The riveting process placed no demands on the steel surface quality and the painting processes were relatively primitive.

The introduction of welding as the primary joining process for steelwork and the adoption of faster processes placed greater demands on the steel quality. The introduction of new cutting technologies, again giving faster speeds and improved accuracy, also required a clean steel surface. Finally, as the building process was completed in a much shorter time, the weathering process no longer left steel in a fit state to be painted, especially as the paint coatings, designed for longer life, were improved.

As a result of these changes, the steel treatment line was introduced into the industry. The line replaced earlier cleaning methods, so-called "pickling", in which the steel plates were dipped into a chemical bath which removed millscale. The treatment line comprises a number of machines, usually linked by a conveyor system.

The sequence of machines is usually as follows. First, the plates are levelled. This process passes the plate through a rolling machine, with several rollers in series. The plate is passed through these on the conveyor system, and first bent, then straightened. The deforming and straightening process leaves the plate level and also has the effect of relieving some of the stresses left by the steel mill rolling process, and subsequent handling. (These can result in distortion later as the plate is heated during cutting and welding.) The rolling also crushes and loosens millscale.

Next the plates are heated. This is achieved by passing the plate through a cabinet, again on the conveyors, and within the cabinet the plate is heated, using either gas flames or hot water. The heating process raises the temperature of the plate, to a point where once the priming paint has been applied, it will dry rapidly. Heating also removes snow or ice, in climates where this is a problem. The use of hot water assists further in the removal of millscale. The washing process in particular also has a role to play in generally cleaning the plate and removing any other debris.

The plate is then shotblasted inside the next cabinet, where impeller wheels throw steel shot (or other abrasive materials) against the plate. This removes any remaining millscale and cleans the underlying surface to a high quality. The surface is then in a good condition for subsequent cutting processes and also painting at a later stage.

The next process is primer painting, where the plate is passed through another cabinet which contains automatic paint-spraying equipment. This matches the speed of the conveyor and covers the plate with an even coating of primer. The primer is designed to protect the plate during subsequent assembly processes, maintaining the high quality surface which has been achieved during the previous stages of treatment.

The previous heating now assists the primer to dry, and this is further speeded up by passing the plate through a final cabinet where hot air can be blown over the painted surface to remove volatiles.

At the end of the treatment line, the plate is generally moved on the conveyor system to a buffer storage location. It is then lifted clear of the conveyors, usually by crane but alternatively by a vehicle, and moved to a storage location in the next workshop, ready for cutting.

The cost of the treatment plant and associated handling equipment is expensive, and many smaller shipyards choose to have the preparation carried out by a supplier, or possibly another third party. This practice raises questions, since the quality of the process is important. There is a potential for abrasion and other mechanical damage to the primed plates in transit. The thickness of the primer coating is important for many modern cutting and welding processes—in particular, too thick a coating can interfere with cut and weld quality.

PLATE AND PROFILE CUTTING

The first stage proper of the hull production process is to cut out the steel piece parts which are required. These range from the major shell plates, which for a large vessel may be 20 metres in length and four metres wide, to the smallest brackets and lugs. The whole of the subsequent assembly and construction of the hull depends on the accuracy of the piece parts. If they are not cut to size, within carefully defined tolerances, then the man-hours and machine times at all later stages will be increased.

In most cases shipyards now use cutting processes controlled by computer numerical control (shortened to NC). The machine consists of a cross-beam, mounted on two carriages. The carriages run along rails, which are aligned with great accuracy, and which incorporate length measuring, usually through a rack and pinion arrangement. The cross-beam supports one or more smaller carriages which can travel in a transverse direction along the beam. These in turn support the cutting equipment, along with the supply of gas and electricity.

The cutting process is usually carried out by an oxygen and fuel gas combination. The fuel gas is usually propane or acetylene. In addition to cutting, the machines can use the NC database to mark the plate, using a powder marking process. The heat from the torch fuses the powder, giving a white line on the plate, for datum lines and other locating marks.

Some shipyards, particularly where large quantities of steel have to be cut, use a plasma cutting process. This has a much faster cutting speed, and a reduced heat input, which makes for less distortion caused by the cutting process. The plasma process is inherently more difficult to use, because it gives off a large volume of fumes, as well as light and noise. In most cases, the cutting process is therefore carried out underwater. This entails the use of a water tank below the cutting table, which then allows the table to be submerged during cutting, minimising the undesirable effects. The extra cost and operational effort are offset by improved piece part quality.

A few shipyards continue to make use of mechanical processes for cutting. The equipment may be an edge mill, in which the plate is clamped in position and a milling head then travels along the length, cutting the plate to size and incorporating an edge preparation for welding. The accuracy is excellent, and no distortion is caused. However the process is slow and only suited to straight plate edges. Only one edge can be cut at a time, so the plate has to be repositioned for each cut, increasing materials handling requirements. The alternative is an edge plane, where the plate edge is sheared by repeated passes of a plane. The process is more limited in edge preparation, and suffers the same disadvantages of slowness and materials handling.

A new addition to the selection of cutting processes is the laser. This has been potentially attractive for some time, and has been the subject of much research since the mid-1970s. It has been introduced into a number of shipyards, primarily those cutting thin plates, for which the current equipment is most suitable. The laser is a fast cutting process, in which the power available is adequate for thin plates. It also results in the least heat input of any of the thermal processes which are available, and consequently does not cause any distortion of the piece parts. The limitation to date has been the limited power available, but development is continuous and the laser may be expected to make more inroads into the shipbuilding business over the next decades.

Profile cutting is largely the cutting to length of the profiles and then making any cutouts which are required (for example for drain holes) and, in the case of longitudinal stiffeners, cutting an edge preparation for welding the ends. The process used is often manual, particularly in smaller shipyards. Simple template-following tractors may also be used to make standard shapes.

In larger shipyards, the process is often mechanised, because there is a high volume of production of relatively standard items. The profiles may be moved into the workshop on an extension of the conveyor from the storage and treatment area. Conveyors then move the profiles to the machinery and subsequently into buffer storage for the assembly workshops.

The cutting process is generally oxygen and fuel gas, but the control may be automatic. This is one aspect of shipbuilding where robotics has found a useful application, with a standard industrial robot used to guide the cutting torch. The conveyor system then incorporates equipment for locating and measuring the length of the profiles to ensure accuracy.

PLATE AND PROFILE FORMING

The hull form required for a ship to give the required hydrodynamic performance also requires many of the shell plates and their associated profile stiffeners to be formed. The processes used are straightforward, and have been unchanged over many years. The primary forming is carried out by a range of hydraulic presses and rolling machines. These may be special, or general purpose, depending on the type of ships built in a particular shipyard and also on the volume of production which is undertaken.

For shell plates, the primary forming equipment is the shell rolls. This is a set of two rollers, arranged with one more roller above them, power driven and with the upper roller capable of adjustment for height. The plate is introduced between the upper and lower rollers and is passed between them. The upper roller presses down on the plate, and, as it passes, the plate is distorted into a curved shape. The shape which is required in the plate is taken from the hull definition and transferred to a template, traditionally of wood, but more commonly now an adjustable steel template. This is placed against the plate after the rolling operation and the operation may then be repeated until the plate achieves the correct shape.

The process is capable of rolling in one direction only, so is used primarily for parallel mid-body plates. A limited capability for two-directional rolling is available from a skilled machine operator.

A more complex shape is usually achieved by rolling the plate to establish the curvature in the main direction, then using heat line bending for the additional shape which is required. In heat line bending, the shape is achieved by heating the plate, using a conventional oxygen/fuel gas cutting torch, from one side along a pre-determined line. As the plate cools again after the heating, there is shrinkage along the line of the heating which causes the plate to bend. The effect can be increased by cooling along the heat line, using water. The process is slow, and may need a number of applications to achieve the required bending. On the other hand, it is a readily controllable process, which gives a result which is accurate. The process was pioneered in Japan, where the ability to achieve the correct shape, albeit slowly and in a relatively labour-intensive way, was considered to be a benefit when the impact on subsequent assembly operations was taken into account. If the shapes are not accurate, then the assembly processes require many additional man-hours.

For pressing the plates into swedges, a form of stiffening popular for superstructure bulkheads and some major bulkheads in bulk carriers, a press is used. This is a similar machine, but the hydraulics are applied to an upper structure which presses onto a support. Different forms of tooling can be used to prepare different forms in the plate. Large presses have capacities up to 2,000 tonnes or more, for the forming of main structure, including bulkheads. Bulkheads strengthened using corrugations are frequently used on bulk carriers. Smaller presses are used for superstructure, and also for the forming of face flats on brackets. Most such forming operations provide an alternative to welding stiffeners and as such avoid distortion problems, although they do present some handling difficulties.

A number of other machines are available. Gap and portal presses are most versatile, but are more usually found in shiprepair, where a combination of relatively lower cost and flexibility are offset against slowness in operation. These machines press the plates locally rather than along a specified line, so are capable of forming complex shapes, for example bulbous bows.

The profiles that are used to stiffen the ship hull plating also require to be formed. As in the case of plate forming, the equipment is relatively simple and has been used for many years. The main item used is the frame bender, which is designed, as the name implies, to bend the ship's transverse frames. A pair of frames, port and starboard, is generally formed at one time. The two stiffeners (usually offset bulb flats or angle bars) are clamped together and supported on mobile tripods. They are then moved progressively through the machine, which has two support arms and a ram. The profiles are held against the support arms, while the ram exerts the appropriate bending force. The process is similar to the forming of a plate in a press.

The shape of the bent frames is derived from the CAD database, and the information is used to produce either a template against which the final shape can be checked, or to mark the straight profile with a series of curved lines. These are the inverse curves of the final shape. During bending these lines become straight, so that the accuracy of the forming is checked by their straightness.

Longitudinal frames are also formed. As far as possible, these are designed to have as little shape as possible, particularly twisting, which is more difficult to achieve accurately. Use is also made of heat line bending to form profiles that have twist, or have only a limited bending requirement.

Other equipment used for profile forming includes a small rolls, which is used to produce curved face flats (for the support of plate edges). A few small shipyards still use more basic methods, where the profiles are bent using mobile hydraulic rams on a floor grid, but this is slower and less accurate.

Again, as is the case for plate forming, time spent on ensuring accuracy of the individual pieces will save re-work later and reduce the assembly man-hours.

ASSEMBLY

The joining together of the various piece parts, formed and flat, into larger and larger units is all part of the assembly process. A number of specific types of assembly can be identified, and are often produced in specialist areas. Minor assembly includes brackets and other small items. A typical minor assembly would have a one metre by two metres flat plate part, with one or more stiffeners welded as supports. Sub-assembly generally refers to small structural items, typically floors and girders, which may be up to 15 metres in length and two to three metres wide. A number of stiffeners are attached. Major sub-assembly is usually a three dimensional unit.

Units are the smallest parts of the hull which would normally be taken to the building area (dock or berth). The units are generally based on flat or curved panels. Flat panels are often assembled on a transfer line, where a number of specialised work stations are linked by a conveyor. Such arrangements were developed with the arrival of VLCCs, where the large proportion of flat panel structures in the parallel part of the hull made investment in the equipment worthwhile. New designs of such lines are available for a variety of panel sizes and configurations.

The transfer line has a sequence of work which is typically as follows:

Work station 1—plate fairing. The plates which will form the panel will have been cut to size, and usually marked with positions of stiffeners, frame lines and reference points for dimensional accuracy. The plates are generally lifted into the work station by overhead magnet crane and positioned approximately. They are then manoeuvred into their exact relative positions using the conveyor equipment. A magnetic, or sometimes mechanical, clamping system is used to hold them in position for tack welding. The part-finished panel is then moved forward by a plate width to allow the next plate to be craned into place over the clamping area, and the process is repeated until the panel is complete.

Work station 2—plate welding. The panel is moved into the work station for welding. This is usually a submerged arc process, and is often completed using partly automated equipment. The welding equipment may be mounted on a carriage which is able to move along a beam which spans the panel. In simpler systems, welding tractors are used, which run along the panel itself to complete the butt welds. Most systems use a single sided welding process, but some older panel lines have a turnover crane which can lift and invert the panel to allow the second side to be welded. The completed weld is inspected and if necessary repaired before leaving the work station.

Work station 3—panel stiffening. In most cases, the panel line is used for large, longitudinally framed ships, and the primary panel stiffeners are the longi-tudinals. These may be introduced onto the panel automatically, from a cassette which has been loaded with the stiffeners required for the particular panel. They are then pushed into place using a hydraulic ram, and accurately positioned. Alternatively the stiffeners may be lifted individually into place using an overhead crane, equipped with a specialised lifting beam to allow the stiffener to be located. Accurate positioning is accomplished using the location marks on the plate, which indicate the stiffener positions. The stiffeners are held in their correct location, and in contact with the plate, using a magnetic, hydraulic or mechanical clamp. This may be part of the semi-automated system or manually operated equipment. Once in place, the stiffeners are tack welded.

Work station 4—stiffener welding. The panel with the tacked stiffeners is conveyed to the next work station where the stiffeners are welded to the plate. The process is often also submerged arc, and in most cases both sides of the fillet weld are made simultaneously. The process may be on carriages running on a beam, as was described for the plate welding system or, again, tractors may be employed in a lower cost system. In some cases, more than one system is used to reduce the time taken for the completion of this stage of the panel production.

Work station 5—secondary stiffening. Once the longitudinals are in place (or the frames for a conventionally transverse framed ship), any additional members are positioned. These are plate webs, transverses or girders. They are moved into position on the panel using an overhead travelling crane, and located using the plate marks. Final adjustments into position and holding are again accomplished using some hydraulic or mechanical systems. The members are then tack welded.

Work station 6—welding. As the panel becomes more complete, the ability to use semi-automated systems and to complete long runs of weld in a short time is reduced. Usually a mixture of MIG welding and tractors is used. This stage is more labour intensive, and in some cases more than one work station may be required to complete the work within the cycle time which is necessary for the production schedule.

A few shipyards, notably in Japan and also at Odense in Denmark, make extensive use of robotics at this stage. The various welds to attach the stiffening members to the plate and to each other are relatively repetitive, and specialised equipment has been designed and built to complete these welds. The equipment is portable and is located adjacent to the weld which is to be carried out. The welding cycle is then completed automatically, leaving the worker in control to operate a second or even third piece of equipment.

Outfitting work stations. In many cases, the bottom panels of tankers being an example, extensive pipe work has to be fitted on to the panels. The structurally complete panel, following an inspection to confirm its accuracy and completeness, and any necessary repair work, is conveyed to the next work station. Here the pipe supports are located and welded into place. Any other fittings, grounds or supports for outfitting are also located and welded into place. The pipes are then lifted into place by crane and secured. Any other outfitting is also completed. Once again, depending on the volume and complexity of the work to be completed, more than one work station may be needed.

The completed panels may also have some or all of the paint coatings applied to them in a further work station. Only those parts of the panel which will be welded to other panels later in the production cycle are left unpainted.

For a double hulled ship, which are increasingly common, additional stages are required. Once a panel has been completed as described (usually including any outfitting and painting), to form the double hull structure it is lifted by overhead crane, turned over and placed onto the plate panel which forms the other part of the double structure. The second plate panel will have been completed only to the point of welding the primary stiffeners into place and any painting or outfitting which is required. The internal structure is then faired into position on the plate marks, and once the alignment of all the members is correct it is welded.

Curved panels are generally assembled from the formed plates, with the addition of formed profiles for stiffening, on a fixed position jig. The typical jig arrangement has a number of steel tubes, arranged on a one metre grid on the workshop floor. Each tube can be extended in height, using an adjustable inner tube. The heights of the tubes which make up the jig are adjusted using data from the computer aided design system in most cases. The stiffened panel is then completed with secondary stiffening to complete the internal structure of the panel.

The accuracy of the jig, and of the plates which it supports, is of great importance. If the plates are incorrectly shaped, or misaligned, then this has important consequences. First, the internal structural members will have been made to fit accurately, and if the plates are not the correct shape, they will not fit. To make them fit closely enough for good quality welding can be laborious and time consuming. The parts have to be forced into position, using hydraulic or mechanical equipment. The second consequence, if the different members have to be forced into place, is that the accuracy of the ship's hull form may be lost.

OUTFIT PRODUCTION

As has been mentioned previously, there has been a steady trend towards sub-contracting much of the outfitting of ships. Where previously a shipyard would have manufactured in-house many of the parts required, now the policy in most cases is to buy as much as possible from outside suppliers. The management of the shipyard is then able to focus its attention on the project management aspects of the ships that it builds, primarily on the construction of the hull and the installation of the outfit which is required. However, some production is retained in many shipyards, because of location or because existing facilities and skills are available. The main production processes are outlined here.

Pipe production is often the second most important aspect of the shipyard after the production of the steel. Tubes are bought from suppliers in the same way as steel plates and stiffeners. A wide range of pipes is required from which to form the ship systems. Pipe materials include steel, various alloys of copper and nickel and some plastics. Depending on the system to be produced, the pipe specifications will also vary. Wall thickness, for example, depends on the operating pressure of the system. The bought-in tubes are normally stored adjacent to the pipe production workshop. Large steel tubes may be stored outside, but increasingly storage is under cover. Apart from improvements to quality, the internal storage allows specialised storage and handling systems to be used. This increases the efficiency of the operation.

Tubes are stored either in racks or pallets. Tubes of similar size and specification are stored together. In many larger shipyards, the racks in which the tubes are stored are served by partly automated equipment for input and retrieval. When a tube is required, the equipment is able to move to the correct storage location, select a single tube and deliver it to a conveyor which is the input to the first production process. A single operator is able to manage the whole operation.

Alternatives include the use of pallets, in which again tubes of similar specification and size are stored. The retrieval of a tube for production requires the correct pallet to be located and moved to a buffer storage area adjacent to the first production processes, where the required pipe can be removed and made ready.

Other means of storage are available. Small-bore pipes, typically defined as less than 25 millimetres in diameter, can readily be man handled, and this is both convenient and practical. Large pipes, typically above 150 millimetres in diameter, may be handled by overhead travelling crane. The tubes are usually bought in lengths of approximately six metres, which is a *de facto* standard, and which simplifies the storage problem. Some large tubes—for oil cargo pipes, for example—may be longer. Once selected for production, the individual tube is moved by the appropriate means from the storage location to the first production process. This is usually pipe cutting, where the tube is cut, using a bandsaw in most cases, to the appropriate length. This may be a separate item of equipment, with a simple non-powered roller conveyor or other pipe support. In conjunction with an automated storage system, in a larger shipyard with a high volume of production which justifies such investment, the saw may be associated with a conveyor system, and with automatic length measuring.

The typical ship pipe for one of the outfitting systems is around three metres in length. Once cut, pipes go to alternative processes. Perhaps 50 per cent of the pipes on a ship will require to be bent. The number to be bent will depend on the ship type. Oil tankers have long runs of cargo pipes which are all straight, whereas smaller ships have many bent pipes to allow the multiple systems to be fitted into a small space in a shaped hull. The number of bent pipes will also depend on the production-kindly nature of the ship's design. If design for production principles have been adopted, then much of the pipework will be developed for outfitting using modules. In this case, many pipes will be straight, which greatly simplifies the production process and reduces the amount of wastage.

Usually the pipes can be cut to size prior to bending. This depends on the effective use of a computer aided design system. The bending machines use the CAD information to manipulate the pipe as it is drawn around a former. The pipe is supported inside to prevent deformation of the circular shape as it is bent. The machines are designed to bend a range of pipe sizes, and most shipyards with a pipe manufacturing facility have two or more machines. The smallest bender will deal with pipes of between 25 and 100 millimetres diameter. A larger bender will generally manage pipes from around 50 millimetres to 150 millimetres. These ranges cover most of the pipes used on ships. Large ships may require larger pipes, and the bending machines can be found with up to 200 millimetres capacity, and in rare cases 250 millimetres. However, the largest machines are very expensive, and most shipyards do not invest in large capacity machines for a relatively small number of large bore pipes. In most cases, the small number of large pipes required are fabricated, that is, made up of preformed bent and straight sections that are then welded together.

The bending process is relatively rapid, and a pipe can be bent in around 20 minutes. However, when a different pipe size is required, the tooling on the pipe bending machine has to be changed and this can take an hour or two. The scheduling of the pipe bending operation is therefore critical, and it is essential to have information well in advance of production to allow the pipes to be batched by size. The pipe bending operation requires a short length of pipe to be left straight at the end of the tube, to allow the machine to operate. This is then discarded. In some shipyards the development of the pipes allows two or more to be bent simultaneously from a single tube, and then cut to provide the separate pipes. This minimises waste material.

Once bent, the pipe is difficult to handle, and the movement and manipulation have to be performed by crane for all but the smallest sizes. For this reason, some shipyards which need to use automated equipment to keep costs down actually put flanges on the pipe prior to bending. Flanges are the means adopted in most cases to join the separate pipes into the longer lengths required for the ship's systems. The flanges are welded to the ends of the pipes and the pipes are then joined by bolting the flanges together. A flange is generally welded directly to the pipe, and has holes for the bolts which join it to the next pipe in the system. Alternatively a smaller flange may be welded to the end of the pipe and a loose flange which can freely rotate is then retained. The loose flanges on two adjacent pipes are bolted together, the benefit being that on complex bent pipes the precise location of the flanges—and therefore the bolt holes—is no longer needed. This simplifies the welding of flanges prior to bending, which in turn allows the welding process to be partly automated.

Once the pipe has been cut to length, bent and has a flange it is in most cases complete. However, the complexity of some pipe systems requires two or more pipes to be joined. There may be pipes with branches, or simply complex shapes. The, usually, small number of pipes which fall outside the range of the pipe bending capability in a given shipyard also require to be fabricated. The fabrication process requires the pipe pieces to be set upon supports, checked for accuracy, then welded together. It is a basic process which is relatively labour intensive. Some use of partial automation is possible, but generally the complex pipe shapes require manual methods.

Other processes include equipment for preparing branches in pipes and for cutting complex shapes to allow pipes to be joined at angles. The use of computer aided design has benefited the pipe production process considerably. CAD allows the shape and dimensions of the pipes to be extracted in a useable form, both for the bending of the individual pipes and also for the assembly of more complex pipe fabrications. The information is a direct output from the computer, eliminating the need for shop floor intervention in the form of pipe sketches and templates.

Completed pipes may in some cases require galvanising. This is a process which is almost always sub-contracted, since the volume required is too small to make it an economic proposition for an individual shipyard. Pipes are generally pressure tested in the workshop prior to despatch to the installation areas. Finally, prior to despatch, the pipes are cleaned.

In addition to pipe production, shipyards require items for installation in a number of areas. These are:

— electrical items;
— furniture and bulkheads;
— heating, ventilation and air conditioning;
— outfit steelwork (such as ladders, gratings and other minor items).

For each of these there may be a small workshop in the shipyard, but increasingly they will be sub-contracted. In the past a large woodwork shop was found in most shipyards. However, there is less use of wood on board, for example for furniture, the ships' crews are much smaller than used to be the case, and it is generally simpler and cheaper for a shipyard to buy in all its requirements.

Outfit steelwork is a similar case. The blacksmith's workshop has generally long disappeared, and most of the requirements can now be bought from specialists. The same is the case for sheet metal, for cabinets, sometimes for furniture and for the trunking for air conditioning and other HVAC systems.

Electrical work in much commercial shipbuilding is largely confined to accurately measuring cable lengths and then installing cables to connect the bought-in items of equipment. There may be a small team of electricians employed to install, connect and test the equipment, though this is often left to specialist sub-contractors, and in the case of some equipment the manufacturer will send personnel for this role.

Where a workshop is provided for any of these functions, it is generally small and has a limited range of equipment to perform basic tasks. Testing and safe storage of the bought-in items is more usual.

A machine shop was a feature of most shipyards until relatively recently, used for making special fittings, large bolts, deck and other equipment and for a lot of work on bought-in machinery. Prior to the last two decades, many shipyards included an engine works, and a large machine shop was a significant part of that facility. Some shipyards retain a large machine shop as a hangover from previous times, but in most cases the need has all but disappeared. Most of the items previously made in the shipyard are now bought, and the amount of machining on bought-in items has steadily declined. Much machinery is now bought as a complete package, including supports, and is ready to install in the ship. At most a small workshop with a few general purpose machine tools is all that is required.

Material storage is a much more significant element of modern shipbuilding than outfitting workshops.

MATERIAL RECEIPT

The steel which is required to produce the hull is in most cases the greatest weight of materials which the shipyard requires, but the number and variety of outfitting items far outweighs this in terms of organisational requirements. The materials bought in to a shipyard typically account for 60–80 per cent of the value. The proportion of items made in a shipyard has steadily declined over the last century, as the costs of production have increased and the technical specialisation has also increased.

The requirement to receive, inspect and store safely materials until required in production is an important element in any shipbuilding operation. The volume of material to be stored depends on a number of factors. First is the size of material stock which the shipyard requires to guarantee continuity of production. If the shipyard is located in a well-developed region, with local industries capable of producing the requirements, then the stock level can be relatively low. On the other hand, a shipyard in a more remote or less well-developed region will need to maintain larger stocks.

Much of the material for shipbuilding is very specialised, and is made to order for a specific vessel. This is the case even when the item is a standard product. Some items are produced only occasionally, and must be ordered when available. In this case, the storage time in the shipyard may be lengthy. The volume of storage will also depend on the ability of the shipyard to plan and manage procurement. In a well-organised company, the procurement programme is closely integrated with the technical information and production. The material can then be procured, not exactly "just in time", but in such a way as to minimise the time in shipyard storage. The importance of this ability to reduce the material in stock lies in the reduction of costs which results from it. The cost saving comes from a number of factors. First, the storage buildings and other areas can be smaller, saving capital costs or releasing space for a more productive function. Secondly, the number of people needed to maintain the stock of materials can be reduced. Thirdly, and perhaps most importantly, the capital tied up in the materials is released, effectively saving interest charges, either in real savings or by eliminating opportunity costs as capital can be invested.

Another factor in minimising stocks is the relationship which is developed with the materials suppliers. If they can be integrated into the shipyard planning cycle and given realistic information on future requirements in advance, then their ability to plan is enhanced. This allows them to make more effective use of their resources and ultimately reduce costs. Some of the saving can then accrue to the shipyard. While that may seem a counsel of perfection, there are some excellent supplier-shipyard relationships to be found, to mutual benefit.

BLOCK ASSEMBLY, OUTFITTING AND PAINTING

In general the outfitting and hull elements of the ship are kept separate during preparation and assembly. Indeed, in more and more cases, large parts of these activities may be sub-contracted. However, once reasonably large assemblies have been produced, they are increasingly integrated into large blocks which are substantially complete before they are taken to the ship construction area.

In the past, outfitting was simply completed after the ship structure was in place and often not until the ship was launched. To reduce timescales and costs, this has changed, as has the past practice of taking individual pieces to the ship for installation.

The first change was to outfit the steel units, although the quantity of such work which can be accomplished may be limited, primarily by the need to joint the units. This results in hot work—cutting and welding which can damage the outfitting. Therefore the outfitting is often restricted to such items as pipe hangers and other foundations and supports, and localised painting.

As large blocks were adopted, the hot work was complete over larger areas of the ships, and more outfitting could be done. In addition to the foundations, pipes, other services and items of equipment could all be installed on the blocks after completion of the structure. The use of a build strategy to pre-identify this work allowed the design and configuration of the blocks to be adjusted to maximise the amount of outfitting that can be carried out.

The co-ordination of the outfitting items with the steel is a complex planning activity, which can be simplified to some extent by building outfit assemblies. These parallel steel assemblies, and each assembly includes the foundations for the equipment, equipment items, pipes and other services, cables and usually painting. The assemblies can be completed independently of the steelwork and then installed, either on a block or on the ship, at the appropriate time.

Whereas a limited amount of painting and outfitting may take place on steel units, the potential for damage during transport and through further assembly activities makes this more difficult to organise. However, large blocks facilitate outfitting.

Many shipyards have the final construction of ships under cover, and this also applies to the preceding assembly stages of work. Where ship size or limits to investment are a problem, the compromise is to assemble large blocks under cover, often in a purpose-designed building.

SHIP CONSTRUCTION

Ship construction includes both the putting together of the hull structure in a final building position (in a dock or on a berth in most cases), and includes also the installation of equipment, and final outfitting. Outfitting includes installation of steel and outfit-interim products, and individual items of equipment, in the larger product (the ship) prior to its delivery to the customer.

Testing of some interim products and systems may take place during assembly, but the major test activity, leading up to sea trials, is carried out after final installation afloat. The testing function is taken to be the process of ensuring at any stage of the production system that the current interim product does, and the final product will, meet specified criteria. These include any specified requirements, and may include weight, dimensions, production tolerances and functionality. Testing may be destructive, in the case of sampling delivered components, or more usually non-destructive as production progresses through its many stages.

The process of ship construction has changed considerably over the last 50 years of the twentieth century. In many ways, the process in 1950 had changed little for a century. Of course the ships were of steel, having previously been of wood, then iron. And welding was rapidly becoming the accepted process for joining the steel parts together. But the basic process of ship construction remained one of making a large number of small pieces and then taking them individually to a building berth to be joined together (see Figure 25).

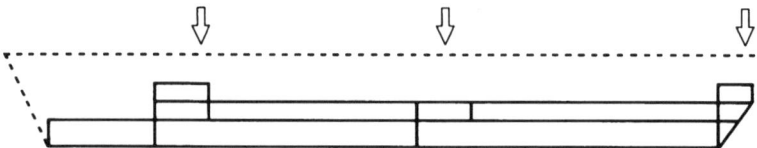

Figure 25.   Ship construction from individual parts—flexible, but slow

The first change was to assemble some of the individual steel parts into small units, in the workshop, and then take these to the building berth. This required both a larger scale transport system than the road (and often internal railway) that had been the usual case. It also required the development of larger cranes, to manipulate and lift the units into position. These replaced the earlier derricks, which rarely had a capacity greater than five or perhaps ten tonnes.

The need to produce more ships, and the need to produce larger ships, grew, along with the need to reduce labour man-hours as labour costs increased. The small units were combined into large units, then blocks. The process of building a ship now had several stages, rather than just piece part production and ship construction. The effect of this was to remove much of the work from the building berth and have it completed in a workshop. The reduced amount of work to be completed on the berth reduced the time required allowing more ships to be built in a given timescale. The

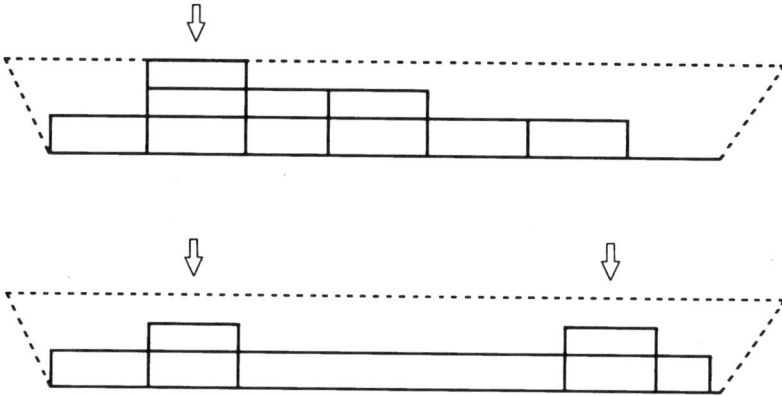

Figure 26.   Ship construction in units, requiring more investment and accuracy

workshop environment also allowed man-hours to be reduced, saving on costs. The impact is clear from Figure 26.

The reduction in time and cost for steelwork resulted in the outfitting of a ship becoming a bottleneck process. Although the ship structure could be produced in a much shorter time, despite increasing ship size, the sequential outfitting still resulted in a lengthy afloat period before the ship could proceed on sea trials. This, and the rapidly increasing complexity of ships, required a change in methods. The same basic approach as for steelwork was adopted. More installation was carried out on the building berth, before the launch of the ship. Some of the items were combined into assemblies, and then installed on a steel unit, or block. Once again, as Figures 27 and 28 show, the result was to introduce more stages of work and shorten the cycle time to complete a ship.

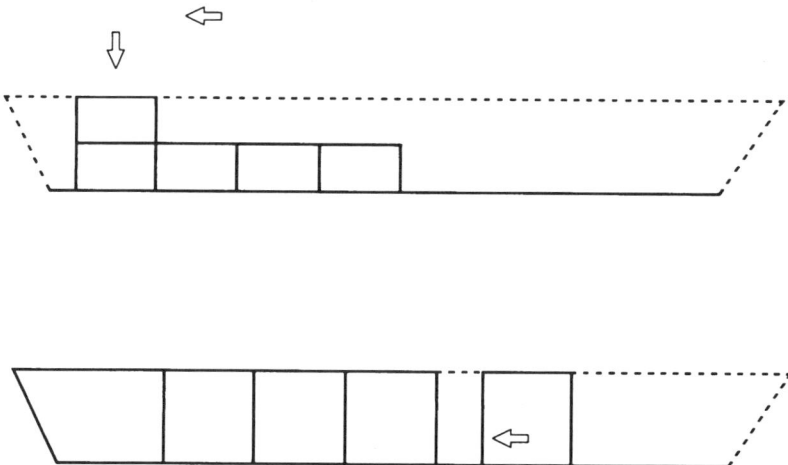

Figure 27.   Ship construction in blocks or rings

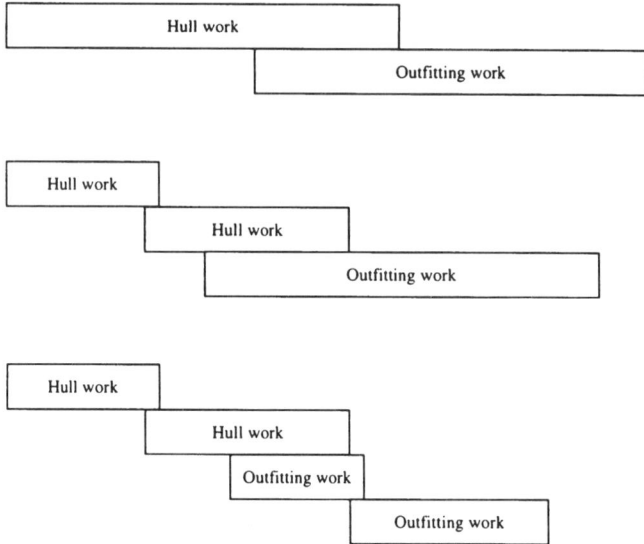

Figure 28. Introduction of additional stages of production to shorten construction cycle time

FINAL OUTFITTING

Historically, the structure of a ship was completed first, and the complete hull was then launched into the river or harbour where the shipyard was located. Outfitting then commenced with the ship afloat. Some work was done prior to launch, but the final outfitting period was often lengthy and labour intensive.

Increasingly, shipbuilders are installing much of the outfitting prior to launch. The installation of pipes at the end of the panel assembly process has been described as an example. Once the panels are joined to form larger blocks or units, further outfitting may take place. The ship on the building berth or in the dock is also available for further outfitting as soon as all the structural work and welding in a particular area has been completed.

As a consequence, the final outfitting period is now often much shorter and the work to be done is limited to completion of systems, installation of more delicate equipment and testing. For standard ships, built in series, the period may be only a few weeks.

The final outfitting period will vary considerably depending on the ship type. In general, the objective is to minimise the period at the quayside, and this is in part to save time. It also results in less work being completed in poor working conditions, and thus saves labour hours and other costs.

However, some specialised ships, for example passenger ships, have a large outfit content, so that the man-hours for outfitting are significantly greater in total than those for steelwork. There is also a large proportion of the finishing work that can be done as effectively on board as on a block. In these cases, the final outfitting period may be as long as the dock time. Other types that require lengthy setting to work of systems will also require an afloat period that is longer.

The key is to have a build strategy for the ship which identifies the resources and times, and makes the best compromise between a minimum dock cycle and a short afloat period, to keep the overall costs of outfitting as low as possible.

NEW PRODUCTION PROCESSES

There have been a number of significant developments in shipbuilding processes in the twentieth century. To some extent these have been required by the changing technology of the ships themselves. But in many ways a shipbuilder of the early twentieth century could rapidly come to terms with the way work is conducted today. The key developments in shipbuilding have been:

— the use of welding as the primary joining process instead of riveting;
— the use of larger structural units and the introduction of outfitting at an early stage;
— the use of computers, mainly for design but increasingly for information management in the production arena;
— the improvements in preparation and cutting technology to produce more accurate piece parts.

But in many areas the changes have been only in terms of scale: for example the sheer size of ships, the use of larger and larger undercover workshops, the increasing size of ship structural blocks. There is also increasing use of automation in the shipbuilding industry.

AUTOMATION

There is no universal definition of automation. One alternative is: "the carrying out of a process without human intervention". This begs the questions:

— When does the process start and finish?
— What human intervention is permissible?
— How can the process equipment be adapted?

So the question "what is meant by automation?" is a difficult one to answer. There are a number of processes in ship construction which are suitable for automation, although the scale of operations, and in particular the size of the final product, makes this a difficult business in which to apply automation. The other question which needs to be answered is "what justification is there for automation in ship construction?".

An industrial operation can be considered to have four components:

— processes: tools and techniques to perform tasks;

— materials handling: transfer of materials between processes;
— control: regulation of quantity and quality of outputs;
— power technology: source of energy for the activities.

Each of these can be at any point on a scale of mechanisation:

— manual;
— power-assisted;
— hand-controlled machine;
— automatic machine, hand activated;
— fully automatic.

A number of examples of automation at different stages of the shipbuilding process can be identified. In all areas, it is possible to find hand tools, which represent the simplest means of carrying out a process. They are used less and less, principally as labour costs increase throughout the shipbuilding world. To improve productivity and give faster production rates, power tools are more commonly used. The guidance and control are still by human intervention.

In some areas of production, where relatively large numbers of items are processed, more complex machinery can be used. One of the early applications, in the area of materials handling, was the use of roller conveyors, particularly for steel materials. These are used for transfer of materials from storage to each successive stage of initial processing—from cleaning to painting to cutting and so on.

One of the simplest examples of automation in shipbuilding is on the steel treatment line, which has a roller conveyor with product detection. The line has a number of limit switches which are tripped by a steel plate moving along the conveyor. As the switches are tripped, they either start or stop conveyor sections, thus avoiding collisions between plates and at the same time ensuring that there is continuity of material passing through the various processes. A more complex example is a numerically controlled plate cutting machine. The machine first has to be programmed: in the past by means of a paper tape containing instructions for machine control and the dimensions of the items to be cut. Then the plate to be cut is positioned on the cutting table, and its precise location is checked. Once the cutting process is initiated, no operator intervention is required until the programme is complete, which could be an hour or two later. An operator may check from time to time that all is proceeding correctly, but essentially the machine runs itself for the cutting cycle. An advance is direct numerical control (DNC) for a plate cutting machine. In this case the nesting of materials is carried out in the technical office of the shipyard and the cutting instructions are generated and sent to the machine remotely. There is still a need for an operator to load and unload steel from the machine, but otherwise the operation is automatic.

A panel line has been described earlier. It has a mixture of automated and manual systems, the choice being determined by the economic factors—in effect whether capital investment or labour use produces the lowest production costs.

Many efforts have been made to use industrial robots for shipbuilding, but many of these have ended with a limited success. The basic technology has been available for two decades, although the effectiveness of the control systems has improved immensely. The cost has also reduced dramatically, along with most other computer-related equipment. But the difficulty in shipbuilding, as so often, is the sheer scale of the operation. There is no reason why a crane cannot be computer controlled, for example in a steel stockyard, to receive and deliver steel plates. But the cost of doing so compares unfavourably in most cases with the use of a human operator. The human can also deal with any physical difficulties which may arise in the process of moving a 10 or 15 tonne mass, up to 20 metres in length.

Cranes for assembly could also be automated, but again, the potential variety of the production floor is such that it is simpler to have a human operator. Where robots have been successfully adopted is for welding processes in assembly. Relatively simple robots, designed to complete a limited range of more or less repetitive welding tasks, are in successful use in a number of shipyards. Other applications include painting and cutting. In particular, the use of robots as part of a profile preparation system is more and more popular.

In this case, the robot is a standard industrial robot, with an oxygen/gas cutting system as the tool it uses. The robot can be in a fixed location, and the profiles to be cut are moved into its range and taken away when work is complete by a system of conveyors. The size of the workpiece, and the operations to be carried out, which include cutting holes in the profiles and preparing the ends for welding, are well within the compass of a standard industrial robot. For large volumes of production, and in a relatively high labour cost location, this is an ideal solution.

COATINGS

Coatings are assuming an increasing importance in marine operations. The need to reduce ship operating costs, the use of more ballast tanks to try and prevent possible environmental pollution and some exotic cargoes are major reasons for this. The coatings are more complex and sophisticated, and also more costly.

Modern underwater paint coatings are designed to provide protection for the ships' structures from corrosion in hostile environments. They are also designed for long life in external hull applications to minimise docking times. For many ships, internal coatings are also important, for example to protect the structure from chemical and other hazardous cargo. They are also essential to maintain ballast tanks, which are very susceptible to corrosion.

The application of coatings in marine production is assuming much greater importance in parallel with the operational importance and the increasing cost of both the coating material and its application in a shipyard. Historically, steelwork was regarded as the most important element in ship construction. More recently, outfitting has been seen to be of at least equal importance in achieving high performance. Current thinking is beginning to give coatings the same importance.

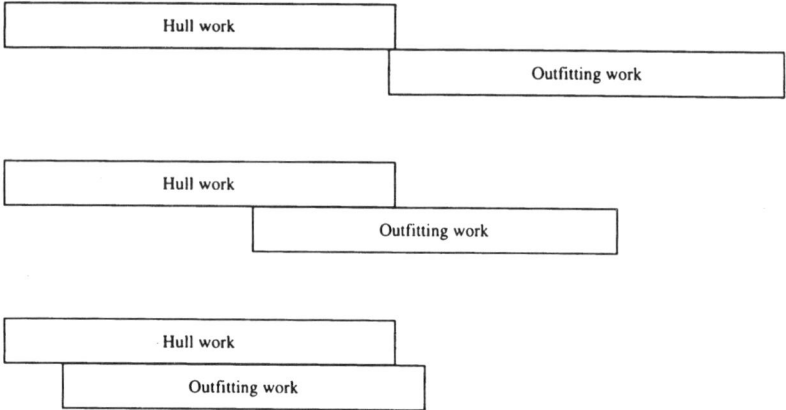

Figure 29. Reduction in construction time by overlapping hull and outfitting work

For a large shipyard, building ships in short cycle times, coating can be a bottleneck process in current shipbuilding conditions. It is the reduction in cycle times for construction which results in the need for improved coating application. Historically ships were built sequentially, and this is shown in Figure 29, which in the first case indicates the sequence of work for a typical ship construction project in around 1950. The second case shows the change in cycle time which occurred through the 1960s and 1970s, with much larger ships being constructed in shorter timescales. The attention of the industry was largely focused on the steelwork, primarily through the use of large blocks to shorten the time for building the hulls. Large cells for painting the hull blocks were introduced, along with the other changes.

The further development of production technology has resulted in parallel outfitting and steelwork, and much reduced build cycle times. Assembling very large blocks, and also outfitting them extensively before they are sent to the building dock, gives very short times at the final construction area.

The block assembly and preceding unit assembly times are extended, but the short time required at the final assembly area has several benefits:

— more vessels can be produced in a given time;
— the utilisation of the most expensive shipyard facility is increased;
— the work done in unfavourable conditions is reduced;
— labour hours are reduced;
— more work can be carried out in parallel.

For very short construction times, steelwork has been extensively mechanised or automated. Outfitting is more difficult to automate, but progress has been made with pipes in particular. Work on board has been reduced by use of outfit assemblies and on-block outfitting. However, coating remains a labour intensive operation, and so it can become a serious bottleneck in the overall process.

Even where large paint cells have been introduced for the final coating of large blocks and units, the labour intensive nature of the work makes it difficult to reduce the cycle times. The required curing time also limits the ability to reduce the overall coating time.

A particular problem is that the painting has to be done after all other activities —in particular hot work—have been completed, to avoid re-work, which is a cause of both cost and time penalties. In practical terms re-work means a painter who has completed a large area of steel having to return, perhaps more than once, to repair the coating where a delayed piece of cutting or welding has damaged the coating. It has been estimated that 25 per cent of all the coating man-hours used in a shipyard may be effectively wasted on what should be unnecessary re-work.

Where coating can be achieved at an early stage of steelwork, there is a potential benefit. Like other outfitting processes, and the steelwork itself, any activity that can be completed early, while the workpiece is in a good environment and is readily accessible, can make savings. Unfortunately, all the succeeding stages of the production cycle are then potential causes of damage. For outfitting, the problem has been recognised. In some cases, outfitting is completed early, in others only preparatory work is competed, and items which may possibly be damaged are installed later. In the case of coatings, the culture in most shipyards does not yet recognise the coating as important or valuable, and care to avoid damage is not always taken.

The coatings used on a modern ship may well account for 5 to 10 per cent of the total ship cost, so if any re-work is required, it can be expensive. The time required for coating can also affect the overall build cycle time, effectively restricting the production capacity of a shipyard.

Causes of coating re-work can be found in most of the operations which are carried out on the structure of a ship during its assembly and construction. The operations include:

— transport, causing abrasion;
— fairing and alignment, where additional hot work is needed;
— tack welding, which damages the coating;
— fillet or butt welding;
— outfitting activities, in particular welding, and fitting of supports;
— block supports causing abrasion and missed patches;
— open air storage, resulting in weathering;
— shotblasting damage and debris inclusions;
— repair of welding defects, causing spatter and burning;
— paint application which is not of adequate standard;
— paint curing in less than ideal conditions;
— lifting, causing abrasion and other damage.

The many problems which can be identified can be solved—or, preferably, the problems can be avoided. There are operational solutions to unavoidable problems by use of improved procedures, which take protection of the coating into account.

It is essential to make sure that the procedures are implemented and then maintained.

Another solution is the use of temporary protection to avoid damage.

The preferable solution is to avoid as many of the problems as possible by addressing the design of the ship to facilitate painting, using the most appropriate facilities and equipment for correct paint application, for lifting and turning units, and so on. The planning and organisation of the work, including the incorporation of a coatings plan, is defined in the build strategy.

The vessel design has to take into account the need both to facilitate painting and to avoid corrosion. A number of areas are important in this respect:

— making it simpler to gain access for surface preparation, for the use of hand tools and increasingly for automated systems;
— providing suitable access for cleaning, for the removal of abrasives and the debris from the blasting process, and also avoiding areas where abrasive can be trapped;
— improving general work access, thus avoiding the need for staging which requires welded or other fixings to the structure. This is partly through design, but can also be managed by minimising work done at late stages of assembly and ship construction;
— designing simpler structures, which can take advantage of double hull and other features, and by designing to automated production.

The use of appropriate facilities and technology is also important. The use of paint cells is a major factor in improving coating efficiency, because they are able to provide:

— protection from adverse weather;
— controlled temperature and humidity;
— an infrastructure giving good access for cleaning and painting;
— faster curing times.

The paint cell, which is a specialised work station in the same sense as a panel line work station or any other conventional work station, provides an opportunity to invest in improved technology. This technology, which is widely available, includes vacuum- or hydro-blasting, both of which avoid clean up of spent grit, and mechanised painting.

Typically shipyards base a build strategy on the requirements of steelwork production. That is, the block breakdown for the ship, and planning of the major structure, are the basis of the whole strategy. The increasing use of early outfitting is now more general, and many shipyards have now built more recognition of outfitting into their planning. In order for coatings to avoid becoming the new bottleneck inhibiting performance improvements, coating requirements must be built into the strategy and subsequent planning and scheduling.

The requirements are for a cleaning and painting programme which is in parallel with the steel and major outfit planning units. A schedule for paint cells, if they are provided, or otherwise for the final coating of structural blocks, is also an important element in the planning.

Quality assurance has a role in improving the efficiency of coatings, along with other aspects of production. This role is in setting finished quality standards, which are the targets for achievement, and also in assisting the stability of the production processes. This involves the adherence to procedures and maintenance of similar standards of finish from block to block.

To achieve the goal of reduced cost, the control of labour expended on coating is required. The planning of the work will assist, provided the actual outcomes are managed by monitoring the hours spent (and thus the cost). The labour force must be adequately trained in preservation of coatings to prevent unnecessary re-work through carelessness.

Any shipyard would like to be able to use a coating which has benign characteristics. The wish list for most would include applicability in any weather conditions, and a paint that can be applied to any surface condition, ideally (but unrealistically) over wet, surface rusted or poorly prepared steel. A paint which will remain attached to the ship's hull after such mistreatment would also perhaps be desirable. A paint which will cure in a very short time, without too much regard for temperature or humidity, is also needed, as is a paint which is abrasion and heat resistant. The coating manufacturers prefer application of their product to take place in good conditions, preferably in a paint cell with a controlled environment. The two sets of preferences are incompatible. Although development work on new coatings is in progress, it is unlikely to lead to a product which meets the shipyards' ideal. The shipyards must take a lead in managing their applications.

ENVIRONMENTAL ISSUES

There is increasing international concern about environmental pollution. As a result, there is increasing legislation to control or ban some industrial activities which cause pollution. A number of marine production processes can cause problems, including painting and surface cleaning and blasting, which can also create a major waste disposal problem. Some of the issues have been considered earlier, and production management has an increasing responsibility to minimise or avoid waste, and then to manage its disposal.

Other production processes can cause problems, including welding, which has potential for causing health hazards, and any process which generates noise. Noise can be both an internal health and safety problem and an external nuisance for adjacent premises. The subject has been reviewed in Chapter 3, and is expected to be an important driver for new technology that avoids or overcomes environmental problems.

OTHER PRODUCTION MANAGEMENT ISSUES

There are other key areas for production management to consider. This includes the management of production capacity. This capacity is defined in terms of the physical facilities, primarily the major investments which control the number of ships which can be built. In particular, the berths or docks for ship construction are a major factor in capacity. In the case of a shipbuilder, once an investment is made, the capacity of a plant will be set for a long time.

Other aspects include the labour force, where the capacity can be varied in a shorter timescale, particularly with the use of sub-contract labour. The capacity can be set for a very short time, in the case of services (e.g. shiprepair), but also in the case of shipbuilding. However, the ability to take on and lay off labour in the short term does depend on a steady supply of trained labour which is always available. In the longer term, this policy may be self-defeating. The ageing workforce and skills shortages, which are identified in Chapter 3, are an increasingly worrying situation for the business of shipbuilding world-wide.

Capacity management is a balancing act. On the one hand there is the cost of providing adequate capacity, which may be difficult to vary in the short term as demand varies, and thus incur more cost than is justified because some capacity is idle. On the other hand, any failure to deliver interim products or particularly the final product—the ship—on time can have dire consequences for the shipyard. The ability to design the production process to meet product mix demands, good planning and quality procedures all assist in determining capacity requirements more accurately, and making capacity management easier.

The need for good and accurate planning and scheduling has been emphasised and the subject considered in another chapter. The importance in production management of organising all the activities to ensure that interim products are on time cannot be over-emphasised. There are variations in the industry. Where a shipyard is building standard ships in a capital-intensive plant, the schedules are largely predetermined. The information on the products and processes allows a rigidity of planning and scheduling which is closer to automobile production than old-fashioned shipbuilding.

In other cases, such as building one-off ships and novel types of vessel, the predictability is much lower, and the scheduling is closer to project management, as found in some large-scale made-to-order industries. Smaller shipyards may also have greater flexibility, and allow short term problem solving to dominate their production style. Ship conversion is also in this area, and the schedules are extremely flexible in many service industries, of which ship repairing is an example.

Quality management is an important element in ensuring the products meet specification requirements. This has also been discussed separately, but it must be embedded in the production management in any shipyard. Ultimately, production is about products which meet specification, built at the lowest practicable cost.

CHAPTER 12

THE DEVELOPMENT OF SHIPBUILDING FACILITIES

THE SCOPE OF RECENT DEVELOPMENT

The size of the industry has been mentioned, but some key statistics will serve to remind readers of the scale of the production of ships. The size of the product has also been considered, and although the dimensions of the largest ships are also repeated here, it is worth remembering that even small fishing vessels are large compared to, for example, road vehicles.

The world produces some 30 million tonnes of shipping annually, measured in terms of its cargo carrying capacity. The largest ship built had a deadweight of 500,000 tonnes; that is to say, could be loaded with that quantity of oil. A typical VLCC of 280,000 tonnes deadweight is some 350 metres in length, 50 metres in beam and 25 metres deep.

The scale of the production facilities required has also been considered, but in this chapter the work required to develop a new facility will be described. Given the excess of shipbuilding supply over demand, it may be wondered why creating new shipbuilding facilities should be considered at all. It may be a surprise to consider just how many have been constructed from a greenfield site, or substantially rebuilt (from a "brownfield" site) in the 1990s.

Expansion in Korea has been referred to in the context of shipbuilding capacity. All the major shipyards in Korea are relatively newly constructed, and even the "oldest", the Hyundai shipyard at Ulsan, has been steadily increased in size since work first commenced on it in 1970. Korea has gone from a minor shipbuilding nation to the possessor of almost one third of the shipbuilding capacity of the world in some 25 years.

China has also substantially rebuilt older facilities and produced one major new shipyard, at Dalian. Other countries where new facilities can be found include Indonesia, with the PT Pal shipyard in Surabaya.

In Europe, too, there have been some significant development, examples of which include the steady growth of the Meyer Werft shipyard in Germany for undercover passenger ship production and the new developments in former East Germany, including Kværner Warnow Werft. Many other shipyards have carried out partial redevelopments as existing facilities and equipment became outdated or reached the end of their useful life. Some of these are normal commercial decisions, based on

227

careful analysis of specific markets and tailored development. Other developments of new shipbuilding capacity can only be described as wildly optimistic.

The reasons for these over-optimistic developments appear to lie primarily in the recent market studies which have forecast a buoyant demand for new ships. The assumptions that were made appear to have been that not only would the market grow rapidly, but also that no other shipyards would address the same market. There is also the desire to develop industry, with shipbuilding seen as a logical industry on which to base industrialisation. (The history of such activity includes the UK in the mid-nineteenth century, Spain and other European countries later in the same century, and Japan at the start of the twentieth century.) More recently, South Korea built much of its enormous growth since 1960 on shipbuilding, and China and other Asian economies are following a similar path, though at the time of writing some of the underlying assumptions about "Asian tigers" are perhaps proving to be false.

At least at the start of such industrialisation and development, the opportunity has been identified to create a major industry, which will require and thus generate a base of suppliers and sub-contractors, and in turn a demand for services. Given some significant commercial advantage, in particular low labour costs in an essentially labour-intensive business, the development path looks particularly appealing. The technology of shipbuilding, at its more basic levels, is readily transferable, as the previous examples over 150 years demonstrate. Even the newer technologies can be assimilated reasonably readily.

Some of the smaller shipyard developments, in developing nations, are motivated by local demand rather than any assumptions about global markets, but some of these are still suffering from the general over-capacity.

The results of over-expansion, particularly where the demand is less than expected, and where commercial advantage is negated by subsidy and other support, have already been described. The outcome, though, is that the world's shipbuilding industry has collectively spent in the order of several billion dollars in the 1990s, essentially on shipyards that were not really necessary.

However, this chapter is about the mechanics, rather than the logic, of the development business. The question how those new shipyards, or major updates, come about is considered as part of the market and the other domains which form the environment of the business of shipbuilding. The objective is therefore to consider the questions of site selection, determination of facilities and relationships between the facilities, leading to a suitable layout and equipment requirement. The typical cost and cost structure of a development are also considered.

SHIPYARD LOCATION

Considering, first, the location of a shipyard, there are a number of factors which dictate the ideal location for a new facility. These can be listed, not in any particular priority order. (In practice, few potential shipyard sites can be described as ideal.

Thus, the final selection is usually a compromise. The first of the factors that are generally regarded as important for a site is a location adjacent to sufficiently deep water, which is self-evident. However, the water depth can be modified by dredging, where a site is suitable in other respects. Many older shipyards which have redeveloped, particularly with recent increases in ship size, have faced this dilemma. Rather than relocate, the existing site has been modified. A striking example is the Meyer Werft shipyard in Germany. Located some 40 kilometres from the sea on the river Ems, it has found it necessary not only to deepen the river locally, but also to deepen and widen the river generally to allow increasingly large passenger ships to be built. The alternative of relocation would risk losing the accumulated skills and capabilities of the shipyard. However, in principle, a site which is suitable *a priori* is preferred. A location with a level site, a few metres above water level (with some dependence on local tidal conditions) is also needed. This is a likely find in a developing nation, but in more mature economies it may be more difficult. A solution which was particularly common in Japan in the 1960s and 1970s was to reclaim land and create the ideal, typically rectangular, site by this means. The major Korean shipyards are also built on partly reclaimed sites. In the case of Daewoo, some of the material for reclamation came from the major site levelling which was required. Once again, the capacity for modifying the site is available, but it is more expensive than finding the ideal.

Also needed is a location with good rock at a suitable depth below the surface to support heavy loads. The depth will depend on the type of construction site to be selected, whether a dock, berth or level site for load-out. The requirements of the civil engineering element of the total package may be the most important. The construction of ships, particularly very large ships, creates many heavy loads and requires very large workshops and other structures. The need to provide adequate support for these may be a primary factor in site selection, and often is also a major factor in optimising the layout.

A location with good weather conditions is preferred. Southern California is one such location, where the climate permits much of the assembly to be carried out in the open air. This is very unusual, and it is normal to complete much of the work in covered workshops. Sites with high rainfall, high winds, very high temperatures and other extremes of weather are not ideal. However, the overriding wish to have the industry in the first place may dictate that a shipyard is developed regardless. The effective modification of the site can then extend to provision of protection against bad weather—generally by enclosing the shipyard, or at least a substantial proportion of it, within a building.

The location which is selected needs an adequate local infrastructure, which includes:

— a readily available workforce, ideally one which is already skilled;
— by implication, local housing and other urban infrastructure;
— local education and training facilities;

— local engineering and other support industry.)

Once again, particularly if the shipyard development is intended to be a vehicle for general industrial development, the infrastructure for the shipyard may be modified. In some of the 1970s Korean developments, the site was remote and housing and the other infrastructure requirements were developed in parallel with the shipyard. Some of the other planned developments in South America, for example, were based on the construction of new urban communities in under-developed regions.

Looking further afield, it is also necessary to have good communications. These will include roads, for local transport and deliveries (at least of small items) to the shipyard. It is routine in some areas to use rail transport, and this is then a requirement for material deliveries. Given the global nature of the industry, an airport in reasonably close proximity is a requirement. Finally, electronic communications need to be considered, although the past dependency on the terrestrial versions is steadily declining.

The infrastructure, like the specific site conditions, can also be modified, particularly where the shipyard is intended as a driver for other industrial development. Co-location of shipyards with steelworks, engineering and other industry has been a feature of some development schemes. The availability of local population is also in some cases arranged by development of new housing and all the infrastructure of a small town. Arrangements to transport large numbers of workers from local population centres to the shipyard are also common. All of this echoes the initial development of steel shipbuilding in the 19th century United Kingdom.

Infrastructure may be created specially for the new development, certainly in the form of new road and rail links. The shipyard site can also provide the necessary port facilities for discharge of imported materials, since few shipyards now expect to manufacture more than a small proportion of the items needed.

Any or, in some cases, all of the requirements can be obtained as the result of modifying the site. Thus, many shipyards are sited on reclaimed land, where the site is created by landfill out into what was water. This approach was particularly seen in the expansions of first Japanese and later Korean shipyards for large tanker construction. The effect of the site selection process can be seen by considering the location of the industry around the world. In fact, few shipyards are in ideal locations. As an example, the West Coast of the United Kingdom can be described as wet and windy, which has implications for productivity. The North East Coast of the USA and Canada suffer from severe winter conditions. The same is true for most shipyards in eastern Europe, including Russia and the Ukraine. Many Japanese shipyards are in earthquake-prone areas. And there are other examples; most shipyards are demonstrably in less than ideal locations, but with adaptation to improve the site to an acceptable situation. Previous acceptance of poor working conditions, and hence lower productivity, has given way to the use of undercover working to minimise the effects of weather.

SHIPYARD FACILITIES REQUIREMENTS

Turning now to the facilities of the shipyard, the decision on what facilities are required is based on a number of factors, which depend to a large extent on the activities described earlier in this book. To some extent, the facilities required are an extension of the site selection outcome, in particular the availability of an industrial infrastructure. The selection of facilities for a particular case can be considered to depend on a number of factors. The first of these is the shipyard product mix, which is an outcome of market research, product development and ultimately successful sales. The size and type of ship which is to be built will clearly have a major impact on the overall facility size, in particular the final construction area. The extent of some of the specialised facilities of a shipyard will also depend on the ship types which it is intended to construct. The second factor is the overall manufacturing strategy for the shipyard, which will dictate, among other major facility considerations, what workshops and other areas are actually required. This is because the manufacturing strategy includes the very important decisions on whether to make or buy specific components for the ships which are to be built. This in turn will dictate the size, number and configuration of ship construction areas, also the size and number of workshops, internal transport and materials handling requirements.

The build strategies for the specific ships which form the product mix will then be based on the overall manufacturing strategy, but may require small modifications for different types. There may also be a degree of flexibility built into the shipyard, to allow it to manage future changes in product mix. These should not be radical, although some facilities have proved to be remarkably adaptable, probably more due to good fortune than prescience. Equally, some shipyards have found that the decision on size and configuration of particular facilities has proved to be a source of problems when their product mix changes due to market conditions.

The factors which are affected by the build strategies include the breakdown of the ship into units and blocks. This will particularly affect the ship construction crane capacities, and also the transport requirements. It will also determine the workshop requirements, including key dimensions and, again, crane capacities. The workshops will be designed to be suitable for the largest units, or blocks, which are to be assembled. The cranes will be sized to be able to lift and manipulate those blocks and units. Since both the buildings and the cranes are very expensive items, their sizing is critical. In particular, they must be capable of dealing with the largest units, so if the unit sizes vary significantly, then for much of the time the capacities which are available will be under-utilised. This represents a waste of resources.

The complete breakdown of the structural units, and also the intended assembly and installation strategy for the outfitting, will provide a hierarchy of interim products. This hierarchy will be the basis for work station design, each specific work station being organised to produce particular products in an efficient manner. The interim products of each type, and for each stage of production, are designed to b similar in size and other characteristics. For example, the units will be divide types, such as double bottom units, side units (which for many doubl vessels will be similar to the bottom units), fore and aft end (more shaped) units, and one-off units, particularly the deckhouses. All the units of each type will have similar dimensions and so on, as far as is possible for the ship design. The outcome will be that the units and the workshop facilities are closely matched, so that effective use of the capacity is assured. At the same time, the investment will be as small as possible.

The product mix will determine the rate of production which is required, and, applied to the interim products, will determine the volumes of interim products which require to be produced. This will underlie the decisions on the numbers of work stations, and also to some extent the degree of mechanisation and even automation which will be adopted.

The hierarchy of interim products will then also dictate the sizes of raw and semi-finished materials. From another perspective, the transport infrastructure may dictate the sizes of materials which can be delivered to the shipyard. This will also have an effect on the work station requirements. For example, it may be necessary to install a specialised work station for joining small steel plates, if these are all that are available. The larger plates which are then produced will enable the shipyard to match their size to the units and the facilities, and so to maximise use of assembly facilities.

The level of technology to be adopted is important for a cost-effective facility. Many shipbuilders are keen to adopt the latest, newest technology. Robots have been particularly popular in recent years. However, a low level of technology may be perfectly appropriate, for example in a low throughput shipyard, or in a low wage economy.

On the other hand, a high level of technology is appropriate for high value products, where the material element is high and quality is critical. It is also appropriate for high volumes of production, where economies of scale are available, and finally in high wage economies, where the substitution of capital for labour can provide a cost saving.

The critical part of a marine production facility is the final construction area. The ability to progress the required series of products through final construction largely determines the performance of a facility. The cycle time required is determined by the product mix. The number of ships to be built will be based on the assumptions about the market and sales potential which have been adopted. The planned capability of the s⊦˙   will also have an impact, with the objective being to find the be⠤t   ⠤ome from the numbers of ships and investment cost for the ⠤e is the time within which each ship requires to be com- oduct mix.

struction facility is very wide. That is, there are plenty of selected may be decided as much by cost and structural ional preference. ip construction is a traditional sloping berth. This is a al wooden shipbuilding facility, where a sloping river ply of timber was the basic requirement. The ship is built on the berth, on fixed supports. When completed, the weight of the ship is transferred to new supports which can move on a system of sliding ways. The ship is restrained from moving during the transfer process, but can be released at the time of launching. The ship is then simply allowed to slide down the berth into the water. The launch is often into the restricted waters of a river or estuary, and the ship, once in the water, must be stopped from further movement. On occasions, damage is caused to the ship, from collision with the river bank or other ships or structures. The restraint is often by use of drag chains, which are large bundles of chain attached to the ship by ropes. Once the ship is in the water, the ropes tauten and the friction of the chains on the berth provides a braking action. The ship is also taken in hand by several tugs, depending on size. Launching was the most common method of moving a newly built ship into the water until relatively recently. However, as ships became larger, an alternative was sought.

For shipyards built since around 1970, the more common choice has been a graving dock. The dock provides a level base for construction, and the float-out operation is simpler and safer than the traditional launch. Ships of up to 300,000 tonnes deadweight have been successfully launched, but the inherent costs, added to the additional problems of rapid construction on a sloping construction area, have dictated a change. The dock is sometimes designed to be of a size which will just accept the largest ship in the product mix. In other cases, and particularly where the planned throughput of ships in the product mix is high (that is, a short cycle time is planned), the dock may be longer than the ship. This allows a part of the ship to be constructed independently. Usually, this will be the aft end, containing the machinery spaces and, for most cargo carrying ships, the bulk of the outfitting work content. The aft end can be built, and partly outfitted, separately from the rest of the ship, while another ship is being completed in the dock. When the previous ship is floated out of the dock, the aft end can be moved into the main part of the dock. The cargo section of the ship is then constructed, while outfitting work continues on the aft end. The deckhouse is then lifted into place shortly before float-out of the ship. This arrangement allows the outfit-intensive part of the ship to have a cycle time which is twice as long as the relatively simple cargo part. For shipyards which rely on a high throughput of ships, the ability to achieve those rates of production is enhanced.

A few shipyards have developed facilities which allow the ship to be built on a flat area at normal ground level. The completed ship is then moved on a transport system for load-out onto a floating dock. A few have also adopted what is in effect a dock, but above ground level. Transfer of large blocks to the construction area is facilitated, and either a sliding system or wheeled transport can be used as alternatives to a crane. The ship is built in the "dock", which has access in the walls. When the ship is completed, the accesses are sealed with gates and the water is pumped into the dock. The water level in the dock is then above ground level. The ship then floats and is moved into a separate section of the dock which is below ground level. The water level is then lowered to that of the surrounding river or harbour. The ship is then outfitted in the lower dock, either afloat or in the dry. In some cases, the lower dock is used as a shiprepair dock. The shipyards designed originally for VLCCs at Setubal in Portugal and Saint Nazaire in France both have this double dock arrangement. The objective is to reduce the dock cost by reducing the quantity of excavation required.

The same principle of construction on a flat area can be combined with a ship lift. The ship lift was developed primarily as a ship repair facility, with the ability to dock and undock a large number of ships, in combination with a number of level repair berths. The ships are transferred to and from the berths on a transport system. The idea was then developed for shipyards which combined both ship repairing and ship construction. The early applications were largely for fishing harbours and for other operations with large numbers of relatively small ships. The lift is made up of a number of beams which run transversely. Each beam is supported by a pair of winches which may be electric or hydraulic. The beams can be lowered and raised in unison, using the winches which attach to the beams with wire ropes or chains. The winches are electronically or mechanically synchronised, to lift the beams at the same rate. The ship to be lifted from the water is manœuvred over the beams and then they bring it up to ground level. The beams also support a platform with longitudinal rails, on which runs a transfer system. Once the ship is at ground level, the transfer system is able to move it into a repair berth. The launching of the ship is simply the reverse process. The ship is transferred on to the lift platform, and then the winches lower it into the water. The system combines the benefits of construction on a level base, and at ground level, with the safer floating, rather than dynamic launching, of the ship. The ship lift, with the associated civil engineering work, is an expensive installation for a single berth, but when two or more berths are used for construction and/or repair, the effective berth cost can be reduced. The ship lift has been applied to larger and larger ships, with the maximum lifting capacity now at some 24,000 tonnes, although the largest commercial operation is smaller than this.

Any of the basic berth or dock configurations described above may be open to the weather. However, in the interests of greater efficiency of production, they are increasingly likely to be partly or completely covered for weather protection. The size of building to achieve this for a large ship is a major undertaking. The largest include the Meyer Werft shipyard in Germany, where the main building over the dock is around 300 metres in length, 100 metres wide and some 50 metres high. This provides complete cover for the ship construction and outfitting in the dock. The build strategy which is to be adopted is then entirely unconstrained by consideration of the weather, and can be designed to give maximum efficiency. This is particularly the case where complex passenger vessels are built, which require the outfitting and structure work to be integrated.

Until the 1980s, undercover ship construction was limited to relatively small ships, since the cost of the additional building could not be easily justified by savings in what was then relatively low cost labour. The need to make cost savings and to speed up production through a reduced cycle time has gradually swung the balance in favour of the larger capital investments. This is the case for high value ships, particularly warships, but also passenger ships, as described. The principle, like so much in the shipbuilding business, is not as new as is sometimes believed. A number of small boatyards have always built under cover, and the Mediterranean galleys of the Middle Ages were largely constructed in enclosed workshops. The application to very large ships is what is a new phenomenon.

Whether covered or not, the final construction area is typically the area of highest capital cost in any shipyard development or upgrading. A covered dock, with its equipment and services, will account for at least 50 per cent of the total cost of a shipyard.

MATERIALS HANDLING AND TRANSPORT

The business of shipbuilding deals with products which are large by any standards. Although the final product, the ship, is constructed in a fixed location, with the possibility of moving to a second location when partly completed, the need to prepare materials and assemble blocks and units in several stages requires a large site. Therefore, the handling and storage of both bought-in materials and units and other assemblies is an important factor in the industry. The ability to move and manipulate large objects is fundamental to efficient ship construction.

The method used to move final assemblies (whether blocks or units) to the ship construction area is a major cost element in any development. There are a number of alternatives which include:

— level luffing jib cranes;
— goliath cranes;
— overhead cranes in buildings;
— self-elevating transporters, in association with cranes;
— ground level systems, which may be either wheeled, sliding or "walking" systems.

The level luffing crane is the most common system, and the sight of the cranes is in many cases the defining aspect of the shipyard. The crane has a tower which can travel on rails. The crane jib can rotate on top of the tower, and also "luff", that is, be lowered from almost vertical to almost horizontal. The combination of rotation and luffing allows a wide coverage of the ship construction area and the adjacent areas which are used for block or unit assembly and storage. The "level" element in the luffing is the arrangement whereby the crane load is kept at the same height above the ground while the jib is lowered or raised. Although these cranes are commonly used, they do have an upper size limit. They are rarely over 200 tonnes in capacity, although examples can be found of up to 400 tonnes. More typically, their capacity is around 100 tonnes. Also, their load capacity reduces as the jib luffs, because as the distance from tower to load increases, so does the force tending to tip the crane. So a crane which will lift 100 tonnes at a radius of 20 metres will be limited to more like 30 tonnes at a radius of 50 metres. There is also a limit to jib length, without excessive cost. The cranes can be used in combination, to lift heavier blocks, but there is some loss of capacity when this is done.

As a result, especially for very large ships, the jib cranes were superseded by goliath cranes. These are effectively a portal frame, which spans the building dock and an area to one side of the dock. The top beam has one or more carriages which have the lifting equipment. The top beam may be arranged as two separate parallel beams, which can permit the carriages to pass each other. This facilitates turning of large blocks, so the crane can move to the location where a deck block has been completed and stored, lift it, turn it through 180 degrees into the correct orientation, then position it accurately on the partly completed ship. The cranes are major items of engineering, weighing several thousand tonnes and with a lifting capacity of up to 1,000 tonnes. The heaviest was originally installed at Kockums in Sweden for blocks on VLCCs, and had a capacity of 1,600 tonnes. The crane has since been modified and sold to the Far East Levingston shipyard in Singapore. The goliath cranes often have their own electrical generation system, so are self-contained structures which can be compared in scale to a medium-sized dry cargo ship. The dimensions of these cranes are specific to a facility, but they may typically have a span of 100 metres and a lift height of 60 metres.

In addition to the crane itself, there is a major civil engineering requirement to provide the foundations for the rails on which the crane runs. These may have a length of 500 metres, to allow the crane to operate over the length of a building dock, and into the block assembly and storage areas.

Where the decision is taken to build ships undercover, the dock is enclosed in a large building. In such cases, the usual choice of crane is an electric overhead travelling type. This is a typical workshop crane—except for scale—consisting of a beam or pair of beams with the lifting equipment on carriages. The beams have end carriages which run on rails, supported upon the building columns. The crane has a lower cost than a goliath, since it does not require the vertical legs to support the beams. The supply of power is also more readily arranged, and the undercover operation is easier. The capacities of such cranes are generally lower than those of goliaths, with 200 tonnes being a large example. They can operate in tandem for large lifts. Undercover construction does not place any premium on very large blocks, since the work will not be interrupted by weather, so the pressure to minimise dock work is less than in the open. Also, undercover building is generally adopted for high value ships, with a large outfitting component, which are generally smaller than the very large tankers and bulk carriers. The need to produce very large structures is reduced, since the ability to install outfitting is of greater significance.

A number of shipyards have tried to operate without the expense of heavy cranage for lifting large structural elements. In general they use either a berth or level construction area at land height, and use some form of ground transport to install very large ship sections. The ship sections are effectively transverse slices through the whole ship, since there is no crane to lift upper units into place. There is a need for a large block assembly shop for the "slices", which are assembled on elevated supports. They are generally extensively outfitted and painted, to be as complete as possible before they reach the building berth.

One transport system is the hydraulically powered, self-elevating transporter.

These have been commonly used in the industry since the development of facilities to build large cargo ships. The vehicle consists of a steel platform, capable of supporting a load which may be of up to 1,000 tonnes. The platform rides on wheelsets, usually four wheels to a set, and in sufficient numbers to support the total load of platform plus ship's block. The wheels are steered and driven hydraulically, and the same power system is also capable of elevating the platform by about half a metre. This elevating capability allows the vehicle to drive under a block, which is supported by trestles or stools, then lift it clear and move it elsewhere. The load can also be set down by driving between another set of stools and lowering the platform. The system was initially developed to allow large blocks to be moved and stored in a shipyard without the huge expense of providing crane rails and cranes to do so. Since their initial use, they have been adapted to position blocks directly on the building berth. The use of electronic steering allows two or more such vehicles to be coupled, so that very large blocks can be handled from time to time. The decoupled vehicles handle more normal loads at other times. This provides a very flexible transport and handling system.

Alternatives for the movement of large blocks include a variety of systems, generally using rails, to either roll or slide blocks into position. These are generally in fixed locations, so have less flexibility than the vehicles. They have been used in docks, and on berths, for ship construction systems which "extrude" the ships, section by section. The large blocks are assembled in a workshop, then transferred to a dock or berth. Once in place, each succeeding block is located and welded, then the ship is slid further onto the berth to allow the next section to be positioned. This lacks some flexibility, but provides a means of covered construction without the expense of covering a complete berth or dock. The Cammell Laird shipyard in Birkenhead is one such example. The system was pioneered at the Arendal shipyard in Gothenburg, Sweden, which closed in the 1970s.

THE WIDE VARIETY OF FACILITIES OPTIONS

In any shipyard, there are a number of specialised facilities which may be sub-contracted. The manufacturing strategy for a facility will determine whether or not these are sub-contracted, or are available on the shipyard site. The decision will depend on various factors, including the availability of specialist sub-contract companies locally, the required volume of production and whether economies of scale in production can be achieved, and the required degree of specialisation. Given the complexity of even the more basic ship types, there are a number of typically sub-contracted items, so that many shipyards do not have facilities for electronics, sheet metal work for heating, ventilation and air conditioning. Painting is often sub-contracted, along with the associated shot-blasting and cleaning activities. In some cases, the shipyard will provide a facility, in the form of appropriate workshop space, but use a sub-contractor who may rent the space, or have free use of it. The sub-contractor will then supply the necessary equipment.

For interim products with a high throughput, a dedicated facility may be required or desirable. Many workshops and work areas are general purpose, and are adaptable to a wide range of interim products. Typical examples of dedicated facilities for high volumes of production are transfer lines for flat panel production for large ships. Although these dedicated facilities often represent opportunities for high technology, they can result in "islands of automation". This is a situation where one area of the shipyard has heavy investment in new technology, typically some automated process, which is considerably in advance of any other areas. Although it will be efficient and produce interim products at low cost, it may not represent such good value to the whole shipbuilding process as spreading the same investment among other areas which are lagging behind in technology. The choice of appropriate production technology depends on both technical and economic factors. Shipbuilding is often described as primarily an assembly industry, and this is true particularly for those shipyards which choose to sub-contract most of the part manufacturing. However, where a shipyard does choose to manufacture in-house, because of location or economies of scale, the decision introduces other aspects of production.

Shipbuilding therefore generally has a mix of types of production, with product or group technology at the initial stages of production changing to batch and fixed position at the final stage. Thus at the start of the shipbuilding production, in the preparation and processing of steel and pipes, there are large elements of mass production industry, with transfer lines and some automation. Assembly has a few specialised systems, such as the panel line, but is more usually a batch production system. As the assemblies become larger, and particularly for blocks, the process switches to fixed position, as is the case on the berth or building dock. The use of the different types, and the technology, can be expected to change over time. There has been a gradual increase in the use of conveyors, transfer lines and automation, although the sheer scale of the product is an inhibiting factor.

THE SHIPYARD LAYOUT DEVELOPMENT PROCESS

There are a number of factors which play a major part in determining the layout. The facility layout process determines the disposition of the work areas on the site. The criteria for a good layout are usually expressed as a list of good attributes:

— uni-directional flow;
— minimum materials handling;
— minimum site area;
— flexibility in operation;
— maximum use of area and volume available;
— easier supervision of labour and processes;
— improved communications;
— capability to provide good quality.

In order to quantify the advantages of a particular layout, a systematic method should be adopted for its development. The basic procedure for developing layout is set out here. There are a number of stages.

First, the requirements to be satisfied by the layout must be identified. These include the volume of production to be undertaken and, from that, the number and type of work stations which are required to produce the required volume; the storage requirements, before and after each work station; any in-process storage which may be required and the proposed flow of work (how the interim products will move from work station to work station). Inspection requirements are determined to ensure adequate product quality, and health and safety considerations, have been achieved. How material will be delivered to the site, how the interim products will be delivered to their subsequent processes and waste disposal requirements to ensure safe disposal are also important issues. This procedure enables all the facilities, and their sizes, to be determined.

Next it is necessary to identify the relationships between each pair of facilities on the site. That is, if two facilities, for example two work stations, require an interim product to be passed from one to the other as the next stage of production, then they need to be close together. "Facilities" includes everything on the site—not only the work stations but also offices, maintenance, storage facilities and so on. It is ideal to quantify the relationships. Some measure of the need for the facilities to be proximate is required. This may be the volume of material (or number of people) which moves between each pair. If the relationship cannot be quantified, then a subjective measure is used—in effect a "consensus" that two facilities need to be close.

In some cases, the facilities should actually be apart. Elements such as gas storage or paint storage are potentially dangerous, and should be located at a distance from other activities.

Once the relationships have been determined, it is possible to optimise the layout against an objective. One which is favoured is minimum travel for materials. A measure such as tonne-metres may be used, and the layout which minimises the tonne-metres of movement may be selected. A relationship diagram is the most common approach (see Figure 30). Using an objective or subjective measure, the relationship between the facilities is determined. In the diagram, A, B, C, D, etc, are facilities, and the numbers represent how close they need to be. A subjective measure, where 10 represents a high dependency and 1 a low dependency, is shown.

Where volumes and sizes are known, the relationships can be quantified. The relationship is then expressed in terms of numbers of journeys which are made by interim products (or people or information) between the facilities. The same approach can be used to identify the best locations for services, such as electrical sub-stations, placing them close to major power users and minimising the cable runs which are required. The information can then be presented in the form of a network, which is the basis of a layout definition. The nodes represent the facilities and the arrows the number of journeys or volume of movement between the facilities.

Figures 31 and 32 show two shipyards, and give some indication of the development over time of layouts and technology.

	A	B	C	D	E	F	G
A	–	10	7	2	–	–	–
B		–	–	10	4	–	–
C			–	–	–	1	–
D				–	–	5	–
E					–	–	2
F						–	3
G							–

Figure 30. Relationship diagram showing interdependence between shipyard facilities.

Notional Tanker Facility. This is a classic layout for the third generation green-field shipyard (see Figure 33). The quay is available for deliveries as well as outfitting. The flow is from the stockyard to the block assembly shop, then to the

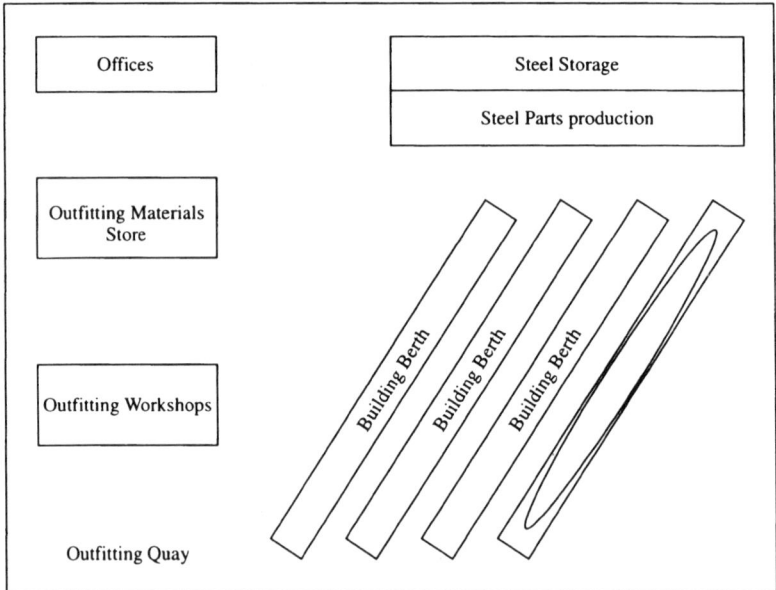

Figure 31. Pre-1950 layout—a direct descendant of wooden shipbuilding:
- *typically on a river bank;*
- *many berths to achieve high production levels;*
- *piece-by-piece construction of ships.*

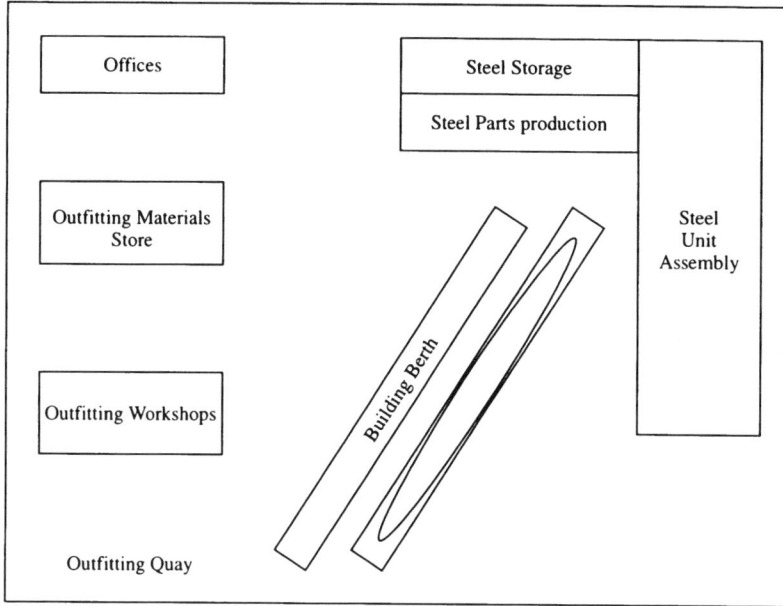

Figure 32.   1960s layout—developed from the older shipyard:
- *fewer building berths, with larger cranes;*
- *unit construction;*
- *still outfitting afloat.*

dock. The outfitting shops are located to serve the block shop (for early outfitting), the dock and the quay.

The largest fourth generation shipyards are Meyer Werft in Germany and Kvær-ner Masa, in Finland. Both can build 100,000 grt cruise vessels under cover. The large investment can be justified by the very high value products. Fourth, fifth and sixth generation developments have focused more on organisation and management than on facilities, to make the maximum use of investments by use of computer aided design and production, materials management and planning.

Other factors which need to be taken into account include the civil engineering aspects. The construction of a major shipyard is a massive civil engineering project. Of the total cost of a new yard, which for a VLCC builder at the end of the 20th century is several hundred million dollars, up to 70 per cent will be spent on the civil works. The lion's share of that will be for the building dock or docks. In addition, expenditure on service provision will be 15 per cent of the total, to provide all the electricity, water and gas supplies to the large site. However the ideal layout turns out, it will be modified by the need to locate docks and other major structures on rock or otherwise acceptable ground. The possible need for land reclamation will also be a factor.

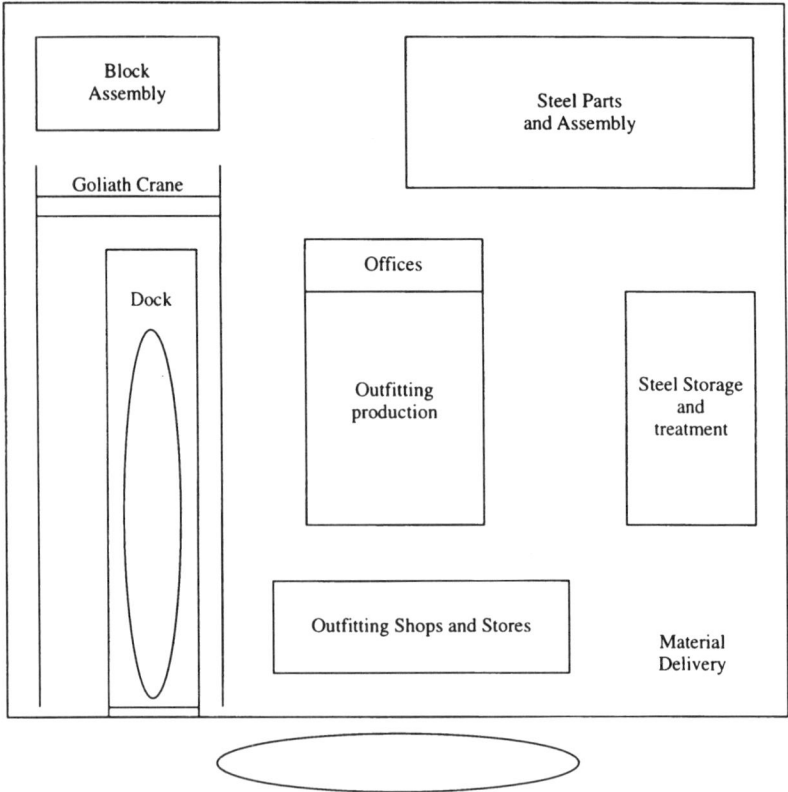

Figure 33.   1960s or 1970s layout—greenfield site:
- *designed for larger ships;*
- *large cranes and large units.*

The workshops are also an expensive item, in particular if a decision is taken partially or fully to cover the building dock. The buildings have to support the heavy, overhead travelling cranes. The layout may therefore be modified to allow several work stations to share a crane, which will then reduce both the cost of providing cranes and also the cost of the workshop buildings.

The final layout (Figure 34) is therefore a compromise between all the factors described. There are some principles to be applied, but in the end each shipyard layout is unique, because of the local factors which affect it.

There is one additional element to be considered. Although the need to determine a product mix for a new facility, from which the production requirements can be identified, has been emphasised, the reality for many shipyards is that the product mix will change.

While many shipyards continue to build standard types of ship, others find that the market they are serving changes over time. Either the demand for the ships decreases, or the price in the market makes production uneconomic, or an alternative

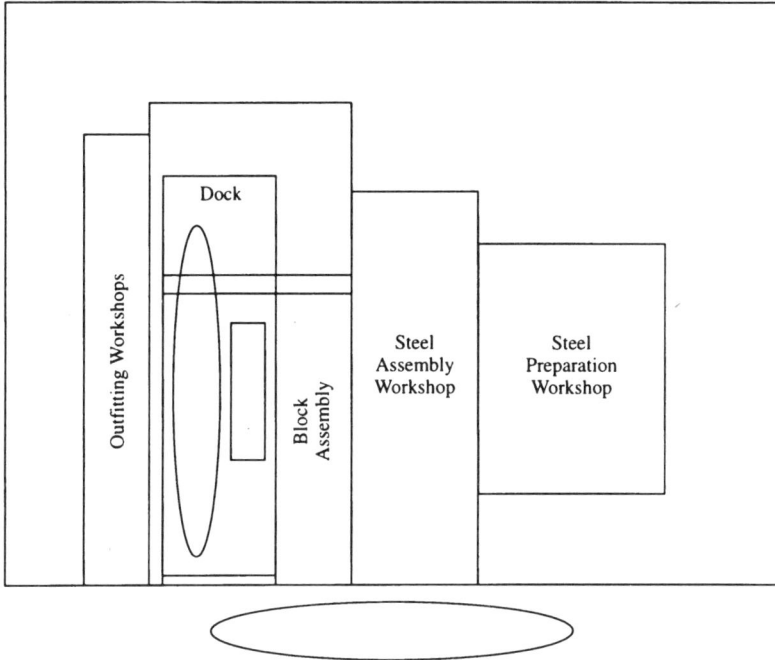

Figure 34.   1970s or 1980s layout—undercover construction:
  • *all facilities in a single building.*

product appears which is more attractive to produce. There is therefore some need for a shipyard layout to provide flexibility. Of course, flexibility in terms of the ability to produce a wider range of products may only be provided with potential loss of efficiency. Or it may be necessary to make an additional investment to change the production facilities to suit an alternative product. Perhaps the key feature is to provide space for expansion or change, and to ensure that the main, fixed facilities will not inhibit any, probably unpredictable, change.

CHAPTER 13

QUALITY ASSURANCE

THE NEED FOR QUALITY

There is a currently massive emphasis on quality in all its aspects, in both manufacturing and service industries. Not only the quality of the finished product, but also the quality of the processes which result in the product, is under consideration. Arguably, the shipbuilding business, whose products operate in an inherently dangerous environment, has always emphasised product quality. The development of classification societies in response to insurance and safety needs is evidence of this.

So quality was initially viewed as the quality of the finished product. It was evidenced by the ability of the ship to operate safely, carry cargoes and generally perform as expected. Unhappily, there have always been ships which can only be described as substandard, and at times there have been quite astonishing losses at sea which led to the development of attempts to manage the quality of the product. These were often enshrined in classification society rules, to determine strength and other critical characteristics, and in safety legislation, a mix of national government laws and international conventions. Most rules were developed in response to losses, perhaps the most notorious being the loss of the *Titanic*.

The other motivation in marine business has always been managing costs. At most times in history, making an adequate return on shipping has been difficult, whether through overcapacity or through the probability of loss of the ship. As a result, there has been a tension between the quality of the ship—at least in terms of safety—and cost. Most of the changes in ship design and regulation which arose from losses of ships have been resisted in some way by the shipowning community. Legislation, or rule changes, have been delayed, exemptions have been sought and rules have been watered down.

The requirements of the shipowner vary, but a low price is almost always a consideration, with quality being effectively fitness for purpose—which may have different interpretations. A bulk carrier has different fitness criteria from a passenger ship. In general, new ships have adequate quality, as completed products, but for the builder of ships that quality has to be achieved at a reasonable cost.

However, the move from a craft industry to newer forms of production has resulted in a need to consider process as well as product quality. The need to

245

minimise costs has led to an emphasis on avoiding unnecessary work. This has several causes; not paying attention to the integration of design and production has already been discussed, as has management of resources. Avoiding re-work—in simple terms doing jobs twice, because they are not correct the first time—is the reason for considering process quality. The benefit of this newer approach is that the quality which is required is achieved at a minimum cost of production, to the benefit of builder and owner.

As a starting point, it is useful to agree what is meant by quality. The word carries some overtones. There is in some views an implication of "high" quality, which implies expense. In these terms, a luxury motor car is intrinsically "better", or of higher quality, than a standard saloon car. But in the world of quality assurance, this is definitely not the case. Perhaps the most useful definition is that quality is determined by "fitness for purpose". That is to say, the product must be "good enough" for the customer's requirements. In these terms, the luxury model car is of appropriate quality if the customer is rich and wishes to make the statement that driving—or being driven in—such a car makes. But if the objective is only reliable personal transport at a reasonable cost, then the standard car is of perfectly accept-able quality. If a quality product is one which is acceptable to the customer, it must also be made at an acceptable cost to the producer. An acceptable cost is one which allows some profit margin within the price available in the current market-place. So achieving quality is about managing production as well as product quality, hence the emphasis on process quality. There are a number of aspects of quality which need to be considered.

Product quality

This is the end result of the production process. Whatever else is involved, the product which is delivered to the customer must meet the fitness for purpose criteria which are appropriate. These criteria can be defined as, first, a suitable specification, i.e. the product development and design process must result in a product specifica-tion which, if fulfilled, will meet all the requirements that the customer sets. Then, conformity to specification, i.e., there must be an adequate production process, which is so arranged and managed that the end-result is a product which does indeed conform to the original specification determined by the design process. Further, the production process must ensure that this is achieved at an acceptable cost, which leads to a mutually acceptable price.

Consistency is another attribute within the production process. That is, the parts and assemblies from which the final product is constructed must be of consistent quality, and, particularly in the case of shipbuilding, of consistent dimensional accuracy. This has been shown to be a major factor in achieving cost-effective production. That this is not self-evident may be a surprise, but first generation, craft-based industry did not regard this as a necessary feature of its production system. This was because of the tolerant processes and the lifting of many dimensions from the ship itself. The need has steadily grown as the business of building ships has progressed to the current, technologically advanced, stage.

The definition of quality can include many attributes of the final product, in terms of its design and specification and the successful achievement of these through the production system. The attributes include:

functionality: whether the final product meets the required operational requirements—put simply, does it work?

reliability: will it operate for acceptably long periods with no more than routine, and minimal maintenance—or will it keep working without breaking down?

durability: will it have a sufficiently long life to pay back its initial investment, retain a resale value and perhaps be convertible for another function later on—will it last?

safety is always important: will the product not only work, but do so without creating hazards, whether to users, operators, others or the environment?

æsthetics may be a feature in some trades, particularly passenger vessels of different types, where appearance may be an important element in attracting customers.

Total quality management (TQM)

The term "quality" has a number of meanings in the current climate. Under the banner of TQM, quality is taken to mean the entire process of specifying, designing, making and delivering a product. So in effect it includes all aspects of the shipbuilding business, to ensure that the ship will be of adequate materials, will be fitted with the most suitable equipment, will have the necessary systems designed to ensure safety and efficiency in operation. Most of these product attributes are ensured by the regulatory systems within which a ship is constructed, notably the classification society rules; and process design—put simply, the ability of the production and business processes of the shipbuilder to meet the design requirements, so that the completed ship conforms to the design requirements. Again, historically this has been the province of the classification society and other regulators. More recently, the need to meet the product quality requirements in the most economical way has been paramount, and this has led to the use of techniques to control the processes themselves, in addition to ensuring, through inspection, that the product is fit for its purpose.

Materials have been specified as suitable for their purpose, but again a testing regime is needed to ensure that they conform. The quality assurance systems are also used to ensure that the production processes for materials are so organised that the quality is guaranteed. The TQM approach also considers employees. Indeed there is a major emphasis on the people, since the human element is a critical factor in ensuring quality. If the employee is content to allow sub-standard materials or interim products to be sent to the next stage of production, then re-work is more or less guaranteed, with all the implications that has for cost and schedule adherence.

The ability of any inspection system to detect large numbers of defects, let alone avoid them, is minimal.

On the other hand, if the employees are given suitable training and motivation, and are properly organised, then they can be enlisted to assist in maintaining quality, multiplying the ability of the organisation to avoid mistakes. The management of the company is responsible for the quality of operations. This includes the planning and scheduling of work, the safe storage and management of materials, and all other operations.

Standards

One mechanism which is used to manage quality is the use of standards. These may be product standards, where the consistency of the output is defined. They may be process standards, where a consistent method is applied to some production process, to ensure quality of the output. The use of standards for processes implies that there will be written procedures, and this is the basis of quality certification. Once standards are in place and are used, there is a consistent approach to production which should go a long way towards ensuring that the products which are made are also consistently good.

Product standards imply using the same items in different situations. This may not immediately appear to be possible, but in many areas different ship types have similar requirements. At the detail level, structural arrangements, outfit items and others can be standardised. This simplifies the production, allowing the standard items to be produced on a routine basis for use when required. While there is a limit to the application of standards, many shipbuilders do not take enough advantage of them.

The use of product and process standards also creates opportunities to develop specialised work methods, which reinforces the product qualilty and also reduces production costs.

Inspection

At some stage it is necessary to inspect the processes and products of shipbuilding to ensure that they are of appropriate quality. Inspection is a relatively expensive procedure, and does not add any value to the product being inspected. It merely confirms that the product is, or is not, fit for its purpose. As will be seen, more than inspection is required if adequate quality is to be achieved at a low cost. Nevertheless, inspection is required at different stages of production, even if quality assurance systems are in place. The shipowner will want to assure himself that the ship will meet his requirements and, however high his confidence in the shipbuilder, he will inspect. Similarly, the shipbuilder will need to carry out some inspection of items from his suppliers. And this will continue down the supply chain for all the equipment which the ship requires.

Inspection is really a check that the procedures have actually been carried out correctly. In a quality assured situation, all the procedures should result in all products reaching the correct standard. But things can go wrong, from inadvertent errors which the procedures do not pick up to, in the worst situation, failure to apply the procedures at all. To some extent the level of inspection is a reflection of the trust the customer has in the ability of the supplier. Different degrees of inspection are appropriate in different circumstances, and it is useful to ask what is appropriate for different products and stages. Inspection may be of a sample of interim products, or in other circumstances may be for all interim products.

For completed ships, there are quay and then sea trials. Even the umpteenth ship of a standard series built in the same shipyard will be inspected and trials carried out to ensure conformity to specification.

One of the major expenditures on any ship is the main engine. This is supplied to the shipbuilder by a specialist engine builder, so the shipbuilder, who has ultimate responsibility for the ship meeting its specification, will need to inspect. This will take the form of trials of the engine at the manufacturer's works, so that its operation has been checked before it arrives at the shipyard. Once it does arrive, all the builder wishes to do is install it in the ship to maintain the building schedule.

Smaller items of equipment, such as winches, may not be inspected. A standard item, bought from a reputable manufacturer, can be expected to operate satisfactorily. And, as the value of bought-in items reduces and their number increases, there is a point at which inspection of everything becomes impossible. Over-zealous inspection requirements can easily become a production bottleneck. So smaller and less critical items, which can be replaced quickly if a problem does occur, will not be inspected. A sample may be, but not every item. Inspection may be visual, simply to check that the item which arrives at the shipyard is what was ordered, and appears to be intact, with undamaged packaging. One or more of a batch of items may be reviewed more carefully, and subjected to some testing.

For items produced in the shipyard in large quantities, for example pipe pieces, the level of inspection and testing will also vary. Pipes for high pressure systems and those which are critical for safety will be routinely pressure tested. A small sample may have any welds checked, using non-destructive methods.

Much inspection will be built into the production processes as part of the quality procedures. The workforce will check its products for dimensional accuracy and other attributes, and if the process is operating properly this will avoid products which are non-conforming. In many cases, this can remove the need for routine inspection and a sampling regime will be adequate. For aspects of production, such as butt welds, which are measured in kilometres on a large ship, complete inspection is not feasible. On the other hand, without some inspection, flaws may occur and be undetected, despite the use of carefully designed and managed quality procedures. In this case a sample of the welds will be inspected, using non-destructive testing. The selection will be representative, with more emphasis on areas of the structure which are known to endure greater stresses. Some destructive testing of samples made using the production processes may also be tested. Provided the samples are satisfactory, the bulk of the welds will be accepted as also satisfactory. There are exceptions to the above. Where safety is involved, or where dangerous processes are involved, a higher rate of inspection will be instituted.

Process stability

In order to be reasonably certain of consistent outputs from a process, the process itself must be stable. In a marine production environment, stability is reached by:

— making similar products;
— using the same work station;
— using the same people;
— using the same procedures;
— using the same equipment and processes;
— monitoring: inputs, the process, outputs.

Stability can be measured. The outputs from a process (products and interim products) can be monitored for correct characteristics: dimensions, strength, shape, finish, pressure, etc. The outputs generally follow a normal distribution—if the process is stable. Both the range and the mean are important.

Quality control

There are a number of ways of reviewing the quality of an operation. This is generally referred to as quality control. Acceptance sampling is concerned with reviewing the acceptability of the inputs to and outputs from a process. In contrast, process control is about managing the process to ensure that acceptable inputs and outputs will be obtained. The two basic techniques of quality control are acceptance sampling and control charts.

Acceptance sampling is the oldest technique. At its simplest, acceptance sampling is carried out for all products. For example, if on trials the ship does not reach required speed then it may be rejected. 100 per cent sampling is not usual practice, except for large made-to-order products and critical items (e.g. for safety, or for military use). In such cases, failure of an inspected item results in rejection, but other items from the batch may be acceptable. 100 per cent inspection is typically not feasible or economic. Usually a sample of a batch of products is tested. There is therefore a probability that batches with defective items will be accepted. The probability can be calculated using a standard formula: for a small sample from a large batch, using the actual number of defective items the probability of finding different numbers of defectives can be calculated. The relative size of the sample from the batch is important. For large samples, a simplified calculation and standard charts can be used. The results of acceptance sampling are used to construct a curve. The operating characteristic curve plots the probability of accepting batches with varying numbers of defective items.

Managing quality

For industrial products, tolerances are set within which small deviations are acceptable. Acceptance sampling will detect out-of-tolerance items, which will not be accepted. Although acceptance sampling will avoid either defective inputs to a process or defective products reaching a customer, they cannot assist in avoiding production of defectives in the first place. In particular for large, made-to-order products, out-of-tolerance items can disrupt production schedules.

Control charts provide a means of advance warning that problems are about to occur. This creates an opportunity to take corrective action. Charts can be applied to any process, e.g. cutting, forming, marking and assembly. However well designed, a process will have outputs with small, random variations and occasional, unusual variations. Unusual variations point to a specific (fixable) problem. Small random variations can be described in terms of probabilities.

In setting up a control chart, six steps are normally identified:

1 decide what characteristics are to be used for control purposes, for example key dimensions;
2 conduct a pilot study to establish mean and standard deviation of the chosen characteristics;
3 design the control charts using the pilot study results;
4 check the control limits for economic feasibility and acceptability in production (that they meet any tolerance requirements);
5 sample the process and plot results;
6 investigate any deviations.

Then, and most importantly, take action to correct any deviations that may be found.

Types of control charts

Control Charts can be used to manage various aspects of process outputs:

Variables, e.g. length, flatness;
Attributes, e.g. percentage defective items, number of defective items;
Capability, i.e. whether outputs are likely to meet tolerance requirements.

The control chart is used to plot the measures taken of actual production outputs against those which were planned. The vertical scale on the chart shows the dimension (or other measurable output), with the required value as the mean of the measured distribution. Unavoidable small variations in the process output result in a distribution of actual values between the lines, which represent the number of standard deviations from the mean. In effect, all the values for a process which is under control and stable will fall within the three standard deviations above or below the mean.

QUALITY ASSURANCE

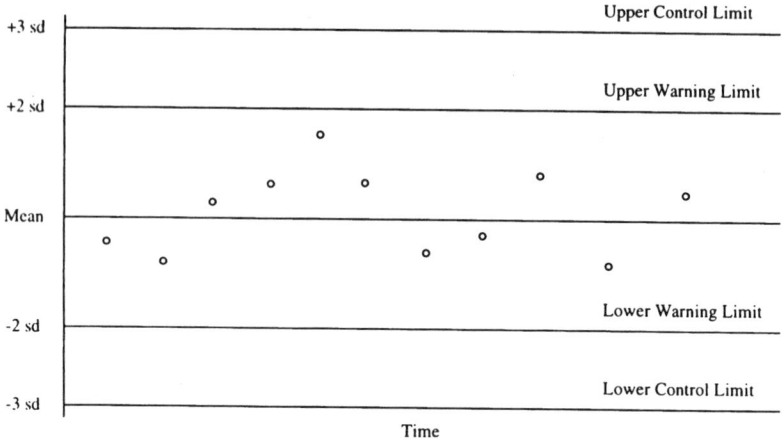

Figure 35. The structure of a control chart. A process in control

Provided the tolerances which the process is required to achieve are greater than the process deviations, all the outputs will be acceptable for production purposes. The three standard deviation line is the action limit, and if the outputs approach this value, something must be done to correct the process. The two standard deviation line is the warning limit, and action may be required if the values reach this limit.

Provided the values remain within the warning limits, the process is satisfactory.

If, on the other hand, the outputs measured over time show any erratic behaviour, such as a trend moving steadily towards the limits, or wide fluctuations within the limits, the process may be going out of control. This could be due to some sort of machine wear, or a gradual deterioration of the process. Identifying the out of

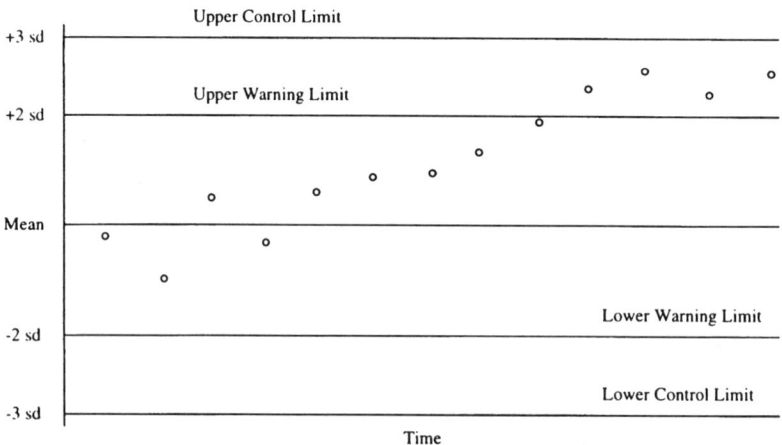

Figure 36. A process going out of control

control process is a trigger for corrective action. In the same way as planning and monitoring are used for managing resources and time, quality assurance is a means of anticipating and then avoiding problems which could disrupt production.

There are more sophisticated methods, which can be used, for example, to manage the sequence of assembly through various stages from piece part to block.

CHAPTER 14

THE FUTURE DEVELOPMENT OF THE INDUSTRY

Forecasting is a dangerous occupation, and since the initial chapter of this book largely dealt with the limited success of market forecasting, this brief look at the future is not going to try and predict very much. Rather, the idea is to try to place such forecasting into a historical context. There has been a lot of change in the business of shipbuilding over many centuries. It was arguably the first global industry, has always been one of international competition and was the first to suffer, if not identify, many of the problems that a global industry must overcome.

In reaching its current status, shipbuilding has achieved some remarkable transitions. Compared to the automotive industry, held up by many as a twentieth century paradigm for global industry and performance, or the aerospace industry, a paradigm for technology, shipbuilding has moved further, if not faster. Any automobile had its basic form defined by the replacement of the horses on a four-wheeled carriage by a motor. It is now, more or less, reliable and far more comfortable, fast and efficient. Any aircraft was basically defined by the Wright brothers, or perhaps more reasonably Professor Langley. It now has a jet, rather than piston, engine, and again, it is far more efficient, safe and comfortable. The materials in both cases have moved from wood and fabric, to metal, to some use of composites.

Ships in the same period have also changed in materials, more radically in form with the development of both submarines and surface effect vessels. Power has changed from sail, still common at the start of the century, to steam reciprocating, steam turbine and then diesel, with electric and other power sources also in use. All the other attributes associated with other industries have also changed as radically. The productivity of the shipbuilding business has also changed dramatically.

So what of the future? The automobile will continue to develop, along the same path as previously, but will perform the same basic, and quite limited, function within the confines of the road systems of the world. The aircraft will develop, although the commercial future is probably already mapped out for 25 years with existing players. As with the automobile, improvements rather than radical new forms will be expected. Shipbuilding looks much more exciting. This may be a source of distress rather than comfort for many engaged in the business, but the last few years of the century have seen some radical changes in ships, in speed, form and size. The industry has managed these through some major upheavals and changes

255

in its own structure. In all these cases, the new technologies which have under-pinned the changes, allied to the changes in economic circumstances, can be traced from inception to implementation. The timescale of change, in shipbuilding as in many other industries, including those which are popularly regarded as radical, is relatively slow compared to the development of available technology. The future should hold some more technological changes which will require more reorganisation of shipbuilding. But most of the knowledge is already in place, and needs refining for application. The potential is enormous. How quickly that potential will be realised and what changes may occur on the way belong in the dangerous realms of forecasting. But the future is there to be seized.

NEW PRODUCTS

The difficulty of forecasting in general, and of market forecasting in particular, has been discussed, and to attempt to do so for the changes in ship products which may be expected is not the intention here. There are a number of trends, which may reasonably be expected to continue. Fast ferries are an important and growing niche market, although not one which will seriously impact on mainstream shipbuilders, particularly those building the larger ships. An interesting question is whether high-speed cargo ships will follow. Bear in mind that the various means of achieving high speed—hydrofoils, surface effects, multi-hulls—and the means to power them have been available for some 20 to 30 years.

There are widely differing views on the subject. Perhaps the most commonly expressed is that high speed ships have no natural market. In this view, high value and perishable cargoes will increasingly be air-freighted, and the lower value cargoes do not justify any increase in speed, especially where this is achieved at high fuel cost. Therefore, the high speed ships will continue to make relatively modest inroads into passenger and car ferry routes. This view, pessimistic from the point of potential builders of such ships, places high speed ships alongside hydro-foils and surface effect ships. That is, they can fill a few selective niches, where the combination of routes and trade is appropriate, and they have some other applications, typically military. Another analogy would be the Concorde supersonic aero-plane, which has been technically outstanding, but commercially unsuccessful.

The alternative view is that these high speed vessels have a significant part to play in the future, opening up potential for new trade patterns. By providing the capa-bility for a different pattern of trade, the latent needs of producer and consumer can be met, and it then only needs an entrepreneur to see the potential and set up the appropriate cargo service. In considering this view, it is worth looking at some of the arguments against large, high speed vessels—for example, that their fuel demands are so much that the usable payload is tiny. This has uncanny echoes of the arguments used against the first steamships in the 1800s, when the size of the coal bunkers would surely make any cargo capacity trivial.

The failure to be a commercial success in the early years of any technology is nothing new. Concorde has already been mentioned, but Brunel's *Great Eastern* was also a financial disaster. On the other hand, 40 years after the *Great Eastern* first sailed, its successors, building on experience and using improved technology, were the new standard. The opportunity to travel relatively quickly and safely across the oceans then corresponded with a wave of immigration to the United States of America. Once the people had moved, trade grew and cargo ships followed.

Of course, we have so much more capable analysis methods than at the turn of the century, both for technical and commercial evaluations, so that any new idea can be tested. Therefore the more radical arguments used against progress in the nineteenth century can be avoided. (These included the contention that metal ships could not float, since wood is generally lighter than water, but metal is heavier!) And also, of course, the failure of any new idea can be anticipated in terms which do not allow for changes in conventional patterns of behaviour.

If the period from invention to demonstration to practical, routine, commercial application of many technologies is reviewed, then a period of 30 or 40 years seems to be the norm. Even the intervention of military needs and the often-expressed view that things change more quickly than used to be the case do not change this. The jet engine took 25 years from invention to acceptance in commercial air travel, and longer to become the norm. So did the steam engine, in a not much longer timescale, in the eighteenth century. In both cases, the application of the technology to routine commercial use required time for improvement and the identification of a new demand—and, of course, a major investment in new ships and aircraft. All of which is a preamble to the suggestion—no more, since this book is not, as explained, in the prediction business—that the time for more high speed ships may be approaching.

The changes in the products of the shipbuilding business are not going to be in absolute size, since the VLCC and its bulk carrying cousins have established the upper limits. Container ships have also grown dramatically in size, for the same reasons of economy of scale. Such economies will not apply in the same way to more specialised ships. This may be an indirect prediction that the various mega-cruise ships and mobile, offshore tax-havens that have been proposed will never be seen. In the light of the development of ships in the nineteenth and twentieth centuries, that may be unwise. The potential is for development of faster ships, of more diverse hull forms and arrangements, of larger ships within the current upper limits, of submarines and of new forms of leisure use.

To return to the safety of not predicting the future, it is perhaps worth simply expecting changes, and looking for them, in ideas that appeared interesting but impractical, or simply not commercially viable, 10 or 20 years ago.

NEW MATERIALS

Allied to the development of new, at least radically new, products is the development of new materials from which they can be made. Until timber was used for shipbuilding, or where it was unavailable, size was drastically limited. The general use of timber for many hundreds of years effectively limited ships to a length of around 70 metres, since longitudinal strength could not be made sufficient for any greater length. Once iron, then steel, became available, the development of larger, longer ships was potentially feasible although, with the exception of the *Great Eastern*, it took many years for that potential to be realised. Part of the change from wood to iron was driven by the sheer lack of trees, with large areas of European woodland having disappeared to build ships.

The benefits of steel have made it the material for shipbuilding in the twentieth century, with some use of aluminium and some higher tensile steels for larger ships. The material has improved in its properties, and in its quality and consistency, so that it is a far superior product at the end of the century than it was at the beginning. Given the properties of steel, its ready availability and low cost, why even consider alternatives?

Once again, using a methodical, cost-benefit approach, the need to change at all appears very limited. Only at the smaller end of the shipbuilding market, and effectively into boat building, for the most part, is significant change seen. Fibre-reinforced plastics have become the norm for small, primarily pleasure boats. A few larger vessels, a good example being mine countermeasures vessels (MCMVs), have been built, because the operational requirements of the ships made it the most suitable material. This outweighed technical difficulties in construction and cost.

Aluminium has been used for high speed vessels, where weight saving is a prime requirement, because of small displacements and the need to minimise power requirements. The use was for relatively small multi-hulls and others, until the HSS 1500 high speed ferries entered service. These vessels are significantly larger than any other previously constructed. That there have been problems is undeniable, but the examples of the *Great Britain* and *Great Eastern* remain. Changes in the generality of ships have always been preceded by some pioneering step change. Often this has not been immediately successful, and sometimes the follow up has been delayed, but if the concept is basically sound the follow up has occurred.

Whether aluminium is the most appropriate material is another matter. The aircraft industry has always had weight-saving as an absolute priority. As a result, once aircraft progressed beyond wood and fabric, aluminium was selected as the appropriate metal. However, in the search for improved performance, in the form of higher speeds and payloads, alternatives have been developed. Fibre-reinforced composites, such as carbon fibres, are an example. As the shipbuilding industry begins to look at larger high speed vessels and seeks similar performance improvements to the aircraft industry, attention is turning to such materials.

Novel materials tend to be of higher cost than conventional metals, but that may only be a function of volume and methods of production. Of course, no large scale change can be expected for a long time. Novel materials, if they are appropriate, will only be applied cautiously in the first instance. They will also require new ship production techniques to allow novel ship types to be built at acceptable costs. A wholesale changeover will not occur, because too much is invested in existing facilities, and the new ideas will need to be proven on smaller vessels before they are adopted.

Even if a material, with all the required strength and weight properties and a comparable cost, is identified, the logistics of production will dictate a lengthy timescale for its general introduction. However, as in the case of the novel products, the search for the next developments in the future should be directed to the immediate past. The seeds have already been sown.

THE EXTERNAL ENVIRONMENT

As in the discussion of the existing environment of the industry, the world within which the business of shipbuilding will have to operate in the future can be usefully looked at as four domains. These are economic, political, social and techno-logical.

The market for new ships lies primarily in the economic domain, although distorted by elements from the political domain as well. As has been identified earlier, any form of forecast of the future of the industry is a difficult operation. Past forecasts, in particular of the market for new ships, have proved either optimistic or pessimistic. Usually the error has been in overoptimism, as a justification for development, although a few pessimistic forecasts can be found which correct earlier optimism.

Until the balance of supply and demand is restored, there is no way in which the market can recover. The restoration of balance has been forecast for the last 25 years, but has not happened. Instead, support has been given to maintain shipyards, and indirectly to continue the production of ships which the shipping industry does not need. Within the overall pessimistic picture, there are a few niches where new ship types, meeting new trade requirements, can be built profitably. In most cases, the relative ease of technology transfer within the industry has ensured that any new market niche rapidly reaches saturation, as more and more shipbuilders enter the market. That many of the new entrants soon fail is of no comfort to the industry, because their intervention serves to reduce prices, and thus stifle new investment and development.

So although there are likely to be opportunities for radical, and less radical, new ship types, making any money out of their production will continue to be a tough proposition. This is due to the political (perhaps with a small rather than a large "p") influence on the market. The shipbuilding business is a model for a market which is hopelessly distorted by intervention, based primarily on political imperatives. The putative agreement, through the medium of the OECD, to eliminate subsidies in the mid–1990s stalled through the attitude of the US major builders—the very group who began the process by sharp attacks on unfair subsidies at the beginning of the 1990s.

There remains a strong desire on the part of most governments to see the end of subsidies, although it is recognised that other governments should really move first to avoid shipyards going out of business. How this situation will develop is again in the realms of forecasting, or even crystal ball gazing. The position at the time of writing is that the European Union has decided to end its 9 per cent subsidy ceiling on 31 December 2000. This will be accompanied by alternative forms of support in the short term, to address the restructuring of the industry and to ensure that it enters the new era in competitive shape. This will include increased support for some specific regions which depend on the shipbuilding industry, and an emphasis on research and development for both products and processes.

The European Union will also address the question of unfair pricing from other parts of the world. With the exception of the USA, which appears to be partly withdrawing from the commercial shipbuilding industry it only re-joined in the mid–1990s, other major shipbuilders have already agreed to abandon subsidies. The South Korean position is very complex, and how it will develop is again something not to be forecast here. What is apparent is that the development of the shipbuilding business in South Korea was built on subsidies in various forms, which is no surprise to anyone else engaged in ship construction. However, the government had previously agreed to stop subsidies, and may maintain that position. Japan is also formally opposed to subsidies, though it has made a lot of use of the research and development route in the past.

An optimistic view can be taken, but with the historical experience (which it will be remembered goes back at least to fourteenth century Venice), and the prospect of China as an increasingly serious competitor, some forms of support may be expected to continue.

Another economic issue is that of ownership structure. Part of the success, and perhaps subsequent problems, of South Korea lay in the large conglomerates —"chaebols"—which own(ed) much of the country's burgeoning industry. Japan also has its industry contained largely within the major industrial corporations. This gives a measure of control of the industry supply chain, allowing some control of transfer pricing within the conglomerates. It also gives financial support to each sector within the conglomerate. Many other industries around the world are government-owned or controlled, which is an indicator of probable support.

In contrast, most European shipbuilders have been relatively small, often single-shipyard, companies. This was identified as a source of weakness in a number of reports in the United Kingdom as far back as the 1960s with the Commission of Enquiry under the chairmanship of Lord Geddes. This and subsequent reports have all promoted the need for amalgamations to assist the process of making the industry more competitive. There have been signs of this process taking place, notably in the development of the Kværner Group (and in the short-lived Bremer Vulkan Group). Vertical integration between shipowners and builders has also been promoted.

The parallel history of both automobiles and aerospace has been of rapid amalgamations of companies, leading to a few dominant, internationally operating companies. In the case of aerospace, this has effectively left Boeing and Airbus Industrie as the two major players for large jets. Arguably, the shipbuilding industry has a similar situation in Japan and South Korea, at national rather than company level.

What is interesting is that the shipbuilding predominance of those two nations was preceded by Japan alone, then by the United Kingdom, and before that the United States of America. If the types of ships being constructed are considered, then it is apparent that European builders are much stronger in the specialist vessels, in several sectors showing almost total market domination. The Far Eastern builders are dominant in oil tankers and bulk ships. The historical parallels would suggest a continuing divergence of commodity and specialist sectors, with a new dominator (China being the prime candidate) in the bulk sector.

The sociological domain, as has been discussed earlier, is apparent primarily in the skills shortages which many parts of the shipbuilding business, worldwide, are experiencing. Reports from the United Kingdom, elsewhere in Europe, the USA and Japan all carry the same basic message: that the business of shipbuilding is seen as old-fashioned, unattractive, dirty and possibly dangerous. The average age of shipyard workers in many cases is over 40 years, and there is an urgent need for recruitment and training of new people, coupled with an increase in automation. This poses perhaps the greatest challenge to the business in those countries which wish to remain engaged in it. There are some encouraging signs, but much remains to be done in improving the image of the industry, so that it becomes an attractive proposition for the 21st century.

THE NEED FOR TECHNOLOGICAL CHANGE

The industry has continued to develop over the last 20 years, despite the problems of over-supply which have characterised the period. The idea of generations of shipbuilding technology has been introduced previously, with each generation exhibiting some significant change over the previous one, in terms of the technology employed. Both "hard" technology—plant and equipment—and what can be termed "soft" technology—dealing with people, organisation and operating systems —have been considered.

The point has also been made that the stage of development of any individual shipyard is as much dependent on its economic position as any technology issues. The most appropriate stage of development, or the level of technology exhibited, is that which produces the lowest production costs. There is another issue, which is that of managing change. As labour costs rise, which is typically symptomatic of developing countries as they industrialise, there is a need to move to newer technology, substituting more advanced equipment for labour. The technology chosen must be upgradeable. In effect the shipyard has to be able to forecast its likely future environment.

Independently of this, the leading shipbuilders continue to develop new technologies. These may be simply improvements to processes, substituting existing equipment or methods with better ones. Examples are the changes from manual lofting of dimensions at full scale to one tenth scale (saving costs), to tape driven, numerical controlled cutting machines (improving accuracy), to direct control from a computer-aided design system.

In parallel, the cutting process has improved, with changes in the cutting gases, development of plasma cutting (increasing speed and reducing distortion) and, currently, the slow introduction of laser cutting (giving even better accuracy with minimum distortion).

Most of the improvements are evolutionary, with occasional revolutionary developments. Each change in one element of the technology of shipbuilding is likely to have consequential effects in others. The ability to produce accurately cut piece parts, on a reliable and consistent basis, has important implications for downstream processes. Accurate parts will simplify assembly, eliminating much re-work. In turn this will allow the assembly process to be improved, with more confidence in the piece parts.

The development of new technologies is led by those shipyards which have the highest production, and particularly labour, costs, and also by those shipyards which have access to money for the research, whether from a parent organisation or a government. Some builders also make alliances with equipment suppliers to develop new processes, from which they can gain the initial advantage.

Therefore in determining what is an appropriate level of technology, attention has to be paid to current and future overall developments which take competitors to new levels of efficiency. This is in addition to the need to manage the balance between capital and labour costs.

CURRENT TECHNOLOGY

The fifth generation of technology, which is approximately where leading shipyards have reached, can be characterised by a small number of significant factors. These build on earlier developments, so may not always be accessible to shipyards at an earlier stage of development, hence the need to monitor progress and try to ensure that new advances can be adopted. The key factors of the technology are that most of the processes are carried out under cover. For smaller ships, this often means a covered "ship factory", although there are some spectacular examples of large, covered shipyards. Meyer Werft in Papenburg, Germany, is one such. Where a completely covered facility is prohibited by size of product or lack of available finance, the protection from the environment is taken to as late a stage of production as possible. Typical is the large, new block shop at the Kværner Govan shipyard. The ships are built from relatively large blocks. The actual size will vary, according to ship size, but the basic rule is that there is substantial completion of the structural work, particularly welding, prior to erection of the block into the ship. The block is of sufficient size to include a significant proportion of outfitting and is painted.

Outfitting is carried out in parallel with the structure. Assemblies of outfitting items, with supporting structure, are built at the same time as their structural equivalents. These outfit assemblies may then be incorporated into the blocks prior to erection, or may be installed separately in the ship.

There is an integrated planning system that co-ordinates all activities. This includes all design processes, purchasing and material control. The planning is centralised, in the sense that all processes are operating to schedules dictated by a master plan. At the same time, the planning at department, workshop or project level is de-centralised, so the best local solutions can be found to maintain the overall schedule. There is an effective system of quality assurance. This subject has been discussed in some detail, but one or two key points are worth reiterating here. First, there must be more than mere compliance with ISO 9000 requirements. It is perfectly possible to achieve quality accreditation, and to comply with appropriate procedures, but not have these effective in improving performance or even product quality. Secondly, the quality system must be contributing directly to improvements in performance, particularly in reducing re-work by ensuring more accurate components and assemblies.

NEW TECHNOLOGIES AND PROCESSES

Having identified some of the key characteristics of current, broadly fifth generation, technology, attention can be turned to what the future holds. Some of the new developments can be more readily identified, since the research has already been done, and some of the relevant new processes are emerging. Once again, there is a mix of radical change and slow evolution. And, as before, the leading producers in terms of efficiency and the highest cost producers (often the same) are leading the development process.

The sixth generation of shipyards which is beginning to emerge builds, as have previous generations, on the past, as well as adapting to changes in products and the operating environment. Many past changes have been hailed as the "new technology" which would revolutionise the business. Most of these have eventually been absorbed, and are now seen as routine, only used when appropriate.

The new technologies which will characterise the shipbuilding industry in a sixth generation are still being developed and introduced into production, but some of the key features can be identified. These key features of the future technology which will define the next generation include:

— undercover construction;
— large, fully outfitted and coated blocks;
— flexible automation;
— integrated CAD and material management;
— integrated planning and scheduling;
— simulation of proposed production to evaluate schedules;
— advanced cutting and welding processes (lasers, electron beam);
— automated materials handling;

   — novel structural arrangements, benefiting from low distortion metal cutting
   or new materials.

Undercover construction is rapidly becoming the normal practice for all but the
largest ships—if not complete cover, then at least sufficient to produce the large
blocks (relative to ship size) which are also steadily becoming the normal practice.
The cost of undercover working is offset by improved working conditions, attractive
to the labour force. These in turn give uninterrupted working and major productivity
gains. The spread of undercover working, with implied high investment costs, will
also hasten the development of ownership changes.

Earlier generations of shipyards led to largely complete ships being launched or
floated out of building docks. The current trend is to large outfitting blocks,
completely painted and ready except for the final welding. Again, this is not new for
some ships, notably large, standard types, but is increasingly the standard practice
for one-off and special types.

Flexible automation has arrived, but its application has not yet become wide-
spread. The introduction of automation has been promised for many years, but the
scale and complexity of ship construction have inhibited its use. Various forms of
automation do already exist, however; and there is indeed no universal definition of
automation. One alternative is "the carrying out of a process without human
intervention". This begs the questions:

   — When does the process start and finish?
   — What human intervention is permissible?
   — How can the process equipment be adapted?

In the past, relatively simple devices, with limited autonomy, have been described
as automatic. The dream has been to have some form of robot which could find,
accurately position, set up and perform some task with no operator intervening. This
is still utopian, but a pragmatic application of automated devices in different forms,
specialised for a limited range of tasks, is a reality. Most are finding applications for
welding and painting, which are repetitive and uncomfortable tasks for human
operators. The use of automation, including anything up to the degree of sophistication of a true robot, has a number of motivations. These are primarily to overcome
shortages of suitably skilled labour, whether due to absolute shortages of people or
shortages of skills, as mentioned, due to the poor image of the marine industry. Their
use is and will be to carry out tasks in poor working conditions. There is also a
desire to improve productivity, so that overall production costs can be reduced.
Therefore, some form of cost-benefit analysis is essential. This is true for the most
complex type of robot, a simpler automated device or indeed absolutely any other
item of equipment. There may be a justification for automation as a pilot project, to
develop a new type of equipment or to extend its use into a new application, but
mainstream use will demand that the cost is justified by the productivity gains.

One of the major themes of the new generation will be integration. This is
primarily in the "soft" areas of the business. Although many shipyard engineers are

excited by "shiny, new hardware", most of the productivity, and hence cost gains, will be made by improving the flow of information around, and indeed beyond, the shipyards.

Computer-aided design is finally coming of age. The promises in the early days of productivity gains in drawing offices, through the use of "electronic drawing boards", were largely unrealised. As in the case of other technologies, there has been a time lag between the technological breakthrough and trial implementation, and the emergence of a commercially viable, fully operational technology. It might seem wholly inappropriate to compare computer-aided design with the marine steam engine, or even the large, high speed ferry. However, the reality of this, and most uses of computing, is that it takes a long time for a practical, easily operated, commercially justifiable product to arrive, in exactly the same way as the other technologies took, and are taking, time to become acceptable.

The theme, though, is integration, and this is where the benefits of the computer will be seen. The ability to model, consistently at all stages, from preliminary design to a fully developed product is part of the benefit. What this allows is the abstraction of information at each stage of development, to support the procurement of materials and equipment. As the supply chain of the shipyard increases in importance, the ability to manage that chain, accounting for most of the value of the ship, also increases in importance. The opportunity is being held out for integration of the supplier with the shipyard, moving on from confrontational, contract-based relationships to a form of "virtual shipyard".

The theme of integration is also apparent in the development of the internal processes of the shipyard. The ability to visualise the complete ship, or any subset of its parts, allows the full impact of the work breakdown approach to be realised. All aspects of the operations can now (almost) be scheduled so that every department, including any that are external—part of the supply chain—can integrate its operations with the others. Thus, all the planning of the ship production process can be fully integrated, and all the levels of planning, from the top, corporate level down to the scheduling of an individual workstation, can be linked.

The total integration of all the processes implies a massive interdependence, and the point has been made in this book and elsewhere that the shipbuilding business is very unforgiving. That is, the failure of any or all the numerous parts which go to make up a ship is a problem. If any item is not delivered, is the wrong specification, is the wrong size, fails to work or otherwise does not perform its allotted function, then the ship is not complete and cannot be delivered. Relying on the integrating capabilities of computer-aided engineering to manage all the processes to deliver, especially to shorter and shorter timescales, has its dangers.

It can be argued that many shipbuilders, notably in Japan, have achieved remarkably short timescales already. Equally, it can be said that that has been done by a process of standardisation of product, of interim product, of process, of method. The new challenge is to achieve that same end for the individual product. However, once the rigid control of the standardised process has been lost, and this applies to the supply chain as well as internal processes, there is an inevitability about variances.

In other words, things will go wrong. Given the complexity of the product, some items *will* be delivered late, be the wrong specification, be the wrong size, fail to work or otherwise not perform their allotted function.

In such a case, what can be done? The solution, which, as with others, has been available but has rarely been adopted is the use of discrete event simulation. This technique has been around for a long time, but was only sensibly applicable with the advent of powerful and accessible computers. It has more recently been available without the need for knowledge of a relatively complex programming language. Finally, it is only recently that readily understandable, graphical outputs have been available. Simulation can now provide the capability for a shipyard, having developed its highly interdependent plans and schedules, to test their robustness in the event of the failures which have been described, so the ability to maintain an overall schedule in the face of some random failures can be evaluated. If some item is delivered late, or if some problem is encountered during the assembly or installation processes, then the impact can be examined in advance. Generalised contingency plans can be made, priorities for expediting supplies can also be decided and alternatives can be explored. In many ways, the use of simulation can make available to production staff what computer-aided engineering technology has made available to ship design staff: that is, the ability to evaluate many alternatives quickly and to determine the optimum solution to specific requirements or problems; in other words, to design and test the production process before committing any actual work.

The emphasis of this look at the way the business of shipbuilding might develop has been on the steady advance of some established ideas, like undercover construction, into new areas, and especially on the potential for improvements in preparation for ship construction. The increasing use of automation, where entirely justified by cost, when compared with sub-contracting or other alternatives, has also been discussed. It is now appropriate to consider what new processes might have automation applied to them.

One is the laser. They have been around for some 40 years, and have been available as a metal cutting/welding tool for about 30 years. Preliminary research into their application for ship construction, because the laser is a very benign heat source compared to other forms, began around 20 years ago. Pioneering applications, which can best be described as heroic failures, were made in the early 1980s, while a solid base of applications research was built. The use of laser cutting for thin steel plate was firmly established in the 1990s, and it is now also a process which has proven applicability for welding. The pioneering research also saw applications for a wide range of processing in the shipbuilding industry, given the ability of the laser to cut most materials. The vision was of a multi-use cutting and welding system, using a single power source and a directed beam, driven by a full CAD model, producing highly accurate parts for both ship structures and outfit installation. The vision had particular applicability to smaller, specialised, one-off ship types. If the lead time from concept to application which this chapter proposes is correct, then the multiple use of lasers should be a major element of the next generation of shipbuilding.

There are other thermal processes, including electron beam welding, which have had a similar lifespan to the laser, and may also be found in application in the near future.

If the use of novel materials is adopted, then for the shipbuilders to be able to produce vessels from them in an efficient and cost-effective manner, new production processes will be required. The scale of the shipbuilding industry, even for the smaller ships which the current high speed market represents, means that the materials will be used in ways, and particularly in quantities, that are novel. So the production processes are not yet available, but the craft level of production which is appropriate to small boats will not be adequate. An analogy might be the mid-nineteenth century steel industry, which moved from small scale and expensive to cheap and reliable large scale production over a few decades.

Finally, the capabilities of new processes and production methods, and of new materials, will have an impact on the design of ships. If parts for the ships' structure can be cut with very high accuracy, then many design features which allow relatively large tolerances for production purposes may be dispensed with. Similarly, design features which reduce the production work content may become more feasible. Many of the compromises which have evolved in a shipbuilding era of weld distortion could be abandoned.

There is of course a large scale development, implementation and training programme for any shipyard to proceed down the development paths which have been sketched out. But the imperatives of competition, labour skills shortages and product variety are all increasingly felt, and the whole history of the industry has been of a need to adopt changes. The new processes and technologies are there; it remains to be seen how rapidly the shipbuilding business adopts them.

This chapter began by shying away from the dangers of forecasting, but inevitably any view of the future has an element of forecasting in it. This is still not the intention. Rather, if there is any message from this final chapter, it is that the business of shipbuilding must review and take note of the lessons of history. Shipbuilding is an older, if not a wiser, industry than most. It has been global for longer, and will still be in business when some more fashionable industries have come and gone. The lessons about adaptation and change are all available in the recent development of the industry.

They must be learned.

INDEX

The word CONSTRUCTION *is used as a main heading in place of* SHIPBUILDING, *and all other aspects of the topic are referred to from there.*

Except where necessary to distinguish the sense, the singular form has been used throughout, and this includes the plural where appropriate.

Acceptance
  sampling, 250
  vessel, of, 110
Accommodation, build strategy, 171
Activity map, construction organisation, 192
Advertising, 87
After-sales service, 86–87, 88
Agreement
  interim, 92
  OECD, 35, 36, 259
Allowance, buyer's, 103
Aluminium, future development and, 258
America. *See* Latin America; United States
American Shipbuilders Association, 19
Approval
  assignment, of, 124
  plans and drawings and inspection during construction, 94, 103–104
Arbitration, 123
Assembly
  block, outfitting and painting, 215
  hull production, 208–210
Assessment
  market, defined, 21
  market demand, 16–17
Assignment
  builder's warranty, of, 117
  contract and, 123–124
  right of, 96
Association for the Structural Improvement of Shipbuilding (ASIS), 19
Association of Norwegian Marine Yards and the Norwegian Shipowners' Association Form of October 1981 (Norwegian Form), 93
Association of Western European Shipbuilders (AWES), 18
AWES Form
  design responsibility and, 93
  exclusion of implied terms and, 111–112
  limitation on builder's liability and, 120
  title to the vessel and, 113
Assurance, quality. *See* Quality

Automation, 12, 219–221
  See also Technology
  flexible, 264
  "islands" of, 238
AWES. *See* Association of Western European Shipbuilders

Bank charges, contract price and terms of payment and, 102
Benchmarking, 188–190
Biocidal Products Directive (EU), 49
Blasting, 50, 51, 203–204
Bonus, builder's, 104
Brazil, 8, 31, 71
Brunel, Marc, xiv
Build location, 168
Build strategy
  See also Construction
  accommodation, 171
  basis of, 224
  bottlenecks, 169
  hull, 169–170
  introduction, 167
  key dates, 168
  labour resource requirements, 168–169
  machinery spaces, 170–171
  main production parameters, 167–169
  main purchasing dates, 172–175
  manufacturing strategy and, 231
  objectives, 166–167
  planning framework, 171–172
  PWBS and, 231–232
  sub-contracting and, 169
Builder
  bonus of, 104
  default of, 118–119
  drawings of, copyright etc. and, 125
  insolvency of, 119
  leading, 60–72
  liability of, 116, 117–118, 120
  lien of, 113–114
  modifications to specifications for the vessel, 108–109

Builder—*cont.*
  owner relationship, 88
  ownership of, 42–45
  rescission by, 121
  risk insurance, 122
  warranty of, 95–96, 115–118, 124
Bulgaria, 69–70
Buyer
  approval required, 105
  default of, 96, 120–122
  modifications to specifications for the vessel,
      107–108
  rescission by, 96, 118–120
  right to rescind, 112
  supervisors, of, 105–106
  supplies of, 97, 118, 125

CAD/CAM, 140–142
  See also Design
Canada, 230
Capacity
  demand and, 35–36
  management, 226
  measures of, 57–59
  world, 57–60
    estimates of, 36–37
Catastrophe theory, 83–84
CESA. *See* Confederation of European
    Shipbuilding Associations
CGT. *See* Compensated gross tonne
Charges, bank, contract price and terms of
    payment and, 102
China, 5, 66
  future development, 260
  market share, 8, 11
  political support, 32
  recent development, 227, 228
CIM. *See* Computer integrated manufacturing
Claims, notice of, 117
Class, description and, 93–94, 98–100
Coatings, 221–225
  See also Painting
Commercial organisations, information sources
    and, 19
Commission of the European Union. *See*
    European Union Commission
Company, reviewing technology in, 78–80
Compensated gross tonnage, defined, 6
Compensated gross tonne (CGT)
  capacity measurement, as, 57
  competitiveness measurement, as, 80
  leading shipbuilders by, table, 62
  performance measurement and, 13
Competition
  builder/owner relationship and, 88
  European Union Directorate (DG IV), 33–34
Competitiveness
  defined, 73

Competitiveness—*cont.*
  measures of, 80
  technology and, 73–74, 80–82
Computer-aided design, 265
Computer integrated manufacturing (CIM), 142
  See also Integration
Confederation of European Shipbuilding
    Associations (CESA), 18
Constant cost lines, 81–83
Construction, xiii–xiv, 3–4
  See also Build strategy; Design;
      Manufacturing; Outfitting; Production;
      Technology
  approval of plans and drawings and inspection
      during, 94, 105–107
  economic conditions and, 11
  organisation
    information flows, 193–197
    key production activities, 192
    key requirements, 191
    maintenance activities, 192
    production technology and, 216–217
    shipyard facilities for, 201
    sub-contracting, 193
    title passing during, 119
    undercover, 234–235, 236, 262, 264
      ship layout development process, 1970s or
          1980s, figure, 243
Contract
  approval of plans and drawings and inspection
      during construction, 94, 105–107
  assignment of, 123, 124
  builder's warranty, 95–96, 115–118
  buyer's default, 96, 120–122
  delays and extension of time for delivery/force
      majeure, 95
  delivery, 95, 112–115
  description and class, 93–94, 98–100
  dispute resolution, 96, 123
  effective date, 125
  effectiveness, 97
  form, 92–93
  interim agreement, 92
  invitation to tender, 91
  legal framework, 91
  letter of intent (LOI), 91–92
  modifications (to the specifications for the
      vessel), 94, 107–109
  notice, 97, 125
  parties/preamble, 93, 97–98
  patents, trade mark, copyrights, etc. 97,
      124–125
  price, terms of payment and, 94, 101–104
  rescission by buyer, 96, 118–120
  right of assignment, 96
  standard terms, summary, 93–97
  taxes and duties, 97, 124
  trials, 94–95, 109–112

Control, quality. *See* Quality
Copyright, patents, trade marks, etc. 97, 124–125
Cost
    inventory management and, 150–151
    labour, 48, 82
    progress monitoring by, 181
    purchasing materials and services, 147–148
Cost-price gap, 34
Courts, dispute resolution and, 123
Crane, 235–236
"Critical path", delivery and, 115
Croatia, 11, 69
Currency, contract price and terms of payment
    and, 102

Damage or loss, risk of, 114
Damages, 103–104
Date
    See also Time
    "drop dead", 104
    effective, contract, 125
    key, build strategy, 168
    main purchasing, build strategy, 172–175
Deadweight
    capacity measurement, as, 57
    defined, 5
Default
    builder, of, 118–119
    buyer, of, 96, 120–122
    interest, 119
Defect
    design, 116
    nature and time of, 115
    ongoing process of review, 106
Definitions
    compensated gross tonnage, 6
    competitiveness, 73
    deadweight, 5
    demand, 22
    displacement, 5
    gross tonnage, 6
    inventory, 150
    light displacement, 5
    local infrastructure, 229–230
    market assessment, 21
    market forecast, 21
    market intelligence, 21
    net tonnage, 6
    planning unit, 176
    quality, 246, 247
    steelweight, 6
    supply, 22
Delay
    excessive, 115
    extension of time for delivery/force majeure,
        and, 95
    permissible, 104

Delivery, 95, 112–115
    purchasing materials and services, 149
Demand
    capacity and, 35–36
    defined, 22
    forecasting, scrapping and, 23, 25–26, 28–29
    market, assessment, 16–17
    short term. *See* Short term demand
    supply and. *See* Supply and demand
Demolition market, scrapping and, 26, 28
Denmark, 13, 35, 67–68, 209
Design
    See also Construction; Drawings; Planning
    computer-aided, 140–142, 265
    conceptual, 128, 131
    detail, 129–134
    faults, 116
    functional, 129, 132–133
    information flow, figure, 194
    new process and production methods and, 267
    preliminary, 128, 131–132
    production and, 127
    production, for, 134–135
        application of, 138–139
        consequences of no, 142–143
        effect of changes in technology, 139–142
        objectives, 137
        planning and engineering and, 158–159
        pre requisites, 136–138
        standards, 135–136
    responsibility for, 98
    scope of, 127–128
    transitional, 129, 133
Development
    facilities options, 237–238
    future, 255–256
        current technology, 262–263
        external environment, 259–261
        need for technological change, 261–262
        new materials, 257–259
        new products, 256–257
        new technologies and processes, 263–267
        undercover construction and, 262
    industrial, shipbuilding and, 4
    materials and services, of, 145–146
    materials handling and transport, 235–237
    scope of, 227–228
    shipyard facilities requirements, 231–235
    shipyard layout development process, 238–243
    shipyard location, 228–231
DG IV. *See* European Union, Competition
    Directorate
Directive
    Biocidal Products, 49
    volatile organic compounds, 50
Discrete event simulation, 266
Displacement
    defined, 5

Displacement—*cont.*
  light, defined, 5
Dispute
  rescission, as to, 120
  resolution, 96, 123
Dock
  See also Facility; Shipyard
  capacity measurement, as, 58–59
  double, 233–234
  graving, 233
Drawings
  See also Design; Planning
  approval of plans and, and inspection during
      construction, 94, 105–107
  builder's, copyright etc. and, 125
"Drop dead date", 104
Drydocking, builder's warranty and, 116
Duties, taxes and, 97, 124

Economics, 11, 17
  "STEP" factors, 41, 42–45
EDI. *See* Electronic data interchange
Effectiveness, of contract, 97
Electron beam welding, 267
Electronic data interchange (EDI), 202
Employment, table, 36
Engineer, guarantee, 88–89
Engineering
  civil, shipyard layout development process
      and, 241
  facilities, 178
  planning and
      design for production, and, 158–159
      production, for. *See* Production, planning
          and engineering
      PWBS and, 161–163, 164–165
  production, 160, 195, 196
Environment
  production technology and, 225
  "STEP" factors, 41–42, 48–53
Europe, 66–71
  See also individually named countries
  docks, 59
  future development and, 260–261
  industry structure, 15
  market share, 8, 11
  performance trend comparison, Japan and,
      figure, 47
  political support, 14, 32
European Union
  See also individually named countries
  Biocidal Products Directive, 49
  subsidies, 35, 260
  volatile organic compounds Directive, 50
European Union Commission
  information sources and, 19
  subsidies, 35

European Union Competition Directorate (DG
    IV), 33–34
Exchange rate, 7, 12, 14
  "STEP" factors, 42, 45
Expenditure. *See* Cost
Exploration, subsidising of, 33
Export
  credit assistance, 38
  licences, 124

Facility
  See also Dock
  engineering, 178
  maintenance, 201
  notional tanker, 240–241
  options, development and, 237–238
  shipyard
      development and, 231–235
      interdependence, relationship diagram, 240
      production technology and, 201
  support, 201
  supervisor's, 106
Far East
  See also individually named countries
  future development and, 261
  prices, 34
Fault. *See* Defect
Finance, to shipowner, "STEP" factors, 42
Finland, 69, 240–241
Flag, registration and, 100
Force majeure, 95, 114
Forecasting
  production levels compared with, 23–25
  short term demand and, 20–22
Foresight Report, xv
Forms, contract, 92–93
France, 14, 68, 234

Germany, 67, 234, 262
  ownership of shipbuilders, 44
  political support, 14, 37
  recent development, 227
  ship layout development process, 240–241
  shipyard location, 229
Globalisation, xiii
  See also World
Government, 2
  See also Politics
  approval of assignment and, 124
  exploration subsidised by, 33
  information sources and, 18
  support measures, 37–40, 56
Graving dock, 233
Great Eastern, 2, 257
Gross tonnage, defined, 6
Guarantee
  performance, 99
  refund, 118

Guarantee engineer, 88–89

Hull
  See also Ship
  build strategy and, 169–170
  outfitting work and, overlapping, figure, 222
  production technology and, 200, 202–203
    assembly, 208–210
    plate and profile cutting, 204–206
    plate and profile forming, 206–207
    steel treatment (levelling, shotblasting,
      painting), 203–204
  PWBS and, 174–175
Hungary, 70

IMO. *See* International Maritime Organisation
Implied terms, exclusion of, 111–112
Indemnity, copyright etc. and, 124
Industry structure, 15
Information
  flow, 193–197
  sources, 18–19
Infrastructure, local, defined, 229–230
Insolvency, builder's, 119
Inspection
  approval of plans and drawings and, during
    construction, 94, 105–107
  quality, 248–250
Instalments, recovery of, 118
Insurance, 96, 122
Integration, 142, 264–265
Interest, default, 119
Interim agreement, 92
International Maritime Organisation (IMO), 50
Inventory
  defined, 150
  management, 150–154
Invitation to tender, 91
Italy, 14, 44, 68

Japan, 5, 60, 62–64
  See also Shipbuilders Association of Japan
  exchange rate, 14
  forecasting and production levels compared,
    23–24
  future development, 260
  industry structure, 15
  inventory management, 150
  market share, 8, 11
  ownership of shipbuilders, 44
  performance, 13
    trend comparison (and Europe), figure, 47
  political support, 38, 39
  robotics, use of, 209
  scrapping and, 28
  shipyard location, 230
  subsidies, 33, 35

Korea, Republic of. *See* South Korea
Korea Maritime Institute, 65
Korean Shipbuilders' Association (KSA), 18, 64
Korea Shipbuilding and Engineering (KSEC), 65
KSA. *See* Korean Shipbuilders' Association
KSEC. *See* Korea Shipbuilding and Engineering

Labour
  coatings and, 225
  cost, 7, 12–13
    performance and, constant cost lines, figure,
      82
    "STEP" factors, 48
  force, 226
    capacity measurement, as, 58
    "STEP" factors, 46–48
  resource requirements, build strategy, 168–169
Laser, 205, 266–267
Latin America
  See also individually named countries
  political support, 32
  shipyard location, 230
Launch conditions, 168
Layout development process, 238–243
Letter of intent (LOI), 91–92
Liability
  builder, of, 116, 117–118, 120
  exclusion of, approval of plans and drawings
    and inspection during construction, 107
Lien, builder's, 113–114
Lift, ship, 234
Light displacement, defined, 5
Liquidated damages, 103–104
Lloyd's Register of Shipping, 18
Location
  build, 168
  changing, 4–5
  delivery, of, 112
  shipyard, development and, 228–231
  works, of, 98
LOI. *See* Letter of intent
Loss
  damage or, risk of, 114
  insurance, 122

Machinery spaces, build strategy, 170–171
Maintenance facility, 201
Man-hours, progress monitoring by, 182–184
Management
  inventory, 150–154
  production, 226
  quality, 226, 247–253
Manufacturing, 199
  CIM, 142
  strategy, 160–161, 231
MARAD Form, 93
Market
  assessment, defined, 21

Market—*cont.*
  current, 15–16, 20
  demand
    assessment, economic conditions and, 17
    models of, 16–17
    short term. *See* Short term demand
  demolition, scrapping and, 26, 28
  forecast, defined, 21
  intelligence, defined, 21
  newbuilding, scrapping and, 28–30
  research, 87
  share
    See also Exchange rate; Labour cost;
      Performance; Politics
    1980–1990, table, 7
    defining, 7–8
    industry structure and, 15
    key factors in fluctuating, 11
    number of ships on order in 1994, table, 10
    world shipping on order in 1994, table, 9
Marketing function, 86
Material
  handling and transport, 235–237
  information flow, figure, 195
  new, future development and, 257–259
  procurement, 179
  receipt, 214–215
  services and
    development, 145–146
    purchasing, 146–147
      cost, 147–148
      inventory management, 150–154
      quality and, 148–149
      supplier relations, 147–150
Mexico, 71
Modification, specification for the vessel, to, 94,
    107–109

National Shipbuilding Research Program
    (NSRP), 19
Net tonnage, defined, 6
Netherlands, 68, 83, 146
Noise, 52–53
Norway, 44
Norwegian Form, 93
Notice
  claims, of, 117
  requirements, delivery and, 114–115
  standard term of contract, 97, 125
NSRP. *See* National Shipbuilding Research
    Program

OECD. *See* Organisation for Economic
    Co-operation and Development
Order
  See also Procurement; Purchasing
  cost, 151
  leading shipbuilders by total, table, 61

Order—*cont.*
  number of ships on, in 1994, table, 10
  securing, 86–89
  short term demand and, 17–18
  world shipping on, in 1994, table, 9
Organisation. *See* Construction, organisation
Organisation for Economic Co-operation and
    Development (OECD)
  agreement, 35, 65, 259
  export credit assistance and, 38
  shipbuilding information sources and, 18
Outfitting
  See also Construction
  final, 218–219
  current technology and, 262–263
  hull work and, overlapping, figure, 222
  measures of productivity, 187
  production, 75
  production technology and, 200–201,
    210–214, 215
  workstations, of, 209–210
Outsourcing, 145–146
Owner
  builder relationship, 88
  finance to, "STEP" factors, 42
Ownership, of shipbuilders, 42–45

Painting, 51–52
  See also Coatings
  production technology and, 215
  steel treatment, 203–204
Parties, to contract, 93, 97–98
Parts, replacement, 116
Patents, trade marks, copyrights etc., 97,
    124–125
Payment
  recovery of instalment, 118
  terms of, contract price and, 94, 101–104
Performance, 7
  See also Production
  CGT and measurement of, 13
  gaps and, constant cost lines, figure, 83
  guarantee, 99
  key indicators of, 180
  labour cost and, constant cost lines, figure, 82
  relative, shipbuilding regions, figure, 81
  technology and, 13, 80
  trend comparison, Japan and Europe, figure,
    47
  world-wide improvement in, 16
Pipe production, 210–213, 249
Planning
  See also Construction; Design; Production
  corporate, 155–156
  detailed, 156
  engineering and
    design for production, and, 158–159
    production, for. *See* Production, planning
      and engineering

Planning—*cont.*
  engineering and—*cont.*
    PWBS and, 161–163, 164–165
  information flow, figure, 194
  integrated system, 263
  resource, 178–179
  strategic, 156, 176
  tactical, 156
  unit, 176–178
Plans, approval of drawings and, and inspection
    during construction, 94, 105–107
Plate and profile, hull production, 204–207
Poland, 11, 15, 69
Politics, 2, 32–33
  See also Government; Market share
  climate, 41
  political support, 14–15, 31–32
  subsidies, 33–34, 35, 260
Pollution, 49
Portugal, 234
Price
  contract, and terms of payment, 94, 101–104
  cost gap, 34
  newbuilding, and current market, 20
  purchasing materials and services, 148
  subsidies and, 34
  typical average ship, 1990–1997, table, 20
Process
  new, future development and, 201, 263–267
  new production, 201, 219
  shipyard layout development, 238–243
  stability, quality and, 230
Procurement, 154
  See also Order; Purchasing
  material, 179
Product
  change, 82–84
  life cycles, 84–86
  mix
    ship layout development process and,
        242–243
    short term demand and, 19–20
  need to adapt for changes in, 82–84
  new, future development and, 256–257
  quality, 246–247
  when to be made, 175–178
  where to be made, 178
  with what to be made, 178–179
Product-oriented work breakdown structure
    (PWBS), 137–138
  build strategy and, 231–232
  hull and, 174–175
  planning and engineering and, 161–163,
      164–165
Production
  See also Performance
  bottleneck, build strategy, 169
  capacity measurement, as, 58

Production—*cont.*
  design and, 127, 267
  design for. *See* Design, production, for
  elements of technology and, 74–75
  engineering, 160
    information flow, figure, 195
  levels compared with forecasting, 23–25
  management, 226
  measuring, 5–6
  outfitting, 75
  over-capacity in, 15–16
  planned rate, 168
  planning and engineering
    benchmarking, 188–190
    build strategy. *See* Build strategy
    hierarchy, 155–157
    how they work, 157–158
      what is to be produced? 158–159
    how will ship be produced? 159–161
    product work breakdown structure, 161–165
    productivity, 184–188
    progress monitoring, 179–184
    when is product to be made? 175–178
    where is product to be made? 178
    with what is product to be made? 178–179
  process, new, 201, 219
  requirements, inventory management and, 153
  set-up cost, 151
  technology. *See* Production technology
  world shipbuilding capacity and, figure, 57
Production technology, 199
  See also Automation; Technology
  block assembly, outfitting and painting, 215
  coatings, 221–225
  environmental issues, 225
  final outfitting, 218–219
  hull production and. *See* Hull, production
    technology and material receipt, 214–215
  new production processes, 219
  other production management issues, 226
  outfit production, 210–214
  pre-production activities, 200
  scope of, 199–201
  ship construction, 216–217
Productivity, planning and engineering and,
    184–188
Profile, plate and, hull production, 204–207
Profitability, measure of competitiveness, as, 80
Progress monitoring, 180–184
Protocol, delivery, 112
"Punch" list, 110–111
Purchasing
  main dates, 172–175
  material and services
    cost of, 147–148
    inventory management, 150–154
    quality and, 148–149
    supplier relations, 147–150

PWBS. *See* Product-oriented work breakdown structure

Quality
assurance, 225, 249–250
control, 250
defined, 246, 247
inspection, 248–250
management, 226, 251–253
need for, 245–246
process stability, 230
product, 246–247
purchasing materials and services, 148–149
standards, 248
total quality management (TQM), 247–248
types of control charts, 251–253

Refund guarantee, 118
Registration, flag and, 100
Rejection, of vessel, 110
Remedies, buyer's default and, 121–122
Repair
manner of, builder's warranty and, 117
productivity and, 188
Rescission
builder, by, 121
buyer, by, 96, 118–120
buyer's right of, 112
Resources
labour requirements, build strategy, 168–169
planning, 178–179
Review
See also Progress monitoring
defects, of, 106
Right
assignment, of, 96
complete works, to, 119–120
rescind, to, buyer's, 112
Risk
insurance, builder's, 122
loss or damage, of, 114
Romania, 70
Russia, 70–71, 230

SAJ. *See* Shipbuilders Association of Japan
Sale, surplus/deficiency in proceeds of, 121
SCA. *See* Shipbuilders' Council of America
Scrapping
actual and expected, 1990–2000, table, 27
demolition market and, 26, 28
forecasting demand and, 23, 25–26, 28–29
main nations engaged in, table, 27
market demand assessment and, 16
newbuilding market and, 28, 29–30
scrap steel from, 28
Service, after-sales, 86–87, 88
Services, materials and. *See* Material, services and

Set-off, contract price and terms of payment and, 102
Ship
See also Hull; VLCC
acceptance or rejection of, 110
change in type of, 2–3
construction. *See* Construction
container, 6, 37
demolition. *See* Scrapping
gap between prices and costs (early 1990s), table, 34
high speed, 256
increase in size of, 2
layout development process, 238–243
LPG/LNG, measurement of, 6
measuring market share and, 7
modifications to specifications for, 94, 107–109
number of, as measurement of capacity, 59
number on order in 1994, table, 10
passenger, measurement of, 6
reefer, measurement of, 6
title to, 113, 119
typical average prices, 1990–1997, table, 20
Shipbreaking. *See* Scrapping
Shipbuilders Association of Japan (SAJ), 18
SAJ Form, 93
acceptance or rejection of vessel and, 110
buyer's modifications and, 107
buyer's right to rescind and, 112
buyer's supervisors and, 106
defects, ongoing process of review, and, 106
design responsibility and, 98
dispute as to rescission and, 120
events of buyer's default and, 120–121
exclusion of implied terms and, 111
indemnity and, 124
limitation on builder's liability and, 120
method of payment and, 103
nature and time of defects and, 115
replacement parts and, 116
rescission by builder and, 121
sea trials and, 110
timing, buyer's approval of drawings, and, 105
title to the vessel and, 113
value of buyer's supplies and, 118
Shipbuilders' Council of America (SCA), 19, 35
Shipyard, 3
See also Dock; Facility
facilities requirements, 201
development and, 231–235
layout development process, 238–243
location, development and, 228–231
Short term demand
factors identifying appropriate product mix, 19–20

Short term demand—*cont.*
  forecasting and, 20–22
  information sources on world fleets, 18–19
  ordering decision influences, 17–18
  prices and, 20
Singapore, 236
Social factors, 41, 45–48, 261
  See also Labour
South America. *See* Latin America
South Korea, 5, 60, 62, 64–66
  current market, 15
  increased construction capacity in, 23, 25
  market share, 8, 11
  ownership of shipbuilders, 44
  political support, 31, 32, 39
  recent development, 227, 228
  scrapping and, 28, 30
  shipyard location, 229, 230
  subsidies, 35, 260
Spain, xiii, 14, 68
Specification
  description and class, 98–99
  purchasing materials and services, 149
  vessel, for, modification to, 94, 107–109
Standard
  design for production, of, 135–136
  quality and, 248
  terms of contract, summary of, 93–97
  work, of, 100
Statistics, short term demand forecasting and,
    21–22
Steel
  cutting, 75–76
  future development and, 258
  scrap, 28
  treatment, hull production, 203–204
Steelweight, defined, 6
Steelwork
  outfit, 213
  production, 75
  productivity, measure of, 186–187
"STEP" factors
  economics, 41, 42
    exchange rates, 42, 45
    finance to shipowners, 42
    ownership of shipbuilders, 42–45
  environment issues, 41–42, 48–53
  political climate, 41
  social factors, 41, 45–48
  technology, 41
Strategy
  build. *See* Build strategy
  manufacturing. *See* Manufacturing, strategy
Sub-contracting, 83
  build strategy and, 169
  construction organisation, 193
  facilities options, 237
  items, builder's warranty and, 116–117

Sub-contracting—*cont.*
  work, of, 100
Subsidies, 33–34, 35, 260
Substitution, approval of plans and drawings and
    inspection during construction, 107
Supervisor
  buyer's, 105–106
  facilities of, 106
Supplier, relations, purchasing materials and
    services, 147–150
Supplies, buyer, of, 97, 118, 125
Supply, defined, 22
Supply and demand, 55–56
  capacity of worldwide shipbuilding business,
    57–60
  government responses, 56
  leading shipbuilders, 60–72
  shipbuilding countries, 60
SWBS. *See* System work breakdown structure
Sweden, 8, 14, 38, 237, 238
System work breakdown structure (SWBS), 137
  planning and engineering and, 164

Taiwan, 8, 30, 31, 66
Taxes, duties and, 97, 124
TBT. *See* Tri-butyl tin
Technology, xiv, 41
  See also Automation; Production technology
  change
    generations, 76–78
    need for, future development and, 261–262
  companies, reviewing in, 78–80
  competitiveness and, 73–74, 80–82
  current, future development and, 262–263
  design for production, and, 139–142
  elements of, 74–75
  future, key features, 263–264
  generations, 75–76
  market demand assessment and, 17
  new, 263–237
  numerical scoring, 79
  performance and, 13, 80
  product change and, 82–84
  product life cycles and, 84–86
  securing orders, 86–89
  shipyard facilities requirements and, 232
Tender, invitation to, 91
Terms
  implied, exclusion of, 111–112
  payment, of, contract price and, 94, 101–104
  standard contract, summary, 93–97
Time
  See also Date
  approval of plans and drawings and inspection
    during construction, 105
  defects, of, 115
  delivery, for, 95, 112–113, 114

Time—*cont.*
  reduction in construction, overlapping hull and
    outfitting work, figure, 222
Title, vessel, to, 113, 119
Tonnage
  See also Market share
  capacity measurement, as, 57
  compensated gross, defined, 6
  gross, defined, 6
  increase in, shipbuilding, 2
  net, defined, 6
Total quality management (TQM), 247–248
  See also Quality
Trade, 1–2
  associations, information sources and,
    18–19
  market demand assessment and, 17
Trade marks, patents, copyrights etc., 97,
    124–125
Transport, of materials, 235–237
Tri-butyl tin (TBT), 49–50
Trials, 94–95, 109–112
Turkey, 27

Ukraine, 70, 230
Undercover ship construction, 234–235, 236–237
United Kingdom, xiv, xv, 4, 43
  environmental legislation, 49
  market share, 3, 8
  materials handling and transport, 237
  political support, 14, 38
  shipyard location, 230
  subsidies, 33
United Nations, information sources and, 18
United States, xiii, 71
  market share, 8
  information sources and, 19
  political support, 32, 37, 38
  shipyard location, 230
  subsidies, 35
  Title XI scheme, 38, 42

United States Department of Commerce Marine
  Administration Maritime Subsidy Board
  (MARAD), 93

Value, of buyer's supplies, 118
Venezuela, 71
Venice, xiii, 33, 37, 43
Vessel. *See* Ship
VLCC, 2
  current market and, 15
  life expectancy forecasting, 25
  scrapping, 28, 30
  supply and demand and, 55
  typical, statistics, 227
Volatile organic compounds (VOCs), 50

War, subsidised shipbuilding and, 33
Warranty, builder's, 95–96, 115–118, 124
Waste disposal, 52
WBS. *See* Work breakdown structure
Welding, 52
  electron beam, 267
  quality assurance and, 249–250
Work
  completion of, progress monitoring by,
    180–181
  electrical, 213
  flow, figure, 196
  location of, 98
  right to complete, 119–120
  standard of, 100
  stations, outfitting, 209–210
  sub-contracting of, 100
Work breakdown structure (WBS), 162–165
Workshop, ship layout development process and,
  242
World
  capacity, 36–37, 57–60
  fleets, information sources on, 18–19
  globalisation, xiii
  leading shipbuilders by compensated gross
    tons, table, 62
  leading shipbuilders by total order book, table,
    61
  shipping on order in 1994, table, 9